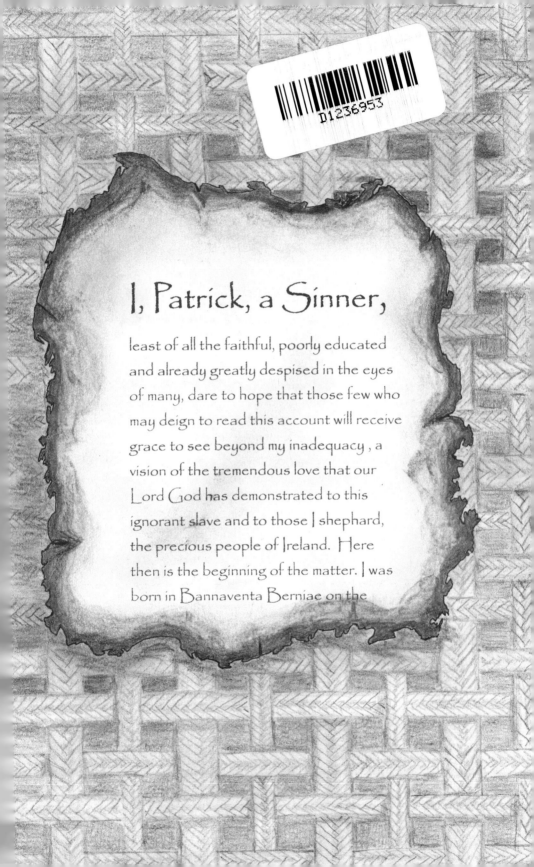

I, Patrick, a Sinner,

least of all the faithful, poorly educated
and already greatly despised in the eyes
of many, dare to hope that those few who
may deign to read this account will receive
grace to see beyond my inadequacy, a
vision of the tremendous love that our
Lord God has demonstrated to this
ignorant slave and to those I shephard,
the precious people of Ireland. Here
then is the beginning of the matter. I was
born in Bannaventa Berniae on the

FACT OR FICTION?

Stories that have survived centuries of telling and retelling are ones that strike a universal chord in all mankind. The story of Saint Patrick is such a tale. For fifteen hundred years people have loved and admired this man of legend and fact. Fantastic myths surround his humble story, which is far greater than all the myths combined. It is the truths woven within the myths, combined with the few actual facts of history and the revelations of Patrick's own character from his writings, The Confession and A Letter to Coroticus that compel me to construct this tale.

It would be impossible to contain all the legends written about Patrick without producing a massive volume. A few that could easily be reduced to their probable roots in truth I have included. Most I have omitted, preferring to devote most of this work to the limited but fascinating record of history. I hope I have succeeded in bringing to my readers, not a true biography, impossible with the limited facts available, but rather the true character of Patrick, with all his faults and failings, strengths and successes, and his heart big enough for all Ireland.

"Thanks be to God."

"I, Patrick, a Sinner..."

A Tale Worth Telling

by

Stephanie Lavenia Swinnea

Aaron Algood Books, Publisher

"I, Patrick, a Sinner..."

First Edition Original Paperback

Published and manufactured in the United States of America.

Aaron Algood Books Co., P. O. Box 177, Terlton, Oklahoma 74081-0177

Library of Congress Catalog Card Number: 99-90442

ISBN: 0-9671060- C-1

Illustrations by Stephanie Lavenia Swinnea

Cover Art and Design by Stephanie Lavenia Swinnea

Cover photography and layout by Steven Tremble

Bibliography – Roman History, Celtic History, Early Christian Church History, Druid History, Legend and History of Saint Patrick.

TABLE OF CONTENTS

Preface   -   Fact or Fiction?   ….…................….   iv
Acknowledgements   ……………………………………..   vi

BOOK ONE – SIN AND SLAVERY

BEGINNINGS   Commentary from the pen of Patrick   ..   3
Chapter 1   -   Flames of Fancy   ………………………   5
Chapter 2   -   Pirates!   ………………………………   15
Chapter 3   -   Slavery   ………………………………   25
Chapter 4   -   Property of the Mad Prince   …………   37
Chapter 5   -   Hope Deferred   ………………………   45
Chapter 6   -   Teller of Tales   ………………………   53
Chapter 7   -   The Potter's Clay   …………………   65
Chapter 8   -   The Curse Causeless   ………………   77
Chapter 9   -   A Voice in the Night   ……………………   85

BOOK TWO – FREEDOM AND FRUSTRATION

Chapter 10   -   A Bitter Bargain   …………………   97
Chapter 11   -   The Brothers of Gaul   …………………   107
Chapter 12   -   Reunion and Remorse   …………………   117
Chapter 13   -   Three Voices of God   …………………   127
Chapter 14   -   The Improbable Priest   …………………   139
Chapter 15   -   An Open Door   ………………………   149
Chapter 16   -   To Ireland   ………………….………   155
Chapter 17   -   His Severed Head   …………………   165
Chapter 18   -   Will you hear a story?   ………………   177
Chapter 19   -   Bishop Palladius   …………………   187
Chapter 20   -   Day of Disaster   ………………………   197
Chapter 21   -   Last Journey Home   ………....………   205

BOOK THREE – BISHOPS, BUTCHERS, & BETRAYALS

Chapter 22   -   The Paschal Flame   …………………   217
Chapter 23   -   Dichru's Barn   ………………………   229
Chapter 24   -   Every Tale Worth Telling   …………   239
Chapter 25   -   Trial by Fire   ………………………   247
Chapter 26   -   No Greater Love   …………………   255
Chapter 27   -   You and Every Other Snake   …………   263
Chapter 28   -   The Noise of Battle   ………………   271
Chapter 29   -   King's Bishop or King's Pawn?   …………   283
Chapter 30   -   The Gift of God   ………………………   299
ADDENDUM   -   No Shrine, No Monument   …………   303
Disclaimer   ………………………………………   305
Audrey's Lament   ………………………………………   306
Map   ………….………………………………   307
Glossary   ………………………………………   308
Bibliography   ………………………………………   311

Dedicated to all my family and friends.

ACKNOWLEDGEMENTS

The inspiration for pursuing this story I owe to Patricius Magonus Sucatus, whose Confession set a fire in my soul. To those who helped and encouraged me throughout its development I owe profound thanks, especially Pam Frasier, Nita Gorman, Arlie Clemens, Judit Makranczy, Eugenia Bethard, Simon Spalding, Gertrude Swinnea, Harry Preston, Dr. Peter Rollins, and Rusty Harding. To Susan Howatch, whose literary efforts set a standard too high for me to meet but challenged me to try harder, and whose recent encouragement gave me confidence in the merits of this novel, I owe most humble thanks. And those of my own family, Sam, Patrick, Kathleen, Erik, and Kyle Swinnea who listened patiently as I read page after page and lived the story month after month, I also gratefully acknowledge. Finally, my deepest appreciation I owe to Almighty God, whose grace enabled me to transfer to the printed page, far better than I was able, the passion, humility, and love I perceived in Patrick through his writings and so admire in our Lord Jesus Christ and in the lives of those who desire with all their heart to imitate him.

BOOK ONE

SIN AND SLAVERY

"I, Patrick, a Sinner..."

BEGINNINGS
from the pen of Patrick

There is a debt that I must pay. A debt of gratitude. My story is a meager payment on that debt. I have put off writing, because my scholarship is so poor as to invite ridicule from my peers. Better that I incur ridicule than my debt go unpaid. I, Patrick, a sinner, am least of all the faithful, poorly educated, and already greatly despised in the eyes of many. It is my hope that those few who may deign to read this account will receive grace to see, beyond my inadequacy, a vision of the tremendous love that our Lord God has demonstrated to this ignorant slave and to those I shepherd, the precious people of Ireland.

Here then is the beginning of the matter. I was born in Bannaventa Berniae on the western coast of Britannia in the year of our Lord, three hundred ninety. It was the eleventh year of the reign of Theodosius I, also called Theodosius the Great, a noted lawgiver and defender of Christianity. He waged a successful campaign against the Goths and Visigoths bringing peace to the Eastern Empire in Anno Domini 382. Then he defeated Magnus Maximus just two years before my birth and Eugenius and Arbogast four years after.

By the time I was fifteen, in Anno Domini 405, Theodosius had died leaving his sons, Arcadius and Honorius, reigning over a divided empire. The Visigoths under Alaric had raided northern Italy in Anno Domini 401, but were driven back by General Stilicho, who had been removed from his post in Britannia to lead that campaign. Now Vandals, Sueves, and Alans threatened to ravage Gaul and Irish Scots harassed isolated settlements along the British coast.

Fiercely loyal to Rome, we in our household were not particularly troubled by the many military campaigns. There had always been uprisings and invasions throughout Rome's history, yet the empire remained. Our country had been part of that empire for over three hundred years. Magnificent towns with villas, parks, baths, paved roads, marketplaces, schools, vacant pagan temples and new Christian churches dotted the major thoroughfares of our island. Roman legions maintained the peace. Roman courts administered justice. Roman religion, Catholic Christianity, was encouraged.

I was privileged, born both a British noble and a Roman citizen. My name, Patricius Magonus Sucatus, was both Roman and British. My family called me Sucat. Well off by any standard, we owned a fine villa in town and another on our vast estates near the sea. My parents worked tirelessly, but my own vacations were frequent, my leisure time abundant, and my religion a mere social and political necessity. Pampered, spoiled, and proud, my moral code was simple. Right was whatever Sucat wanted. Wrong was not having it. Like a skillful predator I closed upon what I wanted and took it. And, among other things, I wanted Audrey.

Here my beginning ends and my end begins.

CHAPTER ONE
Flames of Fancy

Mid-May, Anno Domini 405, the last day of school. I fidgeted on the hard bench seat and stared out the window. Old Euslid droned on and on about the proper techniques of writing. I was deaf to his words. The stately columns, the sculptured gardens, and the inviting pool in the brick courtyard below captured my attention. It wouldn't be heated today. Even so a swim would be welcome after this morning's dull rubrics.

I was not yet sixteen, scarcely above average in height, with sandy brown hair and pale blue eyes that twinkled when I laughed and danced when I contemplated mischief, or so I had often been told. A strong physique and athletic skill added to my charms. I was well liked and believed myself superior to most, my poor scholarship notwithstanding.

It was the privilege of all sons of British aristocrats to enjoy the traditional Roman education. Mathematics, grammar, literary fluency, and debate were the principle subjects, with a fair smattering of philosophy and Roman history thrown in. Mathematics stimulated my mind like a game or a puzzle. History was simply storytelling, an art form Grandfather had taught me to love. Philosophy conveniently provided me with other views of the universe besides Grandfather's Christian perspective. Had our lessons been limited to these areas, my stellar performance as an academic would have been assured. But grammar and composition were my bane.

I did learn to write, but not with fluency. It seemed impossible to reduce the multitude of my thoughts on any given subject to written words, words that flowed with rhythm and style. This chore I had effectively eliminated by hiring Amicus to write the essays for me. Thus I had breezed through this last year of grammaticus training.

Amicus was seventeen, called Ami for short, and almost two years older than I. He was tall, slender, with dark brown hair and deep set green-hazel eyes, a slightly angular jaw and a sharp nose. His refined, thin lips could express a full range of emotions, real or contrived, without the help of any other facial feature. He was nice looking in an academic sort of way, the perfect image of a scholar, and my best friend.

In the school of rhetoric, our next level of education, I anticipated great success in verbal debate. However, unless Ami continued to execute them, persuasive writing assignments continued to loom ominously before me. Why worry about that now?

Total silence called my attention away from the window and back to Master Euslid whose eyes were inimically riveted to mine. Master Euslid must have been seventy, though no one had the nerve or impudence to ask. He was slightly bent, about as tall as I, with balding gray hair, a long narrow nose, and an excessively hairy eyebrow that arched independent of its twin when he became annoyed or suspicious, as it did now.

I squirmed. After reading my exam essay, he was bound to know. What could he do? Could he admit that I had fooled him all this time? He'd look like a complete incompetent. Hadn't he praised my good work to Father only three weeks ago? How could he fail me now? What proof could he offer my doting father that I couldn't deny?

Master Euslid shook his head. "Sucat, you'll remain after dismissal." He looked up at the other boys. "One last comment before you go. The Roman officials suspect that our dear Father Molue's death may not have been an accident." My stomach turned. "Such a senseless tragedy. The boys next year will not have as rich an education as you have been privileged to receive. Father Molue's gifts as a storyteller made us see through his blind eyes the glory of Roman history come alive. That is all. When you have received your letter of merit, you are free to go. Class dismissed."

Coroticus turned around, grimaced, and punched me playfully in the arm. He, like Amicus, was seventeen. They had started school at an older age than I and had been promoted with me each year. The two of them were my favorite companions. Coroticus was less than attractive, stocky, with wiry, straw-colored hair, a large nose, and pockmarks from his purulent complexion. Not particularly exceptional at anything, he lacked the drive that spurs men to greatness. But his father was the highest-ranking noble in the province, and would have been king or governor, had he not fallen out of favor with Rome. The people in the province continued to pay him the highest respect. Accordingly his son, Coroticus, didn't need to compete like the others. What I appreciated was Coroticus's perverse talent for conceiving wicked mischief. Ami usually overruled his suggestions, but it was a thrill just to mentally entertain such things.

I grinned and punched Coroticus back. He was as pleased to be free of lessons as I was, though there was a sadness in his manner. We began hastily gathering our writing tools.

Ami, I noticed, carefully collected his things, as though each item were precious, always meticulous. Ami may have worked hard, but he played hard, too, a faculty I admired. We would enjoy our holiday. As the three of us stood ready to leave, Master Euslid approached Ami.

"Master Amicus, you are possibly the finest student I have had the good fortune to teach," Euslid announced as he presented Amicus a letter of merit. "Thank you, Master Euslid," Ami respectfully responded.

"Master Coroticus," Euslid continued, "Not everyone can be the scholar that Amicus is, but you have applied yourself faithfully, though uninspiringly. I commend you for your effort."

"Thank you," Coroticus responded, taking his letter of merit. "And sir," he added determinedly through clenched teeth, "When they find whoever started that fire, I'll kill him with my bare hands!"

"Yes, and I'll help him!" I added nervously.

"I'm sure that Father Molue would not wish his death to inspire such hate. Was he very special to you, Coroticus?" Master Euslid inquired.

"Yes, sir. He always had time for me, cared about everything I did. My father never…" Coroticus broke off.

"He was a remarkable man, a great loss. But we must leave vengeance to God and the legions of Rome, Coroticus," Master Euslid counseled.

"God and the legions of Rome," I breathed worriedly. Master Euslid frowned then placed a hand on my shoulder and led me to a corner of the room. My stomach churned again. He may have lacked the courage to face Father and jeopardize his position, but he could still take a cane to me for my deception. Master Euslid didn't speak right away, just stood there with his hand on my shoulder, his eyes searching mine, and that eyebrow arched menacingly. My eyes moved nervously from his face to his hands to the floor. Finally he spoke, his voice kind and sad, not railing as I had expected, but more like Grandfather might have spoken.

"Master Sucat, I am disappointed more than I can say. You have played me for the fool, a title you are swiftly earning for yourself. Your gifts, considerable as they are, unused, misused, or abused will evaporate, waste away. Virtue makes us wise stewards of the gifts we possess; honor, honesty, diligence. Regrettably, of these three you possess none!"

A quick glance across the room confirmed that Ami, Coroticus, and the others were enjoying my ordeal. Why was Old Euslid preaching to me? If he were going to fail me or cane me, why didn't he do it? Listening to his grave old voice almost made me sick.

What did I need with his lessons anyway? I had outsmarted him for most of the year. I imagined I could outsmart anyone. A look in Master Euslid's eyes told me he had read in my transparent face the impertinence of my heart. Why couldn't I mask my feelings like Amicus? He could be livid with anger and still smile so politely, you'd think he was pleased instead.

"Will I receive a letter or merit?" I asked haughtily, though I was making every effort to suppress my arrogance. Master Euslid slowly pulled out my letter. "To try to approach your father would be a waste of time for you and unprofitable for me."

Exactly! I thought as I smiled to myself.

"However, tonight at church I will make my confession to your grandfather regarding how miserably I have failed to teach you."

"Grandfather?"

Master Euslid handed me the unearned letter of merit and walked away. My mind was suddenly blank, empty. No thoughts, plans, schemes whirled within. Think about it later, I told myself, why waste a perfectly good afternoon? Ami and Coroticus wore mischievous smiles as their eyes met mine. They had enjoyed watching me squirm, but I was through squirming, at least for now. I'd beat the both of them soon enough.

"Come on, I'll race you!" I shouted as I made for the door. It was still a bit chilly for a swim, but I knew they would join me.

"Sucat, just one length. Then you tell us how you expect to wiggle out of the hole you're in," Ami laughed.

"The water's freezing!" Coroticus complained.

"Fruitless arguments seldom alter the inevitable, Coroticus," Ami orated from a wealth of experience. "Just swim!"

Generously I gave them both a head start. The water stung like ice, spurring me to powerful, swift strokes that rapidly cut through the water, sending a surge of hot blood pumping through my veins. Coroticus swam with the same lack of enthusiasm that marked every other effort. He was easily overtaken. But I began to feel I had made a mistake in allowing Ami an advantage. I hadn't slept well for several... Suddenly I shot forward, propelled by a power and energy absent only moments before as happened in every competition. "The champion!" I shouted as I leapt from the pool.

"As always, Sucat," Coroticus grumbled.

"Yes," I replied cockily, "in swimming, running, chariot racing. But in academics, Amicus wins the prize." I bowed in mock homage to Ami, who tousled my hair, laughing warmly. I did try to think of some area to applaud Coroticus for, but his accomplishments alluded me.

Whenever Coroticus did win at anything, which was seldom, he was unbearably arrogant. Whenever he lost, he pouted as he did now, "I could have won, if the water hadn't been so cold."

"Never mind that! Sucat, what scheme are you hatching?" Ami demanded.

"I'll have to come up with a new one. Old Euslid turned a corner I hadn't anticipated. But I'll think of something."

"If my pocket didn't fare so well from your deceptions, I would suggest you try honesty," Ami chuckled. We threw on our clothes and started for the street.

"Have you heard from Audrey?" Coroticus inquired. Overwhelming irritation gripped me as I turned on him. "Watch how you cut your eyes, Sucat!" Coroticus sneered. "Audrey is the finest girl I know. If she wasn't so overly fond of you....."

Audrey was Ami's sister. She was almost as tall as I and younger by only a few months, adventurous, always open to something new, a childhood playmate. In spite of our bent to mischief Ami had always kept us sensible. He was the thinker, painfully addicted to doing what was right...most of the time. This sometimes annoyed Audrey and me. We might want to climb higher, jump further, or swipe just one turnip from Old Euslid's garden. On the other hand, we were free to entertain endless possibilities, because we knew any stupid or hazardous scheme would be reined in by Ami. Last year her parents insisted, for obvious reasons, that Audrey no longer accompany us on our adventures. Still, we had managed one new adventure without Ami's intervention or her parent's knowing.

"When she comes of age," Coroticus continued, "and I have finished rhetorical school, I intend to marry Audrey. She's smart enough to appreciate what I can give her; rank, loyalty, love maybe. When she discovers the only thing you're loyal to is a good time, you won't stand a chance."

I could feel my cheeks growing hot with embarrassment. Was I jealous? Possibly. Was it guilt? To my increased discomfort, Ami stared with studied curiosity. What was written on my face that fostered the uncertain contempt in his eyes? "Audrey will come home soon," Ami finally suggested turning away slowly. "Aunt Beatrice is much improved."

"After four months I should hope so," I mumbled to no one.

With a loud thud the school doors flew open and the younger boys came pouring into the courtyard. "Sucat! A story! A story!" they clamored as they swiftly encircled and tugged me toward the garden seat. Behind me Coroticus murmured almost outside my hearing, "I'm glad he's going away for awhile. Sometimes I almost hate him."

A good story pushes away every other thought, and that's just the kind of story I told. By the time I had finished telling, Coroticus and Ami had gone. Like the monster in my tale, I chased the boys. They ran away squealing but still begging for one more story. I popped a few playfully with my towel, then sprinted toward home.

Ours was the most impressive villa on the street. Much more so than Ami's a half mile further on. but not nearly so grand as Coroticus's on the other side of town. The ornate doors, mosaic art works, fine furnishings, private baths, and landscaped courtyard of my home gave me a sense of pride and worth. What we had was better than most, because we were better than most, I reasoned.

Sunlight reflected warmly off the glass panes of our windows and lit a smile on my face as I neared the house. I ran through the courtyard. A cat, sunning itself on the warm brick pavement, scarcely flicked its tail. One of the servant children, chasing a grasshopper, darted unexpectedly in front of me, sending me hurtling through the door, struggling to maintain my balance.

Bursting into the hallway I collided with Grandfather and we tumbled together into the wall. Somehow we managed to recover before hitting the floor. Why was Grandfather stupidly standing in the hallway where people could run into him? I quickly bowed my head to mask the disrespect in my eyes. It wasn't the collision that had me flustered. It was Old Euslid and the meeting tonight.

My grandfather, Potitus, was nearly sixty-one and robust for a man of his age. Grandfather was an elder, a priest, of the Church and devoted to his faith. His ministry kept him extremely busy and excessively poor. Still, he always made time for me. Many happy hours had passed while Grandfather told me stories that came to life with the magic of his telling. I loved my grandfather, but his determination to see me a good Catholic Christian didn't sit well with my determination to be free of all religion. Out of respect for Grandfather, I did accompany him, along with my mother and my sister, Lupait, to church once a week. Father never required more.

The study door opened and Father stepped through. "I thought I heard something out here. Come in, Father, Sucat. Have a seat." Grandfather and I walked into the study. Father was holding a number of letters in his hand. He waved them in mock despair. "Every letter another excuse for not paying taxes!" He tossed the letters on his desk.

Calpornius, my father, was a handsome, prosperous noble in the prime of his life. As decurion for the Roman Empire his responsibility was to collect taxes and oversee how those taxes were spent. Of course, the lion's share went to Rome.

His business, almost an obsession, left little time for me, though his love for me was real and generous. Boyhood, he believed, was a time for fun and trivial amusements. The only demands he made were some measure of success in school and respect for Grandfather. I always met his expectations – in one way or another.

Presently I availed myself of the opportunity to read one of Father's letters. "To the most honorable Lord Calpornius," it began.

"What was it you wanted?" Father asked of Grandfather.

"Two things," Grandfather replied in his resonant bass voice as he placed a hand on my shoulder. "First, might Sucat put off his trip for one day and you two join me in church this evening?"

I worriedly put down the letter and began listening in earnest. Father glanced at me with a tired look in his eyes. Day after day Grandfather asked the same thing. Today I certainly hoped he would receive the same answer. I held my breath, as Father sat heavily in his desk chair.

"No," he said crisply. My breathing resumed. Usually that was the end of it, but today Grandfather persisted.

"I don't understand. Are you not a deacon of the church?"

"You ordained me."

"Yet you never meet with the saints."

"Nor will I."

I began to enjoy this discourse. Grandfather placed both hands on the desk and leaned toward Father. His eyes were piercing and his silver-gray hair majestic.

"Your vows, they meant nothing?" he asked piercingly.

Father smiled a half smile and stood to his feet. He held up the letters. His voice was cool and professional. "Those vows were extremely important. They meant I am free from ever paying taxes. Emperor Constantine, you remember, was very generous to self-impoverished deacons of the church. And with Stilicho out of the country I can retain my estates without being challenged. Beyond that, holy vows have no meaning to me at all."

Father tossed the letters on the desk. I watched him in total admiration. His ability to use every legal maneuver to his advantage was inspiring. Grandfather's response was less enthusiastic. He slowly lowered his eyes, as though he had lost forever something very precious. Father frowned sadly. "What was the second thing?"

"Yes, well," Grandfather cleared his throat, "I have something for Sucat." I respectfully stood to my feet. Whatever Grandfather had, it was probably something I wouldn't want. Besides, after services this evening and his conversation with Old Euslid, I doubted I would be allowed to keep it.

"Sucat, you are to be congratulated," Grandfather began. "I understand you have completed the second level of your Roman education. Soon you will begin rhetorical school." Grandfather fished out of his robe a small package. "I hope one day you will put your knowledge of law and letters to better use than your father." He handed me the package, a nondescript object, about the size of my palm, wrapped in plain brown fabric. I mumbled a thanks, but all the while I was wondering how anyone could possibly put knowledge to better use than my father had.

One of the servants appeared at the doorway. Father nodded for him to speak. "Lord Calpornius, Mistress Audrey waits in the courtyard to see Master Sucat."

"Audrey!" I blurted out enthusiastically. "Excuse me, Grandfather." I tossed the little package into my tunic and ran out the door, carelessly bumping into and pushing past the servant. Behind me I could hear Grandfather's sad voice, "Will you go to Hell, Calpornius, and take Sucat with you?" For a fleeting moment I felt sick inside. Why should those words depress me? Father didn't believe that. I pushed them out of my mind.

Audrey was prettier than I had ever seen her. She wasn't beautiful, really. Had that face been on anyone else it would have been almost plain. But Audrey's sweet nature and pleasant personality made what was plain seem beautiful. Her most attractive feature, those large expressive eyes, could communicate almost as well as speech, and complimented her full lips and turned up nose.

"Can we go somewhere private?" she asked haltingly. For four months I had anxiously anticipated this moment. I opened the door to a small drawing room just off the courtyard. Audrey hurried inside. I followed, closing the door behind us. Slipping my arms around her, I pulled her close. Her hair smelled like spring and the gentle curves of her body excited painful desire. She gasped and tried to push me away. Her entire body began to tremble. I hungrily kissed her lips while rearranging the skirt of my tunic.

"Please don't," she uttered fearfully.

"Sh, it's all right, Audrey," I whispered hotly into her ear. "No old priest is going to come along like the last time."

"I wish to God I could forget the last time," she snipped sharply though still trembling. "You can't mean that," I breathed, kissing her smooth white throat. "Yes, I do. I keep seeing Father Molue, his robe brushing against the candle flame."

"That wasn't our fault," I only half lied resisting the rising guilt in the pit of my stomach.

"If he hadn't tried to catch me, I wouldn't have tripped over that candle stand. Please, Audrey, forget Father Molue. Just remember the pleasure we gave each other." I kissed her hard, determined to blot out the memory of those flames in the delirium of passion. Audrey struggled against me as I lifted her skirts, just like she did the first time. Girls were supposed to struggle. It was part of the game. But, like a butterfly in a lion's jaws, her flutters only amused me. Power and virility, a sense of savage superiority, surged through me. Tenderness yielded before my firm advance.

"What other game could be so delicious, Audrey? Even in losing the contest you win the prize," I whispered. And like a skillful predator, I took her again... or very nearly did.

"Stop it!" She shouted breathlessly. "Stop it! Do you imagine this is pleasant? Fun?"

"Could anything be better?" I panted incredulously. The contempt and revulsion in her eyes was like a sobering slap to the face.

"Do you really think that the whole world is merrier when Sucat is happy?" Her voice broke and a tear coursed down one cheek. "Just *you* remember, old *friend*. I gave you *one* kiss. The rest you TOOK!"

"But... It was a new adventure, Audrey. I wanted to share it with you. Maybe you were reluctant. I thought once we... once you..."

"What you took from me, Sucat, I will never have to give again. You didn't even ask."

Passion fled. I reluctantly released her and backed away. She must have enjoyed my body as much as I had hers. If not, why had she come? Just to make me feel guilty for Father Molue's death? "Well it's done," I said becoming irritable. "I promise no one will ever know. You can run after our good prince Coroticus. I'll find someone else to share my pleasures with."

Audrey's eyes flashed, "In three months everyone will know!" Angry hot tears streamed down her cheeks. She gripped my hand tightly and placed it against her belly. "Your child grows in me, Sucat!"

For a moment I was stunned, then jerking my hand from hers I retorted uneasily, "I don't believe you. That one time? What happened? You liked it so much you made yourself a whore?"

Audrey's face became pale as death. She sank heavily into an armchair, her body jerking as great sobs deep within tried to surface. Trembling fingers pressed against her mouth to silence them. I looked away. Those words were unforgivably cruel and absolute lies as well. I was reacting, not thinking.

"Only once! Only with you!" Audrey cried out deliberately, haltingly. "What am I to do, Sucat?"

Why was she asking me? But who else could she ask? The air grew unbearably warm and hard to breathe. I couldn't look at the agony in Audrey's eyes without hurting too. I didn't want to hurt, to feel this pressure, this helplessness.

"I don't know, Audrey. You'll think of something," I blurted out.

Audrey's tears suddenly burst into uncontrollable streams. She doubled over, her face on her knees, and poured out her sorrow. Never had I heard anyone grieve so deeply. My sense of helplessness degenerated to one of worthlessness. All I could hope for now was an excuse to get out of that room. Grandfather's lessons about morality and "the wages of sin" filled my thoughts. I resented hearing those lessons before, and I doubly resented my mind reviewing them now. Irritation and anger crowded the pity from my heart. Couldn't Audrey cry quietly, or better yet, go somewhere else to cry? From outside and across the courtyard I heard the welcome voice of my father.

"Sucat, are you ready to go?"

"Sh-h-h," I commanded Audrey.

"Yes, Father," I shouted toward the door.

Audrey stared at me with eyes full of disbelief. Could I abandon her? For what seemed an agonizingly long time my eyes were held captive by those expressive eyes full of tragic, hopeless despair. Eyes that would haunt me the rest of my life. Tearing myself away I fled out the door and away from all my troubles, or so I presumed.

It had been just another adventure, a harmless flouting of archaic rules, I told myself. Yet in one day, no, in one hour, I had dug such a pit. The multitude of simple, innocent folk who were to suffer dishonor, slavery, even death because of my folly, I couldn't possibly anticipate. What a dreadful, dreadful harvest I would reap from one day's careless sowing.

But I get ahead of myself. Bear patiently with an old man's ramblings, and I will show where folly can lead.

CHAPTER TWO
Pirates!

Our villa on the Irish Sea commanded my love like no other place of my acquaintance. The trip itself was a delight. Only Julia, our servant, and the chariot driver accompanied me. Julia never said anything and the driver was too busy for conversation. I preferred it that way.

We traveled the canopied forest road for a little over three miles. The leaves above were bright green and cast spotted shadows on our faces, as the sun winked in and out through them. Deprived of direct sunlight, the forest air was cooler than elsewhere. When we left the forest road, sunlight flooded our faces, and the rolling hills, sprinkled heavily with sweet smelling wild flowers, carried us a few more miles. Soon our nostrils filled with the smell of the salt sea. For the last two miles we followed the coast road. We weren't actually on the shore, but on the cliffs that towered above. This was the part of the journey that I liked best, especially if the sea was rough, and large white-capped waves crashed against the rocks below. Most of the shore was inaccessible. But there were a few good harbors sprinkled here and there. I favored one abundantly sandy beach, good for wading and building sand towers, but only during low tide.

This particular trip, however, I was finding nature's diversions difficult to appreciate. Why couldn't Audrey have waited until after my holiday to force her troubles on me?

The chariot wheels were still turning when I jumped off with my travel bag. Resident slaves and servants dropped their duties momentarily and greeted me with thin smiles. I barely acknowledged them. For some reason Julia attracted my attention as she stepped off the chariot. She had escaped my scrutiny in the five years she had been our housekeeper. I wasn't sure why she interested me now. Perhaps it was the contrast she presented next to the other servants. My mind was working in strange ways, so I let it wander.

It struck me that just as Audrey's features took on beauty because of her sweetness, Julia might have been beautiful but for her harshness. Julia was perhaps thirty-one. She had alluring pale blue eyes and golden brown hair. Her features were classic. But her lips were always a little pursed and her brow a little furrowed.

She pulled her hair back in the most severe and uncomplimentary way. And I had never seen her smile or laugh, though I had heard a voice like hers laughing when only the servants were thought to be present.

Julia was a free woman, not a slave. Father allowed her far more liberties than servants usually enjoyed. She was given a room in our villa rather than a residence in the servant's quarters, and an apartment at our sea side estate as well. She had authority over all the other slaves and servants. Father even insisted that I avoid crossing Julia. When meals were served, I had better be on time or eat it cold. Julia would not have a meal reheated. I didn't like having to bow to the whims of a servant, even an exceptional one.

What did any of that matter? I handed my bag to Julia and walked out of the courtyard, across the field, to the rocky hills overlooking the Irish sea. Maybe the roar of the ocean would make me deaf to the voices within. But the sea was exceptionally calm, the waves peacefully washing the shore. I perched upon a rock and watched the sun slowly sinking beneath the waves. I had no way of knowing that miles away on another cliff, Audrey stared vacantly at that same sunset.

As twilight fell I stood and walked with heavy steps back to the villa. Had I been more alert, I might have noticed on the horizon the tall naked masts of Irish ships moving toward the coast, like a silent floating forest of limbless trees.

Our sea side villa wasn't as elegantly furnished nor as large as the villa in town, but it was cozy and comfortable. Tonight, however, it felt cold and lonely. A few oil lamps lit the main room. I carried one lamp to the wine storage and filled two large tankards. A few drinks usually made me a merry fellow. Tonight would require more than a few.

I returned to the main room, sat down, and began drinking. But the wine didn't make me merry. The more I drank, the more morose I became. Could I deny Audrey, let her be thought a whore and my child a bastard? What of Father and Grandfather if the truth were known? Ami and Coroticus would hate me. Ami's father was none too fond of me now, if he knew… No, she'd have to find some other way out of this. She was already ruined. What purpose would my downfall serve? She'd waited too long to accuse me without casting serious doubts on her innocence. This was the approach I knew I would take. Even so, my stomach cramped at the thought of the hell Audrey would endure. But Sucat had to come first. Rationalization saved me from my guilt. Maybe it wasn't mine. There was that possibility, had to be. I began railing drunkenly at the tankard, as though it needed to be convinced of my innocence.

"Whore! Can't say it's mine for sure. Probably went off to, wherever she went, and had lots…" Even drunk I knew better. "No, she wouldn't have. Not Audrey. Never Audrey. She's my friend," I continued sadly. "Well, I don't care!" Now I raged. " I'm no old man with a whore of a wife and a brat on my knee! Why did she meet me at the church anyway? Did she imagine I wanted to pray?" I took another few drinks.

I don't know where she came from, but Julia suddenly appeared before me. She looked like an angel with her golden brown hair hanging softly around her shoulders and little more than bedclothes on. My appraisal was far from angelic. Perhaps my father had appreciated more virtue in Julia than I had thought possible.

"Master Sucat," she began officiously, "There's a matter I think…"

"I don't care what your problems are," I quipped drunkenly, "Just deal with them or take them up with my father." I imagined Julia, standing naked before my delighted father, officially reciting a list of grievances.

Julia took a deep breath and frowned, "This isn't about my problems." She waited for a response. When I made none she continued carefully. "You raped Mistress Audrey, Lord Sucat. Now she bears the burden of your sin. God help you if you said all those horrible things to her!"

Raped? I considered dully. "How do you dare to speak to me like that?" I spewed.

"How? Knowledge is power." Julia shrewdly studied me then continued, "Four months ago I was taking a meal to Father Molue who had planned to keep an all night vigil. I saw you in the pouring rain half dragging, half pushing Mistress Audrey from the church, her face tear streaked, her hair disheveled, her clothes unfastened, and yourself equally untidy. I thought you shameless to violate your childhood friend – and in the sanctuary of our Lord!

"An instant later Father Molue appeared in the doorway like a human torch, the entire church blazing around him. There was nothing I could do for him, nothing you could do had you wanted to. Still we both know his horrible death was the result of your sin. You are responsible, and you are responsible for Mistress Audrey. Father Molue you couldn't help, but Mistress Audrey…"

I squirmed uneasily and took another drink. Julia sat across from me.

"Those tragic tears I heard today," she continued, "a familiar experience in the lives of slaves and servants." She paused, then barely whispered, "I still remember my own."

"Why can't you go away? Why can't I just wake up and find this a terrible nightmare?" I slurred.

"Why do I waste my time?" she scolded, studying my face with those perceptive eyes. "You're so drunk, my young Lord, it's doubtful you'll remember any of this in the morning." I rudely turned my back to her. In the long stillness that followed no night birds sang. The calm sea remained soundless. Wind made no music in the trees. Only a dog's mournful howl in the distance penetrated the disquieting serenity. Why didn't she say something? Anything!

"Haven't you any compassion?" Julia's compelling voice softly challenged. "A noble's daughter so degraded will find no mercy among her peers." I turned around. Julia was staring vacantly, distantly at the tabletop, her thumb unconsciously stroking on her wrist the jagged scar of a once desperate attempt. As her eyes slowly met mine, she whispered, "*Think,* you wretched boy. What options have you left her?"

My head started to pound severely. Tears filled my eyes. I couldn't, wouldn't, think about it. "Just leave me alone!" I shouted.

Julia stood up slowly. "You, sir, are a selfish, arrogant, young man with one foot in Hell and the other on a mossy rock. Where will your next step lead?"

I dismally watched as she returned to her room, strangely wishing that she would stay and dispel the terrible loneliness that invited more grievous incriminations from my own heart. She was wrong about only one thing. I *would* remember.

Out of the corner of my eye the flicker of lights through the window caught my attention. A multitude of stars seemed to have fallen from the sky and burned brightly on the coastal plains. Amazed and not thinking too clearly, I moved toward the door for a better look. Throwing it open, suddenly face to face with a large ugly man, a club raised menacingly in his hand, half his body painted blue, I jumped back. He pulled me roughly through the door and into the middle of a circle of equally terrifying faces. Most of them hurried past me and into the villa.

The chill of cold iron pressed against my ankle. Instinctively I kicked my would be jailer and sent the shackles flying across the courtyard. The man leapt to his feet, throwing punches but without skill. I easily evaded every blow and landed several with obvious effect, until, glaring hatefully, he retreated a few steps. I studied him.

My opponent was dressed in richly colorful and finely woven clothing. He was young, not more than twenty, slender, almost frail in appearance, with a thin beard and an unsettling madness in his eyes. I glanced at the others in the courtyard. They appeared to be placing bets. To my disquieting wonder all eyes followed me.

These were rugged, bearded, blood splattered men. More sober now, I recognized their race, Irish Scots! A tremor of fear shook my spine. Pagans! Barbarians! Little more than wild dogs! An older man, about my father's age stepped through the crowd of watching Scots and gave my opponent a hearty pat on the back. He also wore what must have been the clothes of a noble. His bearing was regal, and the warriors deferred to him as he passed.

Violently jolted as my stomach collapsed under a heavy blow, I locked my fists together and sent them crashing down, with all the force I could summon, onto the neck of the mad peacock, whose head plowed into my body. He stumbled and fell back. Furious, and still too drunk to appreciate the helplessness of my position, I attacked him with all the skill and agility my athletic prowess allowed. How many times or how brutally I may have hit him, I can't recall.

I swung again, but my arms wouldn't move. Looking from side to side, the hideous smiling faces of two painted Scots greeted me as they restrained my arms. The older noble stepped up. Within I cowered, but he only smiled slightly, his eyes honest and almost fatherly and there was admiration in them. The peacock, bruised and bleeding, sprang like a cat to his feet, his mad eyes filled with jealous rage. A glint from the blade of his battle-axe flashed before my eyes. Terror paralyzed me as I crumbled to my knees.

"Lochru!" the older man shouted angrily.

On my knees, the searing pain in my head pierced even the sockets of my eyes. Over me stood a man whose powerful arms gripped the head of the battle-axe, apparently reducing the effects of the blow, which I knew should have been fatal. His eyes stared intently into those of the peacock, who still held the handle of the axe.

"Cad e sin duinne cad a dheanfaidh se?" sneered the peacock.

"Ca bhfuil an brabach?" retorted the strong man, as he released the blade.

Gaelic! I couldn't understand a word. The language was in a strange way akin to that spoken by our slaves and servants. Whenever my parents were not present, my nursemaids had spoken our native tongue, as did the slave boys who had been my playmates. But we were more than British nobles. We were Romans! We spoke only Latin in my home, not the language of peasants. Once I had become aware of my privileged status, I rejected my former playmates and the language we spoke in play. It was all but forgotten now.

Hot blood began trickling down over my left eye and cheek. My head was splitting in two, or seemed to be. A wave of heat and overwhelming dizziness surged through me. Vomit filled my throat and mouth, spilling onto the ground. Jerked to my feet, I felt the cold iron shackles once more around my ankles. The will to fight was gone. Lifting my head, the madness in the peacock's eyes, more pronounced than before, bore into my own. He grinned wickedly and stepped away.

Outside my notice until now, my father's slaves and servants stood chained together, wearing only their bedclothes. They huddled, shivering, more from fear and uncertainty than from the chill of the damp night air. Their woeful eyes followed me as I was forced into line.

The peacock, Lochru, a name I was sure to remember, pointed toward the sea and yelled at the slave boy who headed the line. Cringing in fear, the child stared in absolute bewilderment. Did that fool expect any of us to understand his repugnant tongue, I fumed? He might as well have been a dog barking. He began lashing the child with a strap. How dare he strike my father's slave?

"Leave off!" I commanded, as I stepped out of line.

The raiders turned to stare. Loud laughter rolled from the strong man's chest. The others questioned him, and he answered in that foul tongue. Sinell, they had called him. I wouldn't forget that name either. He was obviously the only pirate who understood Latin. Soon every raider was enjoying the humor at my expense. Sinell strolled toward me and with a powerful and painful grip led me by the arm to the head of the line.

"Won't you lead us to our ship, young lord?" he mocked in perfect Latin, bowing low. The pirates roared. The temptation to slam my knee into that barbaric face was almost overwhelming, but good sense prevailed. Sinell's eyes caught mine as he raised himself up. A new horror swept over me. He wasn't the mindless beast that I had believed all Scots to be. Intelligence equal to my own poured through those eyes.

A bright flash of light snatched our attention from one another to the villa, my sanctuary, my best loved retreat, bursting into brilliant flame. My heart leapt into my throat. Tears streamed from my eyes. Hardly more than a boy, I hugged my arms to my chest and cried silently for my mother and father. Formidable realities now crashed upon all my senses. The wailing of babies and little children, too young to bring profit in the marketplace, assaulted my ears, as the pirates tore them from their mother's arms and flung them into the darkness. The stench of smoke, sweat, and blood filled my nostrils, depositing the taste of putrescence on my tongue. In the courtyard the battered, lifeless bodies of our elderly servants bathed in blackened pools of their own blood.

Could Hell be any worse than this?

Yet another fear arose. I could feel my mind striving to withdraw into a safe, comfortable dream or memory, far away from the terror I was facing. I fought hard for my sanity, forcing myself to take in everything and find some meaning in the madness. Sinell eyed me critically once again, then removed his hand from the handle of his knife and motioned with his head toward the sea. I humbly bowed my head and led the captives to the shore, our pathway illuminated, as if by torches, from villas aflame.

Near the shore I froze absorbing the scene before me. Party after party of captives, there must have been at least two thousand, were being led to the Irish ships. The ships numbered at least a hundred. All the kings of Ireland must have shared in that raid with King Niall at their head.

A terrible pain shot through my back. Lochru, club in hand, stood shouting in Gaelic and pointing to the nearest curraugh, or skin-covered, flat-bottomed vessel. I obediently continued on.

The crossing was rough and cramped. The stench of clothing uncontrollably soiled by fear and the retching of those unused to rough seas made the voyage intolerable. We were given nothing to eat and little to drink. Were not allowed to talk, sing, pray. There were no blankets to ward off the chill of night. No shade in the day. Most of the captives, taken in their bedclothes, had little protection against the elements. Still in my shirt, shoes, and tunic, I was somewhat more fortunate than most.

I didn't feel fortunate. My bruised body ached. The blood-matted wound on my head pounded. Around my ankles the flesh was raw from chaffing of the leg iron. My stomach gnawed with hunger, and my tongue was thick with thirst. My mouth tasted sour. My breath and body stunk. Even sleep offered no escape. Nightmares tormented what little I managed. My only diversion from this misery was to think. I listened as the pirates went about their tasks. A number of similar phrases I could now recognize, but I couldn't quite recall the meaning. Occasionally an action followed that made the meaning clear, and I was master of that fragment once again, like the Greek we studied in school, forgotten over the holiday, but quick to return.

School! Invariably all my thoughts turned homeward. Why had this happened? What of all my plans, my friends? How would Grandfather and my parents take the news? Would I ever see home again? Would I die? I would rather die than live like this. But, if I did die, what then? What if Grandfather was right, there really was a God, a Heaven and Hell? Perhaps I was dead already and this was Hell. If not, could I face eternity in a state worse than this? Even my thoughts were miserable.

A little boy began squirming nearby. He was about eight, the bastard son of one of our slave women. The personal lives of our slaves and servants had never interested me. I didn't even know his name. Every vacation he and the other children at our coastal estate would beg to hear stories, which I happily told, not as a favor to them, but for the thrill of commanding an audience. Now he looked to me with pleading eyes. What did he expect, I wondered irritably? I wouldn't be telling any stories here. My lip curled in a sneer. Silent tears fell from his eyes. Turning away, my eyes met the critical stares of the other captives. Only Julia had ever dared show disrespect, and then only fleetingly. I suddenly felt they were all my judges in a trial without mercy. I knew the verdict.

A shrill scream jolted us all. One of the women had smuggled her tiny infant aboard hidden beneath her garments. The baby had been wrenched from her arms and thrown into the sea. She flew in rage at the large, murderous villain, only to be beaten and the clothes savagely torn from her body. Her attacker coarsely gripped her ample breasts, full of mother's milk, and suckled that baby's food, while violently raping the body that only three weeks earlier must have been racked by childbirth.

The other raiders stood threateningly over us, defying our intervention, while Sinell and the older noble, Milchu they had called him, sanctioned the brutality by looking away. I tried not to watch, but I couldn't help hearing. "Please, oh, please, please," surged from the depths of the woman's being, as she writhed in obvious pain and terror. She said nothing else, only this, over and over and over, haunting our ears with the tremor of that refrain. When the brutish beast had satisfied his concupiscence, the other pirates stepped forward one by one to share in her depredation.

Vile, heartless, barbarians! I judged contemptuously. "Who are you to judge?" a firm quiet voice within me challenged. Suddenly Audrey's eyes peered into the eyes of my mind. An icy chill gripped me as I felt once again that surge of power, superiority, and cruel pleasure spawned by Audrey's futile resistance and my superior strength. Pleasure, not from love shared or even the consummation of intercourse, but a monstrously evil satisfaction born of forcing my will violently on another. Pleasure so self-centered I had not only presumed Audrey to have enjoyed her violation, but that she would desire to have it repeated. Perversely at that moment I felt no remorse. I tried to shake that proud, empty coldness, but all compassion, all warmth, all goodness was gone. Audrey's tears no longer moved me. In my mind's eye I could even see poor Father Molue burning alive, and I felt nothing... nothing.

Abandoned by God I looked into the blackness of a living hell, not external, but within myself; a total, chilling absence of love; an abominable inhumanity capable of any unspeakable wickedness; an unrepentant evil greater itself than any sin mankind had ever committed. Terrified to see in the face of each pirate my own, my body began to visibly shake, chilled to the bone from the darkness within.

"Christ have mercy! Christ have mercy!" poured unbidden from my lips. The chill, immediately less intense, slowly faded. The darkness, however, remained. God charitably plunged me back into the realm of human compassion, though pain was all I could feel. Guilt and grief over the lives I had destroyed, anguish and remorse over the demon I knew myself to be cut me in two, slicing my heart so severely that I was certain I could feel myself bleeding within. Excuses, reasons, apologies, nothing would stop the bleeding; nothing remove the guilt; nothing relieve the sense that I was the very equal and worse of these evil, monstrous men. I had hated, despised them. Now I hated myself. In all my life I have never known such absolute, hopeless, despair. Worse than wanting to die, I wished I had never been born.

The poor woman's mind mercifully retreated from reality during her ordeal. When they had no further use for her, the pirates did nothing to prevent her, naked, bruised, and bleeding, from dragging herself to the stern of the ship and plunging into the sea.

"I, Patrick, a Sinner..."

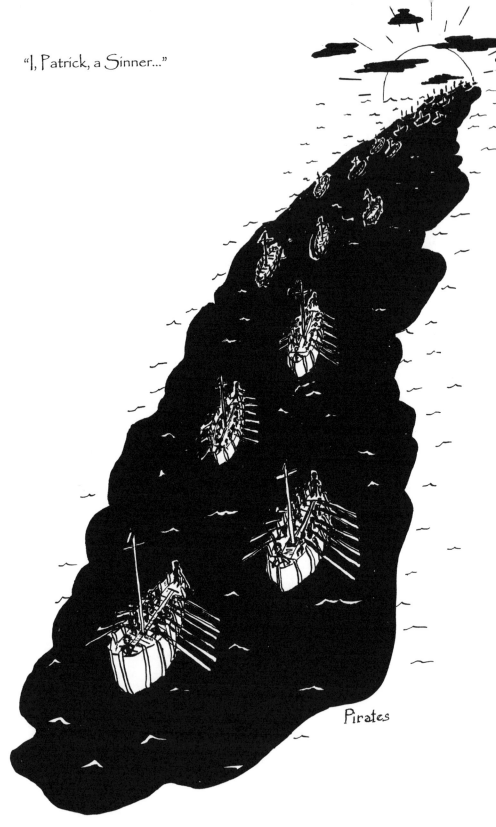

Pirates

CHAPTER THREE
Slavery

The crew became animated with enthusiasm, the captives sullen with dread, as the ship hugged the Irish coastline in search of the harbor. I was relieved. Ireland's majestic cliffs, brilliant green meadows, and dense forests rekindled my love of natural beauty and temporarily alleviated the madness that threatened my mind. Gratitude, both for the splendor that I saw and for the warmth I felt within, brought a small surge of hope.

For the first time since our capture, I relaxed and carefully considered my fellow captives. Many I knew, though not well, of course. A great many more I had never seen; peasants, slaves, servants all. How many nobles might be on the other ships, I wondered? It was early in the season. The sea side estates were seldom occasioned by nobles except on holidays. Most probably none of my peers had shared my misfortune.

What of Julia? Efficient, resourceful Julia, had she managed to escape capture? Her confident demeanor always set her apart. Good for her, I thought, not seeing her among the others. A peculiar manner of gratitude moved me. Julia had known me better than I knew myself and, even despising me, she cared enough to warn me of my own decadence. "One foot in Hell and the other on a mossy rock." You were right, Julia, I thought, but of what value was your warning when there is no help for me? I covered my face with my hands and rocked rhythmically back and forth. I was on the edge, but at least I was still sane enough to know it.

Shouts from the crew snapped me out of my stupor. The boat was docking. On the shore curious people eyed the ships expectantly and greeted the crew with exuberant cheers. The working slaves were led from the ships carrying the plunder on their backs. Our miserable company, along with the new captives from the other ships, was herded into a large circle marked by stone pillars. We stood like animals in a circus being sized up by our future masters. I took this opportunity to evaluate the Irish.

There were no signs of refinement as could be found among Roman Britons; no columned porticos, mosaic tiles, glass windows, or heated pools. The buildings in the settlement were primitive turf and wattle huts with skins or fabric drapes covering the doors and windows. Instead of brick or cobblestone, well-worn dirt pathways served as roads. Numerous fishing nets drying on the rocky beaches attested to their dependence on the sea.

Their clothing was coarse. Most of the men wore trousers laced tightly from above the knee to the ankle and short tunics over loose fitting shirts, more practical than the long Roman robes my father wore and possibly a great deal warmer. The women wore long sleeved tunics over full skirts, belted at the waist or under the breasts. Men and women carried long blankets or tartans slung in a variety of ways. Many were barefooted, and few wore any kind of head covering, even among the women. These were handsome people, though weathered. The peculiar wild hair arrangements and bushy beards typical to most of the men effectively camouflaged their good looks, but the women and children were as fine as any Briton. Most remarkable for such primitive people was their cleanliness. Their clothes, hands, and faces showed signs of regular washing. Even the grounds around the settlement were neat and orderly, and there was no smell of excrement in the air. The most foul smelling feature was the circle of captives. Vicious anger and humiliation suddenly seized me. We stunk because these simple-minded barbarians had reduced us to something less than human. Even dirty and foul I was better than the lot of them!

"Your face betrays you! Hide that aristocratic impudence," a voice cautioned sternly.

"Julia?" I turned to see two women stooped and shrouded moving slowly away from me. Clever woman to hide herself so well from these dogs, I mused. Julia's companion must have been the daughter our family had been spared the discomfort of seeing, due to a disfiguring affliction. Grandfather had visited them regularly as their priest and agreed with Julia's desire to keep her hidden away. Poor thing, what would happen to her now? I had almost forgotten Julia had a daughter. Odd that I would feel pity for her now; pity, an emotion all but foreign to me only three days ago.

A murmur rose among the captives. Following their line of sight I observed a large party of savages advancing toward us. Picts! Naked every man of them, their bodies skillfully painted head to foot with terrifying images. They brazenly pushed through the crowd of Irish Scots and into the circle of captives. Laughing, joking, and gesturing perversely, they fondled men and women alike in mock examination of the merchandise. The obscenity disgusted me.

Most of the captives offered no resistance. I knew that was wisdom, but instinctively the first Pict who groped for me I slammed to the ground. As he lunged in retaliation the crack of a whip startled us all. Moving quickly to avoid the lash, the Picts scurried good-naturedly out of the slave circle. Evidently they had violated local custom and were familiar with Sinell's stinging enforcement of the same. Like rats fleeing before a cat, I thought, sneering contemptuously. Oh, my troublesome, transparent face! Having dealt with the Picts, Sinell turned his attention to me.

Grabbing me roughly by the hair of my head, he spoke humorously to the crowd in Gaelic, shook me like a rag, and tossed me to the ground. I was furious! My head still ached from the battle-axe, but my injured pride was the real source of my pain. Laughter from the Scots and Picts intensified my humiliation. I wouldn't be put down by these dogs! "You PIG!" I muttered through clenched teeth, glaring murderously.

Sinell froze. An audible hush fell over the entire assembly, slaves and freemen alike, expectation in every eye. Warily I studied their faces and rose slowly to my feet. Sinell turned deliberately towards me, his expression neither one of pleasure nor anger, but cold, calculating business. The hair on the back of my neck began to rise as my eyes met his. Smoothly and quietly, in perfect Latin, his voice totally devoid of any detectable emotion, he addressed me. "Before I'm through, you'll beg mercy from this pig." Dramatically, like a well-rehearsed actor, Sinell removed a large, flexible, padded leather paddle from his belt and worked it menacingly. Please, no, I said within myself trembling. "Whatever you were, little prince, you're a worm now," Sinell declared chillingly, "not even fit to be a slave. But that... will... change...!"

Striking with forceful speed my face, my stomach, and the bend of my knees, Sinell skillfully executed blow after blow after blow, like the rhythmic beating of a drum, painfully reducing every muscle to quivering pulp. My eyes stung; my nose bled; my flesh crawled; my knees buckled. I fell, forcing myself to kneel upright, shielding my face with my arms, until my withering back could no longer hold me erect. My trembling arms struggled to keep my face from the dirt. Tears streaming from my eyes, I began to pray, "God make him stop! Please!"

"Give it up, lad." Sinell's confident voice commanded between blows. "You're nothing. Admit it. Beg like a worm for mercy."

Maybe I was nothing, but to admit it, to deny everything I had ever been, what would be left? Uncertainty brought greater fear than Sinell's abuse. I fixed my eyes on his. My voice rang out clearly through my tears, "I am Patricius... Magonus... Sucatus,... British noble... and a citizen of Rome!"

For a fleeting instant remorse seemed to shadow Sinell's face arousing a false hope of mercy. Then anger exploded within his eyes and such vicious beating resumed, that I imagined Hell looming before me.

"Oh God, don't let me die, not without you," I begged.

Black enveloped me in what I presumed was death.

The ground was cool and damp beneath me filling my nostrils with a pleasant, musty smell. My body felt no warm patches from sunlight, the air scarcely stirred. If I were still alive I had to be in a shelter of some kind. I attempted to open my eyes, but the pain convinced me of two things, first, that I might enjoy the darkness a bit longer, and second, that I couldn't possibly be dead.

A cool wet cloth brushed my face and covered my eyes. I tried to sit up, but two hands gently pushed me back to the floor. "You're a fool, but a brave fool," a familiar voice smoothly whispered. Overcoming the pain, I raised myself on one elbow and removed the cloth. My eyelids ached, but I couldn't miss an opportunity to look into a friendly face.

"Julia!" I exclaimed, "Oh, God, Julia, what am I going to do?"

"Start over like the rest of us," she said flatly.

"But I'm so scared, Julia, so alone. Even God won't hear my prayers."

"You pompous Prince," she retorted. "There's little you've ever done to endear yourself to God. But whether he hears you or not, be sure he hears your grandfather praying. As long as Potitus lives, none of us will ever be completely alone or forgotten." It hadn't occurred to me, Grandfather undoubtedly on his knees day and night. Hope flooded my heart. Without thinking I threw my arms around Julia's neck and wept like a child who'd just found his mother. "You've picked a hard place to find your heart," Julia said sadly, her voice like velvet to my ears. She embraced me for a moment. "Rest while you can," She suggested as she slowly stood up.

I searched for the words to express my affection and gratitude, but Julia smiled and shook her head. "Your face says it all." A frown instantly furrowed her brow. "Be sure you hide that face from the Irish. It'll be your death." She walked away.

I reclined again pondering what skills might be necessary to start over, when another voice commanded my attention. She spoke a rude Latin sprinkled heavily with British and Gaelic repetitions. I had no difficulty understanding the woman's message.

"Women, you can survive as I have. Whatever pride you had, you won't be needing it here. Remember that. Take off your clothes and carry them in a bundle under your arm until after the sale, otherwise, expect them to be ripped off at the auction. You'll have nothing but your pride to wear after that."

My eyes searched the room for the source of that matter-of-fact exhortation. There were perhaps a dozen women in the room, but the speaker was easy to identify being the only one dressed in Irish garments rather than British bedclothes. She was a bit older than Julia, her features similarly striking though her skin was more weathered. In her youth she must have been exceptionally beautiful. She had a shapely figure and raven colored hair lightly sprinkled with silver, which she pinned up in the fashion of British women. A small wooden cross hung suspended from her neck. She stood behind a rough-hewn table, a coarse sponge and a comb in her hands. On the table rested a large bucket of wash water, a bucket with drinking water and ladle, and an assortment of turnips, carrots, and dried fish. As the women approached the table to eat, she scrubbed their faces, combed their hair, and allowed them to wash other portions of their bodies, talking all the while.

"You are being sold to Picts," she warned them. "They never lose and are merciless winners. Don't fight them. This will be your first night in Hell, in case you thought you'd been there already. Tomorrow have a good cry, then, with God's help, try to find some spark of goodness in your masters."

Some of the women wept. Some were wide-eyed with fear. Others wore wooden, expressionless faces. Julia, I noticed, allowed the other women to eat and be groomed before approaching the table. Her daughter remained in the far corner of the hut, her face and head still covered. What future could she possibly have among these barbarians, I sadly mused?

Julia's face was neither tearful nor frightened as she stepped up to be groomed. She still looked like a woman in control, the equal or better of the woman in charge. As her hair was being combed she quietly asked, "May I know your name?"

"Liddy," the woman answered briefly.

"Liddy, you're a Christian, tell me, is there anything I can do for my daughter, anything you can do?"

Liddy sighed sadly, "You can't avoid slavery. I'm a slave myself."

"Yes, but the Picts! Can't she be sold somewhere else? She's a virgin for God's sake!"

"We were all virgins once," Liddy declared defeatedly.

Julia, her face drawn and determined, turned to Liddy. Her voice was hushed, but I managed to hear what the others could not. "If you can guarantee that she will have but one master, this night will be tolerable and I will beg nothing else. Should they all desire a piece of her, I will in mercy kill her myself."

What was I hearing? I slowly sat up, confused, convinced I was mistaken. Liddy's deep blue eyes looked warily into Julia's, then glanced toward the poor creature still hidden by her shawl.

"Scothie," Julia beckoned.

The girl, Scothie, approached the table. My morbid curiosity suppressed my pain as I strained to see the nature of her disfigurement. Her back toward me, I saw thick, silky, auburn hair cascade across her shoulders and down her back as Liddy removed the shawl.

"Oh, child!" Liddy gasped in horror, "This is no place for you."

Scothie humbly dropped her head and turned away from Liddy's gaping eyes and mouth. That mysterious face, I could see it now, the flawless, radiant face of an angel. Her crystal blue eyes, framed by deep auburn lashes and brows, were expressive, intelligent. Her lips were a soft rose color; her features classic and so symmetrically perfect that she seemed more an illusion than real. Several seconds passed before I realized that I had stopped breathing.

Why had Julia pretended a deformity existed? Why had she hidden her away? Why had Grandfather concurred? I studied Julia's classic features remembering what she had said about her own tears. Had I known of Scothie... I despaired that my perversity, and possibly my father's, had demanded such deception.

"I'll do what I can," Liddy said doubtfully.

"And if you can't?" Julia challenged.

Liddy's expression hardened as she turned toward Julia and determinedly nodded her head. I shuddered. Scothie searched her mother's eyes questioningly, but Julia's face revealed nothing.

"Quickly now, ladies," Liddy ordered as she turned to the other women. The women obediently finished removing their clothing. Julia kissed Scothie on the forehead and spoke with authority. "Stay with Liddy. I'm a survivor. I'll be all right. You take care of yourself." Scothie's crystal blue eyes filled with tears that spilled silently onto her cheeks, but she stood aloof. Brave like her mother, she didn't cling or make a scene.

A shadow fell across the doorway. As I looked up, Liddy was gently pushing Scothie to the floor behind her full skirt. Beyond Liddy, Sinell! Trembling uncontrollably I drew my knees up to my chest and prayed for him to go away. He motioned to the women who tucked their bundles under their arms and followed him obediently to the auction block. Julia never looked back.

My only friend, if you could call her a friend. At least she cared. Now she was gone. A couple of sobs escaped before I reined in my unmanly emotions. Scothie, sitting quietly on the floor stared at me, to my horror, her eyes even more luminous for her crying.

"Please don't stare," I mumbled. "I hate being such a coward." Glancing back at her, I saw she hadn't looked away. Her beautiful eyes were full of pity and admiration. The pity I could understand. The admiration only made me feel more embarrassed yet strangely ennobled. If I could just remember those enchanting eyes and her angel face, I could call up courage anytime I needed to.

"Get up, lad. Nothing's broken," Liddy commanded. "Sinell knows how to beat a man without even breaking the skin."

Slowly and painfully I stood to my feet. Sinell stepped into the hut and approached Liddy. A shudder coursed through me as I backed away, but I found the nerve to address him. "When will the men be sold?"

Sinell glared contemptuously as though my question had been an insult. "Sold already! You, nobody wanted!"

How much more worthless could a man be, I thought despairingly?

A loud slap and Liddy's faint cry jolted me out of my self-absorption. Sinell had hit her, not nearly as hard as he might have, but sufficiently to bring tears to her eyes. Liddy froze statuesquely and stared at the floor.

"You earned that, woman! I won't tolerate deceit or meddling in my business." He pushed Liddy aside, exposing Scothie's back to his view. "Get off the floor!"

Scothie leapt to her feet and fearfully buried her face in my chest. Instinctively I backed away pulling Scothie with me. Sinell stepped toward us. I didn't welcome another beating. I knew I couldn't protect her, but I couldn't just give her to him.

Liddy moved nearer and gingerly placed her hand on Sinell's arm. "Please, Sinell, sell her to anyone but the Picts."

Sinell irritably shook free of Liddy, grabbed Scothie by the shoulders, and spun her around roughly lifting her face to his. In an instant the irritation dissolved. He silently admired her features from every angle. He took a long breath and exhaled slowly, "If the rest is anything like the face..."

Ripping her gown from neck to ankle in one powerful stroke, Sinell exposed her nakedness to his thorough scrutiny. Scothie gasped and fell against me. Remarkably, Sinell's gaze was not lecherous but full of awe, like one admiring a priceless work of art.

"She'll bring a FAIR price," Sinell whistled as he grabbed Scothie's hand and started toward the door.

Liddy stepped bravely in front of him. "Too fair for one man's purse! Those dogs'll bid together then tear her apart."

"Your soft heart would cost me plenty!" He raged, attempting to push Liddy aside. Liddy didn't budge.

"She's a virgin. Have some pity."

"This goddess? You underestimate your British kinsmen."

"I am a virgin!" Scothie interjected anxiously. "No man's so much as kissed me." Her voice, even as frightened as she had to be, had a musical quality not unlike Julia's.

Sinell grabbed Scothie's hair, jerked her head back, and looked menacingly into her eyes for several moments. "By all the gods of Ireland," he finally whistled.

"In Leinster she'll bring a bride's price," Liddy cautiously suggested.

Scothie's eyes were still riveted to Sinell's. Scowling, he released her hair and shook his head. "Had I known you were on my ship little virgin goddess, I would have thrown you over. Bloody wars are fought over much less... Only a fool would risk carrying you all the way to Leinster to sell as another man's bride."

Their eyes still locked, Scothie bravely whispered, "What am I to expect from the Picts?"

Sinell looked uneasily from Scothie to Liddy. Liddy's eyes bore unflinchingly into Sinell's as she answered for him. "The Picts are barbarians sober and even more savage drunk. It will take six or more to buy you. To satisfy their lust each one will torture your body with unspeakable and cruel perversions. You won't be able to bear it." Her voice breaking, Liddy continued with difficulty. "You'll scream, fight, beg them to stop. That will only excite their frenzy. At the first sight of your blood their appetites will change to blood lust. Like wild beasts they will feed those appetites, whether or not you are still alive. By morning you will be dead, if God is merciful, much sooner. And the Picts will feel their resources have been well spent." Sinell turned away.

Scothie began weeping uncontrollably. Liddy embraced her. I watched in horrified silence as a new dimension of Hell gaped open before me. The morbid agreement between Julia and Liddy now seemed the pinnacle of mercy.

Sinell turned brusquely back toward Liddy with wounded eyes and gritted teeth. "I can see I haven't broken you yet."

"No," she whispered, tears spilling onto her cheeks. "You let the Picts do it for you, remember?"

"Merciful God!" I exclaimed without realizing I had spoken.

Sinell raised his arm to backhand Liddy, but lost the will and struck me instead. He ran his hands distractedly through his wiry hair. The man I thought so impervious to human emotion now looked tragically tormented. Liddy's eyes filled with compassion. She pushed Scothie toward me and stood before Sinell, gently laying her palms on his chest.

"I would have been dead but for you. I am grateful, Sinell. Can't you spare her, too?"

Sinell roughly grabbed Liddy by the shoulders, "Woman this is my *business*. I sell my slaves in good condition. What their masters do to them is none of my concern or yours."

"*Business*?" Liddy glanced briefly at Scothie, then took a deep breath and spoke with seductive persuasion, "Business? Sell *me*, Sinell. Take the virgin goddess to your bed. You won't lose too much, and look what you'll have! Take her, Sinell. You'll never find another like her."

Sinell said nothing. Liddy quickly glided over to us and whispered in Scothie's ear, "He's a bloody pagan but a kind master." She gently shoved Scothie toward Sinell, retired to the table, let her hair down, and began removing her outer garment. With her hair softly framing her face, Liddy's former beauty became instantly apparent. Certainly Liddy wouldn't face the same terror now that she had when she was a virgin beauty, but she did face being diminished, humiliated, and abused. Why would she sacrifice comparative security for an uncertain future among the Picts, and for a stranger? Scothie seemed both puzzled and guilt ridden, but fear of the Picts made declining Liddy's offer impossible.

Sinell gently brushed Scothie's torn gown off her shoulders sliding it to the floor. Her innocent wide eyes revealed her terrible apprehension, but she made no effort to resist him. Instead she peered bravely into his eyes, eyes that no longer viewed her with the detachment of an art enthusiast but with the powerful lust of a pirate captain.

Frustration and anger mounted within me as his mouth caressed those lips that had never known a kiss and his hands explored the gentle curves of breast and thigh. I couldn't bear to see her with him. She should have been worshiped, not abused. Would he be so savage as to bed her right here with Liddy and me watching every disgusting thrust?

Sinell, breathing excitedly, abruptly released his embrace. "You're sweet, little virgin goddess," he said almost smiling. He stroked her auburn hair, kissed her on the forehead, then sighed and glanced toward Liddy.

Liddy was in her underdress, carefully untying the laces of her sleeves. She had more grace than I and had not witnessed any of Sinell's lascivious behavior. She didn't see him now as he left Scothie and walked toward her. Gently lifting her chin with a finger he chided, "A slave doesn't sell herself. But you'll pay for tempting me like that. It's your tender belly I'll be stroking." Kissing her with surprising tenderness, he deftly slipped his hands beneath her skirts. Finesse, apparently born of frequent experience, left nothing to be seen save the expressions on their faces and the complimentary rhythm of their bodies. At least he allowed Liddy that much dignity. Scothie turned her wide eyes away, but I took in everything.

Sinell groaned with pleasure, shuddered, and teased, "Sorry I couldn't have been longer for you Liddy, but it's you that got me all stirred up." He set Liddy on her feet and adjusted his trousers, while Liddy straightened her skirt. Taking her face between his rough palms he caressed every feature with his eyes. "Drunk or sober," he pledged, "I'll never sell you, Liddy. You're mine till I die. ...Still," he sighed with a twinkle, casting his eyes lecherously at Scothie, "a piece of that honey might be awful sweet! But only a virgin brings a bride's price. Keep her face hidden, Liddy!" he ordered, all humor and tenderness suddenly absent, "or, I swear by Dagda, she won't live to see Leinster." Sinell swatted Liddy possessively on the rump and left the hut.

A heavy sigh escaped Liddy's lips. She had gambled everything and won. She reverently bowed her head and made the sign of the cross. Amazed, I felt like shouting, laughing. Scothie would be a bride, not a slave, though I wasn't sure if there was a significant difference in Ireland. Still, she had been spared fatal torture at the hands of depraved Picts.

While I felt the joy of hope revived, the emotional strain had been too much for Scothie. Uncontrollable tremors shook her body. Liddy calmly embraced her. "I've done what I can for you, child. Now get some iron in those bones," she scolded kindly. Then, looking up at me, she shook her head sadly. "But you, lad, only God can help you."

Oddly her words failed to provoke despair. Whatever misery I faced, it was enough for now, no, more than enough, that God had given Scothie a real chance at life. And me? It's impossible, one might say, an irrational response to the terror, abuse, loneliness, and raw sensuality I had been forced to endure. Perhaps, yet the love I felt that day, love for both Liddy and Scothie, never diminished in all the sixty years that followed.

Liddy redressed then stepped through the door and spoke in Gaelic to one of the guards, leaving Scothie in my arms. I held that priceless treasure next to my heart. For the rest of my life I would cherish that moment. There was so much I wanted to say. For once I was glad my heart could be read in my transparent face.

"No point suffering hunger when you can do something about it," Liddy stated flatly as she reentered the hut.

Love and passion, like water raging through a floodgate, poured through me as Scothie surrendered her tender lips to mine.

"I was speaking of food, children," Liddy chuckled. She placed a firm hand on each of our shoulders. With terrible reluctance we released our embrace. "You don't know when you'll next be fed," Liddy continued, taking Scothie by the hand. "Lad, make use of that wash water. There's nothing smellier than a young man in need of a bath."

I could feel my face glow with embarrassment. Scothie's velvety voice sang sweetly, "I like the way you smell, the dirt on your face, the swollen bruises from that awful beating."

"I'm told I can be quite handsome," I said smiling. "I'd rather you remembered me without the dirt."

Scothie smiled radiantly sending my passions into tormented restraint. I plunged my whole head into the wash bucket, scrubbed the dirty, matted hair and the painful axe wound carefully, then raised up and shook like a dog, showering Scothie and Liddy generously.

Liddy gasped in surprise, while Scothie, laughing, propelled a half-eaten turnip into my chest. I caught it, stuffed it into my mouth, and splashed her again. The hut strangely rang with our laughter, as Scothie tossed me a couple of carrots, which I ate before resuming my bathing.

While removing my tunic, a small package wrapped carefully in plain brown fabric fell to the floor. My heart leapt into my throat. Hadn't I despised Grandfather's gift only three days ago? Despised it so much, I had forgotten it completely? Now its value was priceless, the last contact I might ever have with home.

My hands shook nervously as I carefully lifted the gift from the floor. I wouldn't open it, not now. It represented a kind of hope in this hopeless place, an undiscovered blessing yet to apprehend when all other hope had failed. As I placed it on the table, the gut-wrenching grief of losing home and family once again battered against my soul. I finished bathing and washing my clothes in agonized silence. Scothie, sobered by her own grief, did the same.

After Liddy had redressed Scothie in fine garments and arranged her hair, Scothie looked like a goddess in the robes of a British princess. Then her face was veiled, and she was completely enveloped in a great hooded cape before being led by Liddy to a waiting ship.

I stood watching that ship from the slave circle, bound hand and foot to one of the stone pillars. Near the ship Sinell haggled with three men in white robes, their hair shaved peculiarly above their foreheads from ear to ear. Priests, I guessed them to be, but of what religion? I knew little enough of my own religion, the Ten Commandments certainly, most of which I had already broken. Of other religions I knew practically nothing.

Sinell gestured toward me and I knew these were to be my new masters. Sinell took their payment, boarded the ship, and ordered the crew to cast off, taking Scothie out of my life forever, or so I imagined.

CHAPTER FOUR
Property of the Mad Prince

Three warriors approached the slave circle, cut me loose, along with two other slaves, and led us toward the waiting priests, who I later learned were Druids. The priests scrutinized us then began a serious discussion, glancing our way from time to time. I didn't know what use those Druids made of their slaves. I'm glad I didn't know.

The hair on the back of my neck strangely tingled, when over my left shoulder that peacock prince, Lochru, suddenly appeared, grinning wickedly. He sauntered arrogantly up to the Druids and demanded something of them. I concentrated hard on every syllable. In the hut Sinell had always spoken to Liddy in Latin, though she obviously knew Gaelic. Perhaps that was his habit to thereby remain fluent in a language not his own. It certainly benefited me. Now I strained for understanding. The Druids adamantly shook their heads in opposition to his demand and shouted, "Sinell, Sinell." Whatever Lochru wanted, Sinell was entirely opposed to his having it. Lochru's eyes slowly changed from blue to the cold gray of well-polished daggers. He repeated his demand, but the priests stubbornly refused him. With the swiftness of a striking adder, he drew his knife, laying the blade against the uncooperative Druid's throat.

"Lochru!" Milchu shouted as he hurried from a nearby hut and boldly swept between them. Lochru slinked away toying with the blade of his knife. For the first time I saw the resemblance between them, Milchu and Lochru, king and prince. Yet how very different they were.

King Milchu smiled that same, slick, patronizing smile I had seen Amicus use so often to great advantage. He embraced the distraught Druid with one arm and extracted with his free hand a variety of highly valuable and beautifully crafted pieces of jewelry. The Druid's face lit up with amazement. He glanced briefly at me, then selected the finest pieces and nodded his assent to King Milchu. The warriors then separated me from the other two slaves. Insolent with satisfaction Lochru pompously placed himself before me. His mad eyes and thin lips smiled. "Fight me now, brave Briton!" he ordered, pushing me repeatedly backwards, "Fight, you worm!"

Fight? He with a knife and me in shackles? He was insane! Instantly I knew my error. "Hide that face from the Irish," Julia had warned. "It'll be your death." Reading the hasty judgement in my eyes, Lochru's flashed with anger. In an instant his cold, flat, knife blade slid teasingly down my cheek, to my neck, to my collarbone. I didn't breathe, nor did I allow Lochru to see in my eyes the fear and hate I felt. Sharp, hot pain gripped me as the point of his knife nicked through my skin and into my collarbone, provoking a barrage of obscenities from my lips. I smothered the injury with the palm of my hand. Lochru laughed! The fiend! And with his tongue cleaned my blood from the blade of his knife.

Was this monster to be my master? "You, nobody wanted," Sinell had snapped. Nobody but some strange priests and a mad prince. Despair clawed at my throat and sent shivers up my spine. Mad or just plain evil, whatever Lochru was, my survival now depended on humoring him. I dropped my head and grudgingly accepted the degradation of slavery.

The trip around the northern coast of Ireland was pleasant compared to crossing the Irish Sea. It was late spring and the island sparkled with a rich green luster like a rare gemstone. Seals and sea birds played along the coast and added their voices to the rhythmic splashing of the waves. The wet breeze kissed my face, leaving with me the taste and smell of salt. Closing my eyes I could almost imagine I was home. A burst of course laughter intruded upon my reminiscing. One of the sailors was evidently a humorist. Repeating his phrases over and over in my mind, I continued my study of Gaelic as I watched the men at work.

The crew all wore shaggy beards and dressed similarly to Sinell's pirates, minus the blue paint. According to their different personalities, they conversed, joked, or grumbled as they performed their duties, which were few. All the rowing was done by silent, expressionless slaves. Several of the slaves wore the rags of Roman-British garments. Two were dressed in some other foreign design, and the rest were clothed in coarse and rudely constructed garments, pieced together, but of Irish fashion. King Milchu and Prince Lochru were in stark contrast in their brightly-colored trousers and cloaks. Judging by their faces, they were happy to be sailing. Happy to be going home, I guessed.

The unfortunate illness of one of the oarsmen resulted in my being pressed into service. I took my seat behind the oar and carefully wrapped my hands with two of the small towels that I had made from Scothie's discarded gown. I was grateful for the towels, grateful for the memory, and grateful for the exercise. Any athlete would prefer rowing to sitting idly.

The contracting and relaxing of my muscles with every cut and draw of the oar made me feel alive and powerful again. The peculiar looks I received from several of the slaves alerted me to the smile on my face. A few others began smiling as well. Perhaps they were amused by my foolishness, or perhaps they had remembered again, as I had, the joy of the sea.

Light hearts make the heaviest load easier to bear. Soon the curraugh was clipping along briskly. The captain appeared impressed with our improved efficiency. He approached and studied me a moment, then moved on. He mentioned something about the ship and oarsmen. The voice that answered was Milchu's. I couldn't resist the urge to quickly glance over my shoulder. The captain produced some Roman coins and pointed toward me. Might I be sold? The captain seemed a reasonable man. I turned back to my work and began to pray.

The shriek of Lochru's incensed voice terminated the discussion. Why had I allowed myself to hope when sorrow inevitably followed in its wake? "As long as Potitus lives…" Julia's words echoed with in me. Grandfather wouldn't abandon hope. I wouldn't either.

Milchu's Rath or fort was several miles inland. King Milchu, Prince Lochru, and several warriors led our caravan. The other slaves and I formed the body of the train, and three warriors followed. The burden Lochru obliged me to carry hardly taxed my strength. But for my shackles the journey would have been pleasant. I had wound two towels around my ankles, preventing the shackles from rubbing additional sores, but the difficulty of adjusting my stride to the length of the chain still resulted in a few spills and subsequent abuse from Prince Lochru. I remembered Coroticus's sour disposition whenever he lost and determined not to let Lochru's rob me of the few pleasures left.

The Irish countryside was primitive and beautiful. The last of the spring flowers were in bloom. Tree leaves had changed from yellow-green to a rich emerald color, matching the grass below. The air was fresh and just cool enough to feel comfortable to those who kept a lively pace. Not a well traveled and dusty road like most in Britannia, the trail we followed was spongy with green grass which cushioned our feet for a mile or two, giving way to a carpet of leaves as we followed the edge of a forest the remaining miles.

The conversations of the freemen in our party convinced me that my concentration had begun to bear fruit. I was right to be pleased at having put my intelligence to good use. Still, it was one thing to understand what was said, another to speak coherently. So I practiced speaking silently to myself, "May I have some food? Some water? Lochru is a demented slug," and whatever else came to mind. With a little effort I might be understood.

As Milchu crested the hill ahead of us it took no fluency of Gaelic to understand his shouts of anger and alarm. All the warriors rushed ahead, disappearing over the summit. Bloodcurdling screams assaulted our ears as we mounted the hill behind the warriors and came face to face with the obscenely brutal treatment of those who presumed to steal King Milchu's cattle. King Milchu's men sliced, hacked, and clubbed the offenders, who fought with equal ferocity but were disadvantaged by the surprise of the attack. To my utter revulsion each man who fell was immediately decapitated, his head attached by its hair to the belt of the victorious warrior, his mouth still moving, his eyes opening and closing, his eyebrows furrowed, until the last of his life had drained away. Blood streamed from the severed heads down the warriors' legs, spilling onto the ground, mingling with that which flowed from the lifeless bodies. Nothing I had witnessed painted such a visual impression of horror, the blood, everywhere blood. My nights had been tormented by scenes of the pirates' raid at home. This horror guaranteed more sleepless nights.

Prince Lochru, I noticed, had remained just outside the circle of fighting, but managed to steal a trophy for himself by decapitating the victim of another warrior's battle-axe. Holding his trophy by the hair at arm's length, Lochru scaled the hill toward me. Vomit rose in my throat as the warm, scowling head, swinging like a lantern, was thrust into my face, splattering me with blood from head to toe. "I have earned many trophies," Lochru bragged contemptuously, "But you had none in your hall. What kind of warrior prince earns no trophies?" Mercifully King Milchu who had been walking the crest of the hill, intervened, sending Lochru back to the head of the caravan. I breathed deeply to clear away the dizziness and nausea.

"You think us barbarous, young Briton?" he asked, his eyes still fixed on the carnage below. I judged silence to be the safest response. He considered me curiously. "Why do I care what you think?" He grimaced sadly and turned away. My eyes followed and met Lochru's, filled with jealousy, glaring back. I wiped the splattered blood from my cheek and lip, picked up my load, and followed on.

Huge circular mounds within rings of ditches comprised the outer perimeter of King Milchu's Rath. The cleared area in the center of these rings supported several buildings, a corral, a sheepfold, a few huts, a feast hall, and maybe a larger residence, each standing in symmetry one to the other. It was neither a town nor a fort in the Roman sense, but could be an adequate resort for the scattered population for protection from invaders of for the celebrations of local feasts, weddings, and other ceremonies.

Once within the rath, the clansmen were greeted enthusiastically by craftsmen, bards, herdsmen, a brehon (or judge), a priest and others whose occupations were difficult to determine by costume or accouterments. Slaves hurriedly presented the warriors with long sticks, sharpened at both ends. Concentrating on their Gaelic phrases I watched and listened studiously. The warriors carried their sticks to the largest building, the feast hall, drove one end into the ground, then impaled their trophy heads on the other. I closed my eyes for a moment, took a deep breath, and had another look. Hanging from the blood-soaked walls the length and breadth of the building were other, much older heads. Grimacing I wondered if mine would one day adorn some feast hall. No, the head of a slave would hardly be counted a trophy. I determined to study something else.

Turning away from the feast hall I saw several warriors stripped naked, scrubbing the blood, sweat, and dirt from their bodies, while slaves poured generous amounts of water over their heads. My earlier deduction regarding their good hygiene was correct. I only wished they afforded the slaves such luxury.

The feast hall doors opened and a number of slaves began carrying trays of food from the fire pits into the hall. The freemen followed with leisured gait laughing and talking good-humoredly. A tall massive man with deep-set eyes in his overly large head approached the new slaves and ordered us to sit. "Slaves of King Milchu," he began, and continued to address us briefly, but pointedly, in Gaelic. "I am Lord Totmael, your overseer. Those of you who are troublesome will feel the lash. Torture is the fate of those who steal or run. But those of you who work hard will eat and sleep well. King Milchu is a good king. That is all."

Eat well? Until now I had been refused any food. The turnips, carrots, and dried fish I had smuggled inside my tunic before leaving the slave hut had provided my only nourishment for the past three days; the last bite consumed just before dawn. As if to illustrate his point, two slaves began walking among us distributing small loaves of bread. My gratitude for that one loaf exceeded any appreciation I had ever experienced over mounds of feast fare at Coroticus' extravagant parties. I took a huge bite. My fingers stung with the impact of Lochru's foot as he kicked the loaf from my hands. Astonished at his sudden appearance, I instinctively chewed and swallowed lest he rip the food from my mouth as well. "Nothing! He gets nothing!" Lochru shrieked at Lord Totmael and the serving slaves. Then he strode with feigned dignity into the feast hall.

My throat constricted with hunger and emotion. Stimulated by that small offering, my stomach began gnawing unbearably. Why was Lochru not satisfied? Hadn't his abuse already settled the score, my reward for having humiliated him in Britannia?

No. Prince Lochru's intention was obviously more sinister. Getting even wasn't enough. I was to be broken, body, mind, and soul, until I was no longer a challenge but an object of contempt, and he could feel the satisfaction of absolute superiority. My continued, pathetic servitude would be his trophy, a constant reminder of his victory. God, how could I stand it?

Cramping painfully from hunger, I clutched my stomach and felt Grandfather's gift still hidden in my tunic. "Hope," I breathed. Glancing at the others I was convinced they were far too occupied satisfying their ravenous hunger to notice me. I withdrew the package and carefully unwrapped it. A small, hand-bound book fell into my lap. Rolling it open I began to read:

"The light has come into the world, but men preferred
darkness to light because their deeds were evil."

I had seen evil. I knew that darkness. Every time I prayed I still saw it within myself, cold and terrible. But I didn't prefer it. I hated it. I read on.

"Jesus said, I have come into the world as light, so that
no one who has faith in me should remain in darkness."

My tears made it impossible to read further. I folded my hands over the little book and bowed my head in prayer. The darkness within was still terrifying, but as I repeated the words Grandfather had written over and over, the finest pinpoint of light began to glow. Frightened, my eyes flew open. Self induced, the result of hunger and despair on an active imagination, I discounted intellectually. My father's skepticism was alive and well in me. But I desperately wanted to believe the light was there, to believe that God had finally begun to hear me. Prayer was now impossible. Suppose I prayed and saw only evil, only the chilling darkness, no light at all? That faint glimmer had given me such hope; I could no longer live without it.

That evening, hungry and distraught, my sleep was surprisingly not tormented by the scenes of terror that my mind had replayed night after night. I dreamt instead of Old Euslid walking up and down between the tables of students, all hard at work completing an exam. Looking at the table before me, I saw that I, too, was being tested. The test was titled LIFE. Each line was a record of situations and challenges I had faced. My answers were the decisions and actions I had made in response. In almost every case my answer was wrong. Every lie, disobedience, cruelty I had ever done; my deception to Master Euslid; the horrible death of Father Molue; my violation and abandonment of Audrey and our unborn child; and a host of serious but lesser sins; they were all there.

I anxiously searched the head of the exam for the score required for passing. ONLY A PERFECT SCORE CONSTITUTES ADVANCEMENT it read. Oh, God! God! What could I do? Could I go back and live my life over? Even if I did, I might manage a better score, not a perfect one. But I would try, if I could just have another chance. What other hope was there?

Euslid's robes brushed against my chair. His hands lifted my exam from the table. There was something peculiar about those hands. Ashamed and embarrassed, I didn't look up.

"Dreadful, dreadful performance," he remarked in a voice younger than his years. "Such wickedness in one so young. You know, don't you," he said resting a hand on my shoulder, "You can't live it over again."

My heart sank. A long heavy silence crushed the soul within me and magnified the furious pounding of my heart. "Then my life has counted for nothing, and no matter how hard I try, it never will." I confessed brokenly. Cold, empty darkness moved to overtake me.

"It can be erased," I heard softly spoken.

Full of uncertainty, I peered into his face. Not Euslid, but the Lord Jesus Christ stood beside me, his loving eyes blazing with light. Light that illuminated every foul, dark, corner of my being. I wanted to run, to hide in shame, but his kind eyes held me. I summoned all my courage and asked in a voice barely audible even to me, "Erased? You mean by my death?"

"No, ….Because of mine." He laid the test before me and skillfully tore the incomplete part of the exam from that which I had so miserably failed, his hands bearing the scars of his crucifixion. Destroying the evidence of my failure in a burst of brilliant flame, he added, "The record is blank. In the eyes of God you have never lived until this moment. Go and sin no more."

I considered in amazement the remainder of the exam. There were no marks, no answers, no mistakes. It was perfectly clean. "Wait!" I begged desperately as he began to walk away. "Please, I know you've given me a second chance, but this is too hard for me. I will only fail again."

"Do not fear failing," he answered smiling. "I am always with you, ready to give you the answers and able to erase any mistakes that you in humility confess. Only believe and love me with all your heart."

At first light I awoke, thrilled, confused, bathed in the strangest, most intense experience of love, like waves that ebbed and flowed, imprinting my emotions, my body, and my spirit with sensations of exhilaration. Perhaps I was still asleep. Splashing my face with the wet dew convinced me otherwise. My heart pounded as I knelt. The darkness was gone! Light flooded my soul as I pledged my faith, my love, and my gratitude to Almighty God.

I withdrew the book of verses and scrolled to a new page.

"In truth I tell you, unless a man has been born over
again he cannot see the kingdom of God."

My heart leapt. I had been born all over again! The burden of my past no longer weighed heavily on my shoulders. I now had the confidence and courage, *faith*, to face the extreme difficulties of the present. Of course, I prayed for some miracle that could free me from that hell and restore me to my family.

Looking back I realize that God intended my new life should not arise from the ashes of my old. My greatest vice, probably the foremost hindrance to any man's realization of his full potential in God, had to be conquered. Pride! That arrogant, foolish assurance that makes the self God, supreme and infallible, I was still full of it. I can imagine no instrument better suited to annihilate my pride than servitude to Prince Lochru.

CHAPTER FIVE
Hope Deferred

My final destination was not to be King Milchu's Rath, but a cluster of five huts near the Forest of Voclut about a day's stride farther inland. Throughout the journey the beauty of the Irish countryside enthralled me, as if I were seeing the world for the first time.

Of course, it rained, an almost daily occurrence in Ireland, but I found the rain more refreshing than annoying. The load I carried and the swift pace we maintained, now that our shackles had been removed, had warmed my body to the point of perspiration in spite of the crispness of the late spring day. Grateful for the opportunity, I lavishly splashed away in the showers the dirt, blood, sweat and sea salt of the past few day's journeys, arousing peculiar stares from Lord Totmael and King Milchu. Prince Lochru, distracted by a young female slave he had collected from the rath, showed no interest in me throughout the journey to my extreme relief, though by his order food was still denied me. That no longer mattered.

Like a newborn babe might wish to return to the warmth and safety of his mother's womb and avoid the pains and trials of life, so I now looked hopefully beyond death, desiring to be continually enveloped in that light and love which I had enjoyed that morning upon my waking, the ultimate happiness, the ultimate freedom. Facing the experience of dying was still terrifying, but with Prince Lochru as my master what other expectation could I have? And beyond death what better existence could I desire?

For this and more I prayed. When the others stopped to eat, I prayed. While we walked, I prayed. As we rested, I prayed. Before the sun had perched upon the western hills, it had become my habit and my joy that every breath should express a prayer. How my admittedly peculiar behavior might have been judged by others didn't concern me. Slaves were hardly creatures of note. When I had been the master, my slaves could have painted themselves purple and I would have neither noticed nor cared, as long as they served me well. Slavery at least brought freedom from convention.

By nightfall we had reached the cluster of huts. Each slave was given a loaf of bread and a blanket. I was given only a blanket. We were then directed to a hut, very much like the slave hut on the coast, which was to be our sleeping quarters. A creek murmured nearby and stars shone brilliantly overhead. The remains of a dwindling fire sparkled at my feet. As the other slaves entered the hut, I remained by the fire gazing upwards at the breathtaking map of the heavens.

"May I sleep here… by the fire?" I asked, hoping my British-Gaelic was truly comprehensible.

Lord Totmael froze; a puzzled scowl on his face. I wasn't sure if he was surprised at my Gaelic or shocked that I had presumed to speak. He grunted disdainfully and walked away. I wandered the few steps to the creek and, collecting water in the cup of my hand, drank heartily. After gathering an armful of firewood, I rose to return to the fire and was startled by Lord Totmael's fierce glare as he towered above me.

"Firewood," I explained. Lord Totmael snorted, then grabbed up several sticks of dead wood and returned with me to the fire. From that day, and for as long as I was a slave, I enjoyed the freedom to sleep beside the fire every dry and temperate night, a pleasure also shared by Lord Totmael. We rekindled the fire, wrapped our blankets around us, and settled down for the night. The last sound I heard, as I bid goodnight to the stars, was Lord Totmael's sarcastic mockery, "Holy Boy! Humpf!" My unconventional behavior had been noticed after all.

The following morning Lord Totmael assigned all the slaves specific duties. I was given charge of twenty-seven addle-headed sheep. An obnoxious grunt was the only instruction I received. However, in Britannia I had known fools with pudding for brains who made their livelihoods as shepherds. What little I needed to know could surely be apprehended in short time. Tossing my blanket over my shoulder, I confidently strode to the sheepfold and opened the gate. My confidence wilted as sheep scurried out in every direction. Arms flung wide, racing frantically from one side of the green to the other, I endeavored to contain the sheep. Had I possessed more humility, I might have appreciated the comedy of the spectacle. Slaves and freemen alike roared with laughter as they left their duties to watch. Their amusement only angered me. To seal my humiliation I stumbled headlong over Prince Lochru's strategically positioned foot and sprawled face first into the dirt. The audience cheered. My cheeks grew hot with fury and embarrassment.

Prince Lochru, screaming snidely that I was an unprofitable slave lacking even the intelligence of his dumbest animal, kicked me soundly then ordered the release of the hounds. Within seconds the dogs had herded the sheep into a well-ordered flock, to the generous applause of all the onlookers. Like the fool in a farce, jeers, hisses, and obscenities assaulted me, as I slowly rose, collected my blanket, and led the sheep to the mountain pasture. With every step my self-pity and misery multiplied, becoming my companions for the remainder of the long, long day. Angry with God, I didn't seek his comfort.

The vigorous early morning exercise had sharpened my hunger. The pains, that I had easily ignored the day before, now gripped my stomach so violently that my throat ached from the contraction. For as long as I lived, I fumed, this primitive settlement was to be my home, this hunger my bread, these animals my work, and these barbarous pagans my family. I imagined all of them decapitated by another savage tribe, or extinguished by plague, or conquered by a victorious British king. And, if I couldn't be freed by their annihilation, I'd escape. I scanned the crest of the mountain, determined to find a route. Prince Lochru surely anticipated that possibility, even counted on it, I thought, my wits overcoming my madness. Among civilized Britons, the prolonged and cruel tortures of those who were unsuccessful in their attempts discouraged other slaves from escape. What might I expect from these barbarians? I could only shudder and determine not to give Prince Lochru any excuse to make an example of me.

Sulking indulgently, I paid almost no attention to the sheep who were so skillfully controlled by the dogs, until late afternoon, when Lord Totmael, shouting angrily up at me, signaled my return. Grudgingly obedient, I herded the sheep back down the mountain, across the valley, and into the sheepfold. After patting the dogs appreciatively, I walked toward the creek.

Livid with anger and yielding a lash of several long, leather straps, Lord Totmael intercepted me. "You worthless, lazy, sluggard! Bastard son of a parasite! Witless worm!" he shouted. He hauled me to a post, unloosed my belt and jerked the shirt from my body. I was paralyzed with fear and outrage. I had witnessed flagellation but never experienced it. "Pretentious holy boy! You who waste the land our gods have made!" He sneered hotly, tying my hands securely to the post. As the lash ripped across my back, I screamed, marveling that some men could endure, with dry eyes and in silence, what I could not. Every stinging blow took my breath and forced me to cry out. Sinell's beating had been punishing, but designed to preserve the merchandise unmarred. Not so the lashings of Totmael.

"Prince Lochru is right to starve you; you who would starve the lambs," his voice boomed.

The last blow was especially brutal. Almost speechless with pain, and choked with tears, yet unable to accept the injustice, I bristled, "What have I done wrong?"

Lord Totmael grabbed me by the hair of my head and turned my tear stained face toward the mountain. A large brown patch of totally barren earth was all that remained of the field where I had pastured the sheep. They'd eaten blade, stem, roots, all. "Barren until next spring!" Lord Totmael blasted, releasing my hair with a jerk that slammed my head into the pole. He untied my hands then turned away.

"I didn't know," I protested vehemently. "I didn't mean to waste the land." Lord Totmael turned back, scowling. "Teach me!" I demanded through my tears. "I'm not a fool. I can learn without a beating."

Lord Totmael smartly backhanded me across the face, knocking me to my knees, then turned toward the fire pit where the evening meal was being distributed. I knew better than to expect anything to eat. Frustrated and furious I remained on my knees and, looking up toward heaven, I vented my rage against God, careless of anybody or anything.

"Why do I have to endure this?" I shouted at the top of my voice. "I hate them! I hate them all! Had I the power I would damn them all to Hell and you with them for allowing their evil!" I hurled stone after stone toward God in his heaven. "It's all a lie! I hate myself for having believed any of it. There is no Heaven, and Hell is right here!"

Before another venomous word could spew out, an icy chill violently shook me from head to foot. I fell on my face perspiring in fear. "God, oh, God," I groaned, "I'm sorry. Please, I can't help my anger or my hate. I hurt so badly, and I'm so scared. I know I'm failing again, but this is too hard. I do believe. Please, don't abandon me. Don't leave me all alone." Waiting on my face in agonizing silence, my blasphemous words echoing in my mind, I hoped for some indication that God had heard me. Nothing! Nothing at all! Rising to my knees I struggled to determine what I could do, should do. Nothing came to mind, only a hopeless silence. The last rays of the sun disappeared behind the mountain, plunging the valley into the diffused glow of twilight. Darkness was about to fall, and I could feel it in my soul. A cool breeze swept across the green, prickling the heated lacerations on my back and sending shivers from head to foot. "Lord Jesus, have I failed so badly, that you have turned away from me forever?" I barely whispered. "......Where else am I to go?"

Through the stillness a gentle voice whispered, "Precious boy, it isn't your Lord who turns away. Nor will I ever."

Consoling love bathed and filled every part of me. I embraced that bloodstained punishment pole and poured out my fear, doubt, and sorrow to God, my only, my dearest friend, and I knew instantly that my virulent outburst had been forgiven.

After gingerly belting my shirt and tunic I rose wearily and made my way to my fireside bed. The stares and smirks of the others made no impression on me. Lord Totmael watched me with unsettling interest, but I was confident he couldn't have understood my incriminating railings, my prayers having been made in Latin. I said nothing but rolled my blanket around me and immediately fell into a fitful sleep.

Rising before dawn, in spite of the misty rain and determined never to start another day without prayer, I located a natural stone altar at the bend of the creek and sought the Lord again. Opening the little book of verses to a new page I read:

"All things work together for good to those who love God."

There was purpose in this misery?? My meditations were interrupted by Lord Totmael's irritated shouts, "Holy Boy! You son of a worm, show yourself!" Before I could respond he had jerked me to my feet, causing the flesh adhering to the back of my shirt to tear loose. I wilted in pain, bracing myself for a blow that didn't come. Lord Totmael carefully released me. His eyes scanned the place where I had knelt, my altar, and lingered studiously thoughtful for several moments. As I waited, I bent down and brushed the wet dirt from my knees, praying silently that God would remove Lord Totmael's contempt.

"You are a 'holy boy'," he pronounced with curious reverence.

"No," I countered, "I'm not at all holy. That's why I'm a slave, I think, and why I need to pray."

Disregarding my confession, and looking seriously bewildered, he queried, "Are you never hungry, Holy Boy? Do your prayers fill your belly?"

"Not hungry!? For six days Prince Lochru has refused me food," I retorted. "How could I not be hungry?" I looked away, frustrated by the stupidity of his question.

"Then why don't you beg for bread?" he bristled, looking at me as though I were the fool. At least his response proved I had clearly communicated. His had been an honest question, prompted by an admirable desire to understand a very peculiar stranger. But at not quite sixteen I couldn't appreciate his sincerity. I had thought him stupid, and he had read it in my eyes. He had a right to be irritated.

Carefully framing my words in Gaelic I answered respectfully, "To beg would only satisfy Prince Lochru's perverse pleasure, not my hunger." Lord Totmael grimaced uncomfortably, but amazingly showed no anger at my criticism of the prince. "Besides," I sighed heavily, struggling to contain my emotions, "When I die from lack of bread, I will no longer be a slave. Maybe then I will be holy."

Lord Totmael turned his eyes slowly from mine to the huts thirty yards away just visible through the trees. "Milchu is a good king. He will not permit your death, Holy Boy. Nor will he allow your value as a working slave to be diminished." His eyes met mine once again. "But beyond that, however much he admires you, King Milchu will not interfere with Prince Lochru's vengeance. You have a powerful enemy."

"Admires me?"

Lord Totmael bent down meditatively and placed a hand on the stone altar. "Pray, Holy Boy," he commanded, then raised up and returned to the fire circle. As I knelt weighing his words in my mind, my eyes lighted on the altar, where a crust of bread marked the place his hand had lain.

From that morning on Lord Totmael taught me the skills I needed to be a good shepherd; the eating and watering habits of sheep; the care and training of the sheep dogs; how to dress against the heat, the rain, and the cold; the best defenses against wild boars and other predators. He personally dressed the wounds from that beating and all the beatings to come. He even corrected my Gaelic from time to time. But his training was not pleasant.

Lord Totmael remained a hard man. He only spoke to me kindly that one morning by the altar. From then on his voice and manner were gruff and sharply critical. He never smiled and avoided me altogether unless some training or a beating was in order. In many ways he was a just men, yet even when my punishments were undeserved, he soundly administered them, even insisted he be the one to do so. I found it hard not to hate him; impossible not to hate the others.

At first I was daily favored by Prince Lochru's special attention. On one occasion he exchanged my blanket for another infested with fleas ensuring several miserable nights and days. He finally insisted that I be given something to eat, then kicked the tin from my hands before one morsel had touched my lips. He even urinated on me publicly.

His small-minded pranks would have been irritation enough, but, being the prince, his behavior gave other small minds the license to treat me with equal contempt, multiplying the abuse. Of course, every mishap became my fault, the consequential beatings by Lord Totmael my lot. No one dared befriend me.

Thankfully, my responsibilities as a shepherd were not to be compromised. There I was left in complete solitude to do my work, so what others saw as a lonely and unpleasant job became, for me, a sanctuary. With the help of my two fine sheepdogs, I could take a little time to bathe, wash my clothes, read from the little book of verses, meditate, and pray. As many as a hundred times every day and almost as frequently every sleepless night, I sought the love and companionship of God in prayer. And I was never disappointed. I say this, not to my credit. It was the Spirit of God glowing within me, helping me to accept my pain as necessary to my reformation, to see the virtue that God was working in me, and becoming my companion, confidant, and friend in this friendless place.

Spring had changed to summer since leaving home four weeks and a lifetime ago. It was my birthday. I was now officially sixteen, though I had claimed to be so for several months. As I knelt at my altar in the early light of dawn, the warmth of my tears distinguished them from the cool rain that fell. I thought of home, the parties, gifts, well wishing I might have received. In my mind I saw the faces of my family and friends. Then I saw Audrey, ghostly pale, and Father Molue.

"You can't live it over again," I heard within myself. No, I could never go back, and if I did it would never be the same, not that I would want it to be. Committing my new life to God once again, I ended my prayers.

The sun had now risen and the glint of metal caught my eye. Lord Totmael's knife lay next to the altar. I could never presume to own a knife. Only the most trustworthy slaves were so privileged, yet what I could do if I had it! The wild rabbits my sheepdogs caught and presented to me for praise, I could skin, clean, cook, and dry during my long days on the mountain, never lacking for food again. I could whittle a needle and sew some rabbit fur boots and a hat to stave off the cold this winter. I might even carve a pipe to play. It was as if God had given me a birthday gift.

My rejoicing came to an abrupt halt as it occurred to me that what I contemplated was theft. But wasn't it justified? I was starving! No, that was a lie. Every day a bit of food had miraculously appeared on my altar. My heartless disciplinarian was paradoxically my benefactor as well. I was hungry but not starving. And could I steal from him?

Perhaps the knife had been planted to make me out a thief? Beyond depriving me of food, Prince Lochru had shown little interest in me for more than a week. But he and King Milchu had become so angry with one another the night before, that King Milchu had struck him. My harassment always followed these rows. I need no further motivation to restore the knife to Lord Totmael. Slaves were beaten for their mistakes, but criminals could be tortured or mutilated.

When I approached him, Lord Totmael became indignant. "You think me a fool? No man with any brains in his head would be so careless with a knife! I should beat you for your insolence!"

But it was his knife, why did he deny it? "Better to be beaten for insolence than judged a thief." I countered anxiously.

Lord Totmael's eyes swiftly met mine, then fell to view the coals of the dwindling fire. "There is a hollow tree halfway up that mountain, where a knife that no one claims might be discarded until a good cause demanded its use," he gruffly suggested while stirring the coals to flame.

Did I dare trust him? I stood to gain little and lose.... A shiver coursed through me. With a trembling hand I held out the knife to Lord Totmael, slowly shaking my head. Lord Totmael reclaimed it, his expression unreadable.

That afternoon while herding the sheep, I noticed for the first time the large hollow tree near the creek and halfway up the mountain. My boyish curiosity led me to explore it. Peering inside, to my absolute horror, I saw Lord Totmael's knife. If this were Lochru's doing....

With knife in hand, I slipped behind a tall tree, and after searching the valley below for eyes that might betray me, I climbed to a squirrel hole about fifteen feet up and deposited the knife. It suddenly occurred to me that the knife might not be the only bait in this trap. Further search of the hollow tree produced only a pipe or whistle. It had six holes and a mellow tone born from the richness of the wood. The temptation to make music was too alluring to resist. I hid myself among the lambs and began to play the pipe, to soothe myself with the magic of its melody, to hope and pray that my fears were unfounded, that Lord Totmael was at least one Irishman with a heart.

CHAPTER SIX
Teller of Tales

The missing knife and pipe were never mentioned. By the time Prince Lochru had given up his efforts to break me by hunger, near the end of the next month, I had the meat from five rabbits dried and hanging high in the branches of a secluded oak tree. There would have been more, but the dogs and I had already enjoyed the meat from the others. Not surprisingly, the daily deposits of food on my altar had ceased.

Allowed for the first time to eat with the slaves, I found the experience repulsive. There were three men, two women, two boys about five and eight, and a little girl I guessed to be three. The ages of the men were hard to determine with their shaggy beards and weathered skin. The mother of the children was possibly twenty-eight, and the younger female, Caitlin, they called her, was close to my age. Prince Lochru had taken special interest in Caitlin on our journey from King Milchu's Rath. At the time she seemed shy and childlike. Now there was a hardness around her mouth, and I pitied her for having suffered a kind of humiliation from Lochru that I would never know. Or would I? My stomach turned. I drove further contemplation from my mind, stepped up to have my plate filled, and took a seat around the fire.

The manners of my companions, I quickly determined, were beneath the dignity of any of the slaves in my father's house, let alone the nobles. The men's language and gestures were coarse and suggestive, reducing the women to the status of whores, with no regard for the presence of children. The older boy had already mastered addressing his mother with vulgarity and contempt. The women's responses were equally lewd. Treated like a leper I ate to myself but within earshot of their insults, which were profuse. As Prince Lochru's fool I shouldn't have expected any better. I couldn't imagine what they had to talk about before I arrived, other than their experiences of carnal gratification.

Slavery had left me too tired, too hungry, too beaten, too isolated, and too devout for sexual appetites to trouble me. But now, the presence of ladies and the unbridled discussion of their pleasurable attributes gave rise to a misery that could not morally be relieved. Thankfully the opportunity would hardly present itself, as long as I was shunned by those I was now forced to acknowledge as peers.

I tossed down the last bite, determined to quickly end the ordeal, when I was arrested by a tug at my elbow. The little girl standing beside me had long tangled hair and big innocent eyes. Though she was dirty, there was evidence her mother had tried to keep her clean.

"What's your name?" she asked quizzically.

"Sucat, what's yours?"

"Ciara," she responded, climbing without reservation into my lap. "Do you know any stories, Sucat?"

"Dozens," I answered, glancing at her mother for reproof or approval. Her mother only stared warily. Already thought a fool, I launched zealously into a tale, capturing Ciara and her brother in the web of my words, a web much harder to spin in Gaelic.

"Once upon a time there was an old woman who lived in a bucket. A fairy passing near heard the woman sighing, 'It's a shame and a shame and a very great shame indeed that I live all alone in this bucket. I ought to live in a nice little cottage among other little cottages, with curtains on the windows and people outside all merry and cheerful.'

'Very well,' said the fairy, 'turn round three times and in the morning see what you will see.'

The woman turned round three times, and in the morning there she was in a nice little cottage among other little cottages with pretty lace curtains and people outside all cheerful and merry.

The fairy went north and south, east and west. After a time she thought, 'I will go see how happy the old woman is now.' When she flew near the little cottage, she heard the old woman complaining, ' It is a shame and a shame and a very great shame indeed that I live here with these common people. I ought to be a noble and live in a great house with slaves and servants to do my bidding.'

The fairy was annoyed but said, 'Very well, turn round three times and in the morning see what you will see.' The old woman turned round three times and in the morning there she was in a great house with slaves and servants to do her bidding.

The fairy went north and south, east and west, and after a time thought, 'I wonder how the old woman is getting on?' No sooner had she flown within earshot of the great house than she heard the old woman complaining in a very genteel voice, ' It certainly is a shame and a shame and a very great shame indeed that I am only a noble lady. Why, I should be queen.'

The fairy was angry, but said, 'Very well, turn round three times and in the morning see what you will see.' The woman turned round three times and in the morning there she was in the feast hall of the great rath sitting in the queen's seat with a golden crown upon her head.

The fairy went north and south, east and west, and after a time she thought, 'I wonder if the old woman is finally satisfied?' Nearing the feast hall, she heard the old woman. 'It's a shame and a shame and a very great shame indeed that I should only rule this little kingdom, when I might rule the whole world. Why can't I have a kingdom the size I am fit to rule?'

'Very well,' said the fairy, smiling, 'turn round three times and in the morning see what you will see.' So the old woman turned round three times, full of proud thoughts, and in the morning, there she was, back in her little bucket, the largest kingdom she was fit to rule."'

"Another," Ciara squealed with delight. And another I told, surprised that the joy I received from the telling was no less here than at home.

"More!" the children chimed. "Tomorrow," their mother, Meagan, I heard someone say, quickly insisted, "if… Sucat will share another with us."

I wasn't surprised that the adults had enjoyed the tales as much as the children had. Good storytellers are always appreciated, especially in Ireland I was to learn.

I stood, swallowed the last bit of brew in my cup, nodded politely to the ladies, and left their company. One of the men quipped loudly, "Who's he think he is, lord of the island?" The simplest manners of a British noble, even my poor practice of them, had further isolated me from the rest of the slaves, at least the adult slaves.

Children recognize no class distinction, They only know what they like, and all children like good stories. It wasn't but a few days until, not only the slave children were at my knee, but all the freemen's and noble's children as well. Calling to memory all the stories I had known, the Roman myths, the Hebrew tales, the recently gathered Celtic lore, was such a delight. For a week or two I felt as though I wasn't a slave, but back in the courtyard of the Roman school entertaining the little boys, or on the coast at our sea-side villa enchanting the slaves and servants. It was good to laugh and tease and feel like a boy again. My sense of humor returned along with that athletic spirit of competition, which had me practicing the training exercises I remembered from school, racing up and down the mountain, and leaping sheep like hurdles.

Prince Lochru's absence the next few months, due to problems with a warring tribe, and the upcoming celebrations at King Milchu's Rath, couldn't have been better timed.

King Milchu had a foster child, a little boy of five named Gosacht, the son of King Madden from the north. Such fosterlings insured peace and good will between the clans. Prince Gosacht was bright and energetic, full of information and questions. He became a regular at story time. "Sucat," he called one evening shortly before Samhain, as he raced across the green. "Sucat, come. King Milchu wants to hear the silly story."

"Silly story?" I puzzled as he pulled me by the arm.

"The one you told last evening."

King Milchu was seated at his table in the small hall he kept at the settlement. Several other nobles were sharing his hospitality. Lord Comnach, a skilled horseman and warrior, and Lord Totmael were among them. Judging from the enthusiasm of Prince Gosacht's introduction, I might have been a famous dignitary. King Milchu smiled, motioned Gosacht to his seat, then commanded, "Amuse me, boy."

I swallowed nervously then, pretending that I was telling for the children rather than the king, I began.

"A young noble, desiring marriage, went to court a maiden. He found her with her father and mother weeping in the cellar. 'Why do you weep?' he asked.

'Look up,' she moaned, 'at the beam over our heads. Do you not see the axe stuck there? Suppose we are married and have a fine son, and he should be sent to this cellar for ale. Suppose the axe should fall and kill him? Could anything be worse than that?'

'Could anything be sillier than you, young woman? Why not remove the axe now and save those silly tears?' He reached up and removed the axe. Having second thoughts about the marriage, he said, 'Until I can find three people even sillier than you, I'll not be back to marry.'

He rode away. At day's end he found a kindly old man to share a fire with. In the morning the old man tied his trousers between twin oak trees, stepped back several paces, and sprang forward, trying to leap into his trousers. The young noble watched in amazement then finally suggested, 'Why not put your trousers on one leg at a time, as I do?'

'Why, I never thought of that,' remarked the astonished old man

'That's one,' thought the noble, and off he rode. It wasn't long before he happened upon an old woman straining every muscle to shove a cow onto her roof.

'Old mother, what is it you're doing?'

"Haven't you eyes, young man? Can you not see how tall the grass is growing on my roof and how my cow could be the better for eating it?'

"Why not cut the grass and throw it down to the cow?' he queried, but she had tired of the conversation and resumed heaving with all her might the uncooperative cow.

'That's two,' he thought.

By nightfall he had come to the outskirts of a small settlement, but the people were not in their beds as one might suppose. They stood around a small pond and with brooms, rakes, shovels, and sticks skimmed the water's surface.

'Good people,' he called, 'what is it you are doing?'

'Have you no good sense? See for yourself. The moon has fallen out of the sky and landed herein our pool. If we don't get it out, everyone who drinks from this pond is sure to go mad.'

'Could it be that you are mad already? Lift up your heads, for the moon remains in the sky. It's only the reflection you are seeing.'

But the people had heard nothing after, 'Could it be that you are mad already?' and took their shovels, rakes, brooms, and sticks after the young noble; who owed his narrow escape to the fine horse he was riding. 'That's three,' he sighed. Realizing that to the wise all men appear foolish, he returned with new patience to the silly maiden, who he happily married. And if I'm not wrong, they're married still."

Somewhere during the tale I had lost my nervousness and spun that yarn as was fit for any king to hear. I was pleased with the telling; pleased with all the good-humored smiles it had generated.

"Do you know other stories?" King Milchu asked.

"Oh, he knows hundreds and hundreds, The old Woman and the Fairy, The Proud King, The Fox and the Crow, Noah and the Great Curraugh, David and... " King Milchu held up his hand to silence Prince Gosacht.

"I won't have all your talents wasted on sheep and children. Every evening after we return from the Samhain Festival, if you are not otherwise employed, you will entertain at my table. Pick a longer tale next time, something violent or erotic, a tale of heroes, gods, lovers. Now you may go."

"Yes, King Milchu," I responded agreeably. Yet I was confused by the sudden cloud over Lord Totmael's expression.

King Milchu, Prince Gosacht, and most of the other nobles and clansmen left for King Milchu's Rath to celebrate the Festival of Samhain. Lord Totmael, though encouraged by King Milchu to appoint another overseer and join them, insisted on remaining at the settlement. I was glad he did.

Two of the slaves in our settlement, Adomnan and Ceolfrid, were disturbingly lazy and would have slighted their work without Totmael's oversight. Another, Comgan, was earnest, but simple-minded, and would have been a catastrophe without just the right instruction. And Meagan, feeling as she did that we were all beneath her, would have been content to serve up hog food for our meals. My concern was purely personal. It was my back that would feel the lash if any disaster occurred. Perhaps I should clarify that I was not the only slave to be treated miserably. The others were beaten when caught in their errors. Perhaps some felt the lash more frequently than I did, but never for another man's mistakes or because of another man's vicious lies. Lord Totmael wouldn't stand for it. He might have taken up for me, had the prince not always sided with my accusers.

My life, however, seemed to be turning around. Because of Prince Gosacht's affection and King Milchu's obvious appreciation, the other clansmen stopped despising me, at least as long as Prince Lochru was absent. The irritating pranks and false accusations ceased. The entire winter season passed without Lord Totmael laying the lash to me, though he still remained gruff and aloof.

Determined to put my energy to better use than playing the bard or filid, Lord Totmael frequently set me at a number of tasks well into the evenings and made excuses to King Milchu regarding my absence. I enjoyed those challenges. The cold of winter limited the boring hours of tending the sheep, so I learned the requirements of forging tools, building turf and wattle huts, making and repairing tables and chairs, and whatever else Totmael felt inspired to teach. I crafted some wooden pieces and game boards for two of my favorite games as well.

Long hours and constant activity helped keep my mind off the unending cold. The warm villas, warm beds, and warm clothes, which I had enjoyed without a thought in Britannia, I would have given all my food for a month to have now. Even so, the cold didn't prevent me from rising before dawn in rain, wind, sleet, and snow to pray. It wasn't such a sacrifice, meeting as I was with my only friend.

Prince Lochru would return to the settlement only briefly, then depart for King Milchu's Rath again. King Milchu and Prince Gosacht spent much of the winter at the rath as well. And so the winter passed.

Spring arrived and though the sheep could now be pastured for long hours on the mountain, Lord Totmael also put me to work with the horses and chariots every evening. The urge to feel the wind in my face just once more was beyond my power to resist. I might claim that I was checking the balance of the wheels or the alignment of the tongue or thrace. I put the horses in harness. Grossly underestimating my self-control I raced recklessly, but skillfully, from one end of the valley to the other. It was glorious! The horses were magnificent!

Driving back toward the chariot house I could see Lord Totmael, lash in hand. My lies were no good now. Checking the tongue or wheels does not require racing like the wind. As thrilling as the ride had been, I was now full of dread.

"Cool down those horses!" Lord Totmael shouted. I nodded and gradually pulled the animals down to a trot, a slow trot, a fast walk, then I slowly walked them around the chariot house two more times before pulling up beside Lord Totmael. Normal coloring had returned to his face, but he still scowled threateningly. "What did you mean to do, Holy Boy? Escape?" he barked.

"No! Lord Totmael. I meant to have fun," I answered honestly, "and I was wrong." I stepped unsteadily from the chariot, unharnessed the horses, and stabled them, then returned the chariot to its housing. All the while Lord Totmael stood fuming. Finished with my task I stood before him. Usually when I faced punishment, there was a sense of indignation at my unjust treatment that made me bold. But I deserved to be punished this time. (Not that the lash is ever deserved.) Lord Totmael's angry silence was unnerving. Well rehearsed for this role, I slowly untied my belt and began removing my tunic.

"Holy Boy!" Lord Totmael snapped so unexpectedly that I jumped. "Harness the horses. I'll teach you to drive like an Irishman!"

The next two weeks were the most pleasantly exciting weeks I spent in slavery and the most exasperating. The sun seemed to take forever to cross the sky each day, while I herded the sheep. But once they were secure in the sheepfold, I darted off to the horses, missing every evening meal to lengthen my lessons.

Lord Totmael's language was crude, vulgar, abusive and loud as he shouted instructions at me and screamed obscenities at my failures. He even hit me over the head with a horsewhip a time or two, but I didn't let any of that dissuade me from learning, nor rob me of the joy of the ride. By the middle of the second week Lord Totmael would race against me, crowing like a rooster every time he won.

Standing on the thrace of the chariot while driving, as the Irish did, provided much better control and the possibility for greater speed, but it was extremely dangerous. I determined to focus on skill and let the speed take care of itself. By the end of the week it was Sucat who did the crowing, or would have, had he not been a slave. Lord Totmael only grunted, but a time or two a smile briefly swept his face, when he thought I couldn't see.

I missed my father and my grandfather so much. Why couldn't this man be just a little kind? He was always a puzzle, a painful puzzle. Sadly, the lessons stopped when Prince Lochru and King Milchu returned, and Lord Totmael avoided me once again.

The other slaves never quite treated me with equity, but by the middle of spring their insults did give way to acceptance. I was teased but not ridiculed for my good manners, and I learned to accept their coarse behavior with as much charity. As welcome as this new cordiality was, it presented me with a new conflict, Caitlin. She was far less beautiful than Scothie, and lacked the sweet innocence of either Scothie or Audrey, but she was pretty and pleasant enough, slender, yet well developed. Prince Lochru had, for the most part, lost interest in her. Two male companions had returned with him from King Milchu's Rath, more like parasites than friends. Their company occupied most of his time. He did still take Caitlin on occasion, but rarely.

At first I thought it was my stories that attracted her to me. I knew what it was that I was attracted to. I spent hours in prayer trying to convince myself, and God, that a slave couldn't expect to remain sexually moral. What choice, after all, did Caitlin have?

"Will you add to her abuse and father another bastard? This one born to slavery? Can you bear the grief this pleasure will spawn?" the voice of Wisdom surely, but I equally doubted that I could bear for long the turmoil my denial had already generated. The manner of these slaves was not subtle, and Caitlin's infatuation with me was no secret. It was expected that I would bed her.

"What's the matter, little prince, don't know how to please a woman?" Ceolfrid teased, as I stood to have my plate filled one afternoon.

"Maybe our Holy Boy hasn't got what it takes." Meagan suggested.

"Naw, I've seen him hard as an old oak poking right through those fancy clothes," Adomnan chortled. "Look here, didn't I tell you? Hard as an old oak."

Their kindly intentioned good humor was impossible to take without obvious embarrassment. "Excuse me," I managed to say, as I took my food and left the circle.

"You've made him uncomfortable," Caitlin scolded.

"It's you that makes him uncomfortable, little miss. Why don't you try relieving his discomfort?" Comgan chortled. The slave circle broke into riotous laughter, which I could hear long after I had left their sight.

Caitlin sought me out. "They're horrible," she volunteered. I nodded and nervously ate a few bites. She sat beside me. "It's all right. I wasn't always a slave either."

She surprised me. It hadn't occurred to me that other slaves might have had former lives, like I had. Slaves were just slaves. I thought I was the exception.

"My father is a freeman in Ui Drona to the south," she continued. "We came to trade at one of the celebrations at King Milchu's Rath. Prince Lochru took a fancy to me, his eyes always seeing what my garments should have hidden. He frightened me. But marriage to a prince would have pleased my father. Marriage was not Prince Lochru's intention. He claimed his most valuable ring was missing and had everyone searched. The ring was found with my brother's belongings. Sucat, my brother is not a thief. Rather than allow my brother to be mutilated, I was given in slavery to Prince Lochru." Caitlin tried to hide a tear by quickly looking away.

"I'm sorry, Caitlin."

"We all have our sad stories," she chirped, trying to sound casual. "I just wanted you to know that, if you felt I was beneath you, just a slave girl, I used to be something more. Not as noble as you, a British prince, but not as low as a slave or servant either."

"Who told you I was a British prince?"

"Prince Lochru. He hates you, because you're better than he is. He knows it, and King Milchu knows it. He thought he could prove his father wrong, make you into a cringing coward like he is, but you're…"

"Shhhh, Caitlin, be careful." I stopped her lips with a kiss. My scalp tingled as her fingers ran through my hair. Her firm breasts pressed hard against my chest inviting me to take her, an invitation I was anxious to accept. Suddenly the hair stood up on the back of my neck and a shiver coursed down my spine. Glancing away from Caitlin's tender mouth, my eyes met the searing glare from Prince Lochru's. He and his companions moved on, but his scheming eyes made me sufficiently wary. I held Caitlin close. Just embracing another human being was a comfort, and her body felt so warm and tender against mine. Reluctantly, most reluctantly, I released her. "You're not beneath me, Caitlin. You're so fine, that I don't want to use you like Lochru does," I only half lied. "But if you keep pressing yourself against me, I'll most likely forget what I really want and take what's offered."

The hardness around her mouth dissolved. She giggled in the same silly way common to most girls her age, a slight irritation to me. But to see her be a child again was a delight. "Finish your supper," I teased, tossing her bread to her.

She caught it, laughing, "I will, if you will tell me about Prince Sucat, and explain why you talk to yourself or a god or whoever so much."

"First, I'm not a prince and..."

"I don't believe you."

"All right, now I'm a prince and a liar."

Caitlin laughed so merrily that I had to laugh, too. "Did the fairy think this old bucket the biggest kingdom you were fit to rule, Lord Sucat?" Her words rang truer than she intended, but I received them in jest.

"Have you been ruining your mind listening to the mad ravings of a storyteller? Storyteller, liar, prince, ah Caitlin, you've fallen in with a sorry lot."

"Don't forget Holy Boy," Caitlin added.

Loud laughter rolled from the heart of me. "Am I really as peculiar as all that?"

"Yes," Caitlin giggled, "even more so."

We laughed, talked, and teased for over an hour, planting memories I would enjoy far longer than the immediate pleasure I had denied myself. I had made my first friend in Ireland. Still, her friendship only made me more uncomfortable in her presence, not less.

Late that evening Prince Lochru took Caitlin to his bed again. She was late for breakfast. When I saw the bruises she had tried unsuccessfully to hide, I found myself unable to eat. I immediately herded the sheep to the high ground and remained on the mountain until well after sunset, avoiding them all. This I did every day for a week, hoping my absence would cool Prince Lochru's jealousy and my lust. But long, lonely days on the mountain afforded me endless opportunities to entertain intimate fantasies. Had fantasies been sufficient to satisfy my sexual appetites, perhaps they could have been justified. But anyone who travels this road becomes only that much more obsessed, until the mind is constantly and insatiably tormented. After a week of fasting I was in a worse state than before. Day and night, waking and sleeping, erotic scenes played on my mind.

One evening, it must have been nearly midnight, Caitlin came to me in my dreams, a misty vision in the diffused light of the full moon. Smelling like spring flowers, her hair, silky and long, flowed over her shoulders and around her young, firm breasts. She was entirely naked. Instantly overcome with physical desire, I longed to pull her body next to mine and feel the satisfaction my fantasies had been unable to provide. But the sadness in her eyes moved me to temper my lust with compassion. I remember turning away from her, trying to force this vision from my mind.

Suddenly every pore of my body tingled with fire, as I felt her slip beneath the blanket beside me. My resistance crumbled. I turned and feasted on the object of my hunger. Her mouth and breasts were sweet in mine, her stomach soft, her thighs firm. I slipped between them; delirious with a pleasure seldom afforded by dreams.

Chillingly cold, the night air swept over my feverish body, as Prince Lochru, laughing hysterically, jerked the blanket from us, exposing and terminating my passionate invasion. I leapt to my feet, naked, confused. Was I asleep or awake? Prince Lochru pulled Caitlin to her feet, pressed her body against his, and teasingly caressed her bare skin.

"She's a good lay, Holy Boy. Too bad you didn't get to find out how good. But I'll be sacking her tonight." Gesturing at the hard evidence of my painful desire, he sneered, "Save that for your sheep."

The sniggers of a half dozen others alerted me for the first time to the publicity of my humiliating exposure. I wanted to crawl into a hole, to hide forever from their leering eyes and degrading insults.

"I'm sorry," Caitlin whispered sadly, as Prince Lochru guided her past me and toward his hut. Hapless girl, to be Lochru's toy, used and humiliated in his effort to strike at me.

By the time I had wrestled through this ordeal in prayer, I accepted that serious decisions had to be made regarding my relationships. Did I wish to enrich the race that kept me in bondage, increasing the slave population and cursing my offspring to a life in Hell? No. Nor did I wish to feel pain or to be responsible for the pain that others, like Caitlin, might know because of me. Obviously any relationship, either filial or intimate, that was dear to me was sure to be severed by Prince Lochru, and in the most painful and public way possible. So, depending heavily on the help of God, I determined to distance myself from the others, to avoid intimacy, for as long as Prince Lochru was my master and slavery was my lot; a difficult choice for a boy of sixteen, but the only wise one.

"I, Patrick, a Sinner..."

Near the end of spring Lord Totmael ordered me to accompany him to the Beltane Festival as his personal slave; a welcome break from my harassment by Prince Lochru and my increasingly awkward relations with the other slaves. I looked forward to an adventure beyond this valley. I was unsure what the responsibilities of a personal slave entailed, but I could count on Lord Totmael to ruthlessly teach me.

CHAPTER SEVEN
The Potter's Clay

Prince Lochru left for King Milchu's Rath several weeks before Beltane to oversee the enlargement of the feast hall and other improvements to the ceremonial grounds. We were to follow later.

Beltane, I discovered, was an enormous event by Irish standards, and King Milchu was hosting the celebration this year for several kingdoms. All that was of minor interest to me. What really mattered was Prince Lochru's absence from the settlement and my reassignment to look after the horses. Lord Totmael prepared himself for the Beltane races by allowing me to challenge him almost daily. My thanks to God was unending.

The excitement, as we rode into King Milchu's Rath the week of Beltane, was contagious. I drove the chariot for King Milchu, while Lord Totmael and Lord Comnach rode the two most magnificent horses in King Milchu's herd.

Games of every kind were being assembled on the ceremonial grounds as we crossed toward the stables. Most were athletic contests, and I yearned to feel the thrill of competition again. The smell of rich meats and sweet breads filled my nostrils. Colorful banners and flags fluttered gloriously. An abstract but skillfully and artistically created sculpture of a man made entirely of wicker, stood just shy of fifteen feet tall and dominated the center of the field.

Totmael's uncharacteristic laughter alarmed me, and I spun my head to see him. He was laughing at me, at my broad silly smile and gaping stares, not a mean spirited laugh but a happy one.

The corral was filled with horses. In all my life I had never seen such an array of beautiful animals. Horse racing, I was told, was the biggest competitive event at Beltane and every other major festival, and all these animals were there to compete. Lord Comnach was to ride in one race and Lord Totmael was to drive in another. My job was to guard King Milchu's horses and chariot, to exercise them daily, and to insure that everything was in good working order. Great! I thought. What better job could I wish for? Were I a free man, I might have volunteered.

I was probably the most conscientious slave at the stables. The others didn't seem to appreciate the privilege they enjoyed, perhaps because it was their usual job, but I relished every moment. I even studied the variety of ways they worked with their animals and the various types of feed used. Most were more than willing to discuss their great skill and knowledge with a beardless boy. By the end of the week my horses were the fittest in the lot, my chariot in the best condition.

Lord Totmael relieved me of my duties one afternoon, so that I might wander among the booths and watch the competitions. I was ordered to learn something useful from anyone who would teach me. Delighted, I started for the green. I watched the competitions first. Most were won with brute strength rather than skill or cunning, but when the two combined the athletes were admirable for their power. I turned to the booths.

The potter attracted my attention. There were plenty of pots, jars, all sizes, exquisitely and colorfully painted with peculiar animals, whose body parts became ropes twisting and twining around and through one another, until it was unclear where one animal began and another ended. The potter was working diligently with a fresh lump of clay.

"Why do you work so hard, when you already have plenty to sell?" I inquired.

"Am I here to answer the questions of a slave, no doubt shirking his work to dawdle in the market?" the potter barked.

"Lord Totmael ordered me to learn something useful," I countered subserviently.

"Totmael? Then work and learn. King Milchu wants a container this large," (he held his hands about knee high) "and decorated with racing horses. Making such a pot would be easy if I hadn't run out of good clay, but this dirty clod I dug is barely workable. You're to take it from the water, pound it, knead it, then wash it. Do this again and again."

"Yes, sir." I took the lump of slimy, cold clay from the water and began to pound it. Muddy water splattered me from head to foot. The potter laughed then took another lump, covered it with a towel, and pounded so brutally, that I imagined the clay would turn to water and disappear in streams down the table legs. He tossed me a towel, and I imitated his actions.

"Why do we wash the clay?"

"To remove the dirt," the potter answered shortly.

"Why do we pound it?"

"To drive out the dirt still hidden within before we wash it again," he patiently remarked.

"And kneading...?"

"...removes the air that will leave holes in the pot when it is fired. To make a vessel fit for a king we have to drive out everything but the very best in each lump, shape it skillfully, fire it long and hot, then add the fine lines and colors of the images he desires to see."

We both worked hard for several hours. Finally the potter put the clay on his wheel and began spinning and shaping, cutting and carving, until I could see vaguely the shape that it was to become. I shared the joy of that creation. It would be impossible for an artist not to love, at least a little, any object that he created, I thought.

"You've seen enough. Return to Lord Totmael and give him this for his kindness in sharing your labor." The potter handed me a small but finely painted jar and lid.

Lord Totmael frowned angrily when I approached. I had been gone for a good while. But after inquiring about my activities his scowl faded. The jar convinced him that my time had been profitable rather than a waste. He grunted approvingly and left me to my work.

That evening, as every evening at Beltane, there was feasting and drinking and fighting, followed by unbridled copulation by those not too affected with drink to master it. The debauchery was not limited to the nobility, but ran rampant across every segment of society. Walking from the lot to the well of latrine required skillful navigation around the inebriated couples in their pleasurable recreation. I ought to have been grieved at seeing men become little more than animals, but I confess I was amused, until the depravity reached a depth I hadn't imagined possible.

The kings had all been drinking but none were drunk, when, en masse, they approached a corral, a large crowd at their heels. King Milchu stepped into the corral along with Lord Totmael and two brehons (judges) from another clan. King Milchu carefully looked over the horses and selected a fine, spirited mare. Stripping off his colorful kingly robes, King Milchu powerfully gripped the mare's haunches and leapt onto her, his hard muscles glistening in the evening light. The enthusiastic crowd cheered vigorously. The mare kicked over the mounting box, but King Milchu rode her securely between his muscular legs, brutally lunging in rhythm with the mare's agitated dancing, until the king's violent tremors signaled a successful insemination. The brehons raised their arms. The crowd cheered. King Milchu released his vice-like grip, dropped to the ground, and swiftly rolled out from under the mare's flaying hooves. Naked, bruised, and dirty he looked less like a king than any of the slaves present. The embarrassment I felt for him didn't diminish my revulsion at his perversity or my disgust at the similar behavior of the others.

One by one the kings entered the corral, reenacting King Milchu's performance, each time with a different mare. They endured injury after injury, but never gave up, until all had satisfied the rite and were judged fit to reign another year.

Swiftly moving through the crowd, I reached an open space and, bending well over to avoid the splatter, vomited. The rapacious glances that I received from two noblemen illuminated the folly of imagining any of this to be amusing, especially for those who were unwilling participants, human and animal alike. I quickly lost myself in the crowd.

The next morning I woke early as usual, but not to pray. I had been far too engrossed in the festivities to entertain any but the fleeting thoughts of God. This was the day of the races, the one competition I was determined not to miss. After lightly exercising the horses, I rubbed them down, brushed their coats, manes, and tails, and fed them a light breakfast. A slave girl distributed my morning meal. I attempted to eat, but my excitement made more than a few bites impossible.

"Should a man eat like a bird?" a voice barked.

"Only if he wishes to fly," I quipped merrily without thinking. Lifting my eyes, the sight of King Milchu with Lord Totmael startled me. I leapt to my feet and dropped my head.

"So, you wish to fly, Holy Boy?" Lord Totmael began gruffly. "You will get your chance."

Lord Totmael informed me of the row at the feast hall that night. Lord Comnach had been insulted, as someone invariably was, at the portion of meat he was allotted. The more celebrated the warrior, the better the cut of meat. A contest had ensued to establish just who deserved what, and Lord Comnach had lost his hand in the fighting. Some nights men lost their lives, and over meat! Without a champion King Milchu's clan would forfeit the race, and a poor rider would bring humiliating dishonor. King Milchu had seen me ride against Lord Totmael. Now he wanted me to ride for him. A win would be preferable, but at least, if I didn't place, it wouldn't bring dishonor to a noble. After all, who would expect anything but mediocrity from a slave? Lord Totmael's irritation at this arrangement was impossible to comprehend.

I was dressed in the king's colors and led to the course. All the joy and energy of athletic competition surged through me as I mounted the finest of King Milchu's steeds, not an overly large horse, but quick and agile. His tawny coat rippled in the stiff wind, and his brown mane whipped, as he tossed his narrow head.

The other riders barely gave me a glance, but I studied them. They all looked to be formidable opponents. Still, the athlete only wins who keeps his eyes on the goal. I maneuvered my mount into position in the line-up and focused totally on the course.

I saw the arrow fly, then nothing except my horse and the track before us. The smell of fresh-turned earth and horse lather filled my nostrils. Cool wind burned my face and whipped my hair. The rhythmic thunder of hoof-beats resounded in my ears. The manes of my competitors' mounts came into view, as they attempted successfully to overtake us. Hot blood raced through my veins at the insistence of a pounding heart. Beneath me the power and energy in my steed flowed through his muscles and into mine. Lather flew from the neck and withers of the horse just ahead, as we methodically closed ground and overtook him. The finish in sight, and without a cue from me, King Milchu's steed burst forward in an all out run, overtaking our only remaining rival just four feet before the finish. The spectators cheered and banged their spears against their shields. We soared past. I have seldom felt more completely alive. Not only did I ride, I won! The only beardless boy in the contest.

Still exhilarated, I carefully cooled my mount, trotting then walking her around the course. Lord Totmael met me on the track and ordered me to dismount. I leapt from the horse's back. Totmael gripped my forearm with one hand and pounded my back affectionately with the other. "Well done, Holy Boy! Well done! Now come, let us do as well in the chariot race." Lord Totmael gave the reins to another slave, who led my tawny champion to a well-deserved rub down and a treat of barley, while Totmael and I hurried to the chariot. Lord Totmael drove. I applied the whip. We came in second by a nose. In the King's box Milchu beamed with pride and received enthusiastically the congratulations of those around him. My satisfaction, no, I admit it was pride, was even greater. I was better than the lot of them, I mused.

The tingling sensation I always felt when danger lurked, alerted me to Prince Lochru's dagger-like eyes, glancing furiously from his father to me. This was the first I had seen of him at the festival and the end of two weeks of peace.

"Why do you stand here grinning like a prince?" Lord Totmael barked, his eyes moving from Prince Lochru's to mine. "Have you no work to do?"

He had been so full of praise before. Was it because we had only come in second? King Milchu seemed to be satisfied. With a heavy heart I returned to my duties at the stable.

A bardic competition followed the races. Riding high on the crest of his success and feeling generous, King Milchu commanded that I be appropriately dressed and attend the bardic. "His attire is already appropriate for a slave," Lord Totmael insisted hotly. King Milchu dismissed him with a glare. I was ordered to bathe. The humility of slavery slipped away with my old clothes, as I donned both the arrogance and the colorful tunic of a noble.

It was the first time I had seen the inside of the feast hall. Well polished swords, shields, spears and battle-axes adorned the walls along with the ghastly, shriveled heads of their most notorious victims. The nobles and their ladies added color in their artistically painted and embroidered garments of fine wool, linen, and silk. Golden torques, finely beaten and cut, resembled sparkling lace collars around the necks of the richest women, a contrast to the solid gold torques worn by the men.

The loud, low thump of a staff struck against the wooden table top signaled the noisy crowd to silence. The first competitor was announced and the stories began.

"Long ago, so the ancients tell us, King Connor's sister, Dichtre, was wed to the powerful Setanta of the Knights of the Red Branch," the filid began. "Such a celebration has never been nor ever will be again. But the joy was short lived. That very night the beautiful bride was snatched away by none other that that mischievous god, Lugh the Longhand. It was a year before she was found again nursing a wee son at her breast. But was her child the son of a knight or the son of a god? Or possibly he was both as we shall see.

"Dichtre's mind was forever fragile from living so long among the gods, so she determined to raise her son far from the Rath of Connor, in the quiet, lonely countryside. Some say Lugh teased her there, tempting her to return with him to the Otherworld. Her body refused, but her mind slipped over a little more every day, until at last only the body remained.

"Her son, Cuchulain as he came to be called, left in search of his father, intent upon joining the Knights of the Red Branch. When he approached the Rath of Connor the sons of all the nobles were wrestling roughly on the green. Cuchulain challenged the champion. Instead of answering his challenge, all the lads fell on him at once. This ignoble and unjust treatment filled Cuchulain with rage, transforming him miraculously into a savage beast of a boy with the power of ten strong men.

"Flung bruised and bleeding onto the grass, the boys began crying for their fathers to save them. King Connor and Setanta hurried to the green. They recognized the lad, who, in his rage was attacking friend and foe alike. A harper and ten naked virgins were quickly called to fill his eyes and ears with beauty and bring calm to his raging soul. That they did.

"From that day forward, whenever there was danger in any corner of Connor's kingdom, Cuchulain, the champion of Connachta, was the man to set it right, often single-handedly, driving his glorious chariot, his charmed spear, the Gae Bulgae, in his hand. But that's another story altogether."

So ended the filid to the loud cheers and applause of everyone present, myself among them. Hearing the master bards and filids weave their fantastic and remarkable tales caused every other concern I had to evaporate. I marveled at their artistry in substance and in telling. Every word and gesture I committed to memory.

There were other tales of Cuchulain, telling how he came to be called Hulain's Hound, how gloriously he beat the army of Queen Mauve and King Allil, and how tragically and heroically he died. Tales of giant fairy folk, pesky little people, great heroes, beautiful heroines, and evil villains filled the hall alternately with the ring of laughter or the sighs of sorrow.

Tales of Macha and her three persons as goddess of war, prosperity, and fertility were heard with superstitious awe, and her ill-omened appearances as a raven soberly attested to. Equally compelling were tales of a kinder goddess, Brigit, who also bore three faces and three functions, healing, crafts, and poetry. She was a real favorite among the bards.

"Holy Boy! On your feet! Your king commands you play the filid," Lord Totmael barked with sarcastic irritation. I looked quickly toward King Milchu, who was full of Irish brew and smiling like a proud child with a new toy. He nodded. I stood uneasily before these masters, feeling more the fool for having to compete in a language not native to me. A short story would have to suffice. I would tell a fable.

"A kindly man, though none too wise, was trudging home along the forest road when he spied a snake, beautiful for color, frozen with the cold. Moved with pity he carried it underneath his cloak and hurried to his hut. As soon as a warm fire had been kindled, he lay the snake beside it. He watched eagerly as the snake began to wiggle once, twice, three times. The old man stretched out his arm to place another stick on the fire, when the snake bolted up, sinking its poisonous fangs deep into the old man's wrist.

"'Why?' asked the dying man, 'am I not the good man who spared you from a frozen death?'

"'Indeed, Good Man,' hissed the ungrateful serpent, 'and am I not a snake?'"

For a moment the hall was silent. Sudden applause and approving nods and laughter from all the gifted bards delighted me and eased King Milchu's confused frown. Only two remained stoic, even hostile, Lord Totmael and Prince Lochru.

When the awards for the week's competitions were presented, I didn't expect to place in the bardic. But I did look forward to the race winners being announced. I was jolted out of my arrogance. Slaves don't win awards.

"King Milchu is a wise man to own such a noble horse, but Prince Lochru is even wiser to have such a profitable slave," the brehon announced. Prince Lochru bowed graciously, a grimace where a smile should have been. Prince Lochru was presented a banner and a beautiful saddle. Beaming with a superior air, he moved toward me and threw his arm around my shoulder in pretended affection. "To the slave prince!" King Milchu shouted merrily. "To the slave prince," everyone obediently imitated as they lifted their cups. Prince Lochru smiled broadly and squeezed my shoulders like a proud big brother then walked me toward the door. Quickly glancing around the hall I located Lord Totmael, watching but aloof.

"Come, I have something special for you," Lochru crooned enticingly. Outside the hall Prince Lochru's two parasites joined us as we crossed the green, all of them reeking of too much drink. Whatever it was, if it was mischief they had in mind, I could easily outmaneuver them, I thought. We entered a hut. Lochru instantly slammed his fist into the pit of my stomach. The leeches joined in the sport, knocking me to my knees.

"What am I guilty of?" I demanded.

""Impersonating a noble," Lochru jeered snidely.

"I am a noble!" I shouted defiantly. I jerked one villain to the ground and throttled the other. Cold, biting metal pressed against my throat. Lochru's knife! I should have remembered.

"A noble?" Lochru mocked. "You presume to be my equal?"

"I would never stoop that low!"

The blade bit into my skin.

"Wait! Your father, the king, would…" one of his companions cautioned. Lochru's eyes flashed from blue to an icy gray. "Strip him! Strip off those noble colors!" he raged removing the knife.

"King Milchu commanded I wear these clothes!" I protested as the parasites stripped the colorful garments away, leaving only my aristocratic arrogance.

"And *I* command that my inheritance and my father's affections will not be usurped be a wretched slave," Lochru seethed.

"I've taken nothing from you!"

"No? Father finds you amusing. You like amusing kings? I'll be king one day. Perhaps you can amuse me."

His statement brought peels of laughter from the miscreants hanging on either side of me. Lochru drained his mug and began critically appraising me from head to toe, smiling thinly. I took care to mask my apprehension. A calculating shadow crossed Lochru's face. He stroked my back with the flat of his knife blade. "All those lashings and no stripes?" he mused. "How odd. Had I been wielding the lash a permanent maze of interesting knot-work would have transformed this flesh into a work of art."

"A monument to your maleficent skill," one of the men chortled.

"An even more interesting design might be carved with that knife," the other suggested.

"Yes, that would be amusing." Lochru hissed, his gray eyes gleaming. "Even a slave should have *something* decorative to wear." The three sniggered grimly as Lochru scraped his knife against a whetstone.

"You are mad!" I anxiously whispered then bolted for the door. Yanking me by the hair, Prince Lochru breathed into my ear, "Mad? No, I'm not mad. But you may be soon enough."

They slammed my chest against the door post. I screamed as the point of Lochru's knife penetrated my flesh. "Shut him up! Gag him!" Lochru demanded. Obediently his depraved henchmen stuffed and tied my mouth with the trouser leg I should have been wearing and haphazardly lashed my wrists to the post.

Like the fangs of a viper the blade bit again, then slowly began slicing a shallow, circular pattern. "God!" my heart screamed out with every torturous twist of the blade. But it was hate, not God, I chose to embrace. By imperceptible increments I began working the laces.

"Dagda's balls!" Lochru exclaimed shortly. "How can I see to carve with all this blood?" The drunkards roared with laughter. One poured the dregs from his mug over my lacerated shoulder. I gasped, nearly sucking the gag down my throat. "You fool!" Lochru grumbled, "you've soiled my knife!" His words fell on deaf ears as the culprit slumped in a stupor to the floor. Prince Lochru sighed in annoyance, his speech beginning to slur as he took another drink. "This is impossible. What do you think? If the blade were fired, white hot, would there be any blood?" There was no answer from either of his nearly comatose companions. "And you?" he queried, jerking the gag from my mouth.

He was too muddled to see the murder in my eyes or to notice how nearly untangled my restraints had become. "Ah, well," he sighed. He tossed the knife on the table and refilled his mug. "You don't seem to enjoy amusing princes."

Lochru began aimlessly wandering about the hut, drinking heavily, and blithely spewing his narrative. "Do you think I'll make a good king?" I didn't answer. "Milchu doesn't," he continued. "He says you would make a better king than I ...only when he's drunk, of course. You! A slave! Even that slut, Caitlin, would rather bed you than a real prince." His sudden laughter grated against every nerve. "But she won't be worth having once I've used her up and tossed her to the dogs. Woof! Woof!" he barked, patting my head. He thrust his taunting eyes and thin lips scarcely an inch from mine. "Shall I tell you how amusing she can be?" Smugly and tediously he recounted all the bestial and demeaning abuses he had forced Caitlin to suffer, perversely excited by his own monstrous recollections. My murderous passion doubled as I wept for her. "Oh, don't be sad," he slurred patronizingly, his hot, pungent breath brushing my face. "She's just another whore." My heart pounded with fury.

Lochru drained his mug and tossed it on the table where the bloody blade waited. He blotted the blood from my shoulder and gently ran his hands over my back, like a scribe smoothing his sheepskin. My fingers worked the remaining knot frantically. Lochru pressed closer. Only one twisted lace remained. "Caitlin bores me now," Lochru whispered, his hot breath on my neck. A shiver ran up my spine. "At the moment I have a more exotic whore in mind..." He pressed his lips to my ear. His fingers *touched* me. "...a British prince."

Jerking free, I spun around, knocking Lochru against the table. He lunged for the knife. The victory was mine. The cold blade in hand, I threw my knee against his chest; my arm poised to slit his wicked throat from ear to ear. He was right. I *was* mad, mad with rage, committed to kill that bastard and rid the world of his evil.

"Holy Boy!" a voice barked. I froze, trembling with hate. Lord Totmael stepped carefully through the doorway, alarming the demon within me but not disarming him. Totmael scanned the scene. "By all the gods of Ireland!" he swore. His troubled eyes met mine. "You... you weren't born to this, Holy Boy. You have a right to your hate. But if you murder the prince... I will have to kill you. What good can come of this?" He slowly turned and stepped out of the hut.

Good? "All things work together for good to those who love God..." The words from my little book of verses pierced my memory like knives. I looked into Lochru's face. His eyes were wild with fear. If I let him live, what possible good could come from his depravity and my being stripped of everything human? But to kill him, to commit murder? Had I become his equal? Had I sunk that low? My eyes clouded with tears, and my body jerked convulsively, almost like one in the throws of death.

"Why, God?" I demanded, "What good?" That simple, bitter prayer caused the demon to shudder. Still, hate was overpowering. I couldn't drop the knife. With every second it moved tremulously nearer Lochru's throat. "Totmael!" I shouted weakly, "Help me."

Lord Totmael reentered. Reaching over my shoulder he took my trembling hand in his. Steadily he forced my arm to bend and relax. The knife fell to my feet. Prince Lochru slid, unconscious, to the floor. Lord Totmael, supporting my weak limbs, collected my clothes and led me out of the hut and away from the rath to a clear spring.

I bathed and bathed. The lacerations stung. The bruises ached. And every thought of Lochru made my stomach turn. Floods of hot tears warmed the water. I imagined I was running and running, forever running, devoid of any thought. It took several efforts to do something as simple as belting my tunic. My mind wouldn't stay focused. My limbs trembled. My book of verses was gone! Lord Totmael watched in silence.

"Say something, damn it! I'm going mad!" I yelled through my tears.

"Do you imagine you are the only slave to suffer his masters depravities?" Lord Totmael scolded sternly. "Be thankful you were not born a woman."

"I would be more thankful," I barely managed to whisper, "if I hadn't been born at all." My eyes lost their focus. Dullness numbed my mind. I drew my knees up to my chest and began aimlessly rocking forward and back, the rhythm recalling a warm, safe memory from long, long ago.

"Pray, Holy Boy!" Lord Totmael commanded sharply, placing a firm hand on my shoulder.

"I can't," I mumbled like one in a fog, rocking against his hand. "I tried... wanted ...to murder a man. Still wish he were dead. How can I pray now? How can I ever pray again?"

"He needed killing," Lord Totmael gently asserted. "No shame in that. This time you will pray in Gaelic so I can understand." He handed me the little book of verses.

Grandfather's book! The touch of reality startled me awake as if from a dream. Faith flowed from its pages and into my soul. I lifted my eyes toward Heaven.

"Father... Father God," I prayed through my tears, "I know I've failed again. I know it. It was King Milchu's favor I sought this week, not yours. Now fear and hate consume me. Father, if you love me, forgive me and let me die now in the peace of Christ before I fail again. How can I live? Can I be free of hate and fear, when I'm to be treated so shamefully and hurt so badly? Poor Caitlin, how does she bear it? Help her, Father, won't you? God I don't want to suffer, not like that, anything else. What good can come of this, Father? What good?"

With my mind's eye I immediately saw the blood from Christ's nail-pierced hands spilling into and mingling with mine, identifying me with his suffering and washing away all my shame. Whatever my body suffered, whatever Caitlin had been made to endure, I was assured that no shame could mar the soul made clean by Christ.

Then I saw those same hands pounding, kneading, washing, caressing, and shaping a raw, dirty lump of living clay into a beautiful work of art. That was the good! Lochru wouldn't break me, nor would God promise to deliver me. As with Christ, God would share my sufferings and somehow make me all the better for it.

"Is there no other way?" I wept. "None?" A soft, heavy blanket of love, God's own Spirit, wrapped around me. I can't say all anxiety flew, but for the moment there was calm. God was with me. In solemn resignation I whispered, "Then stay close to me, Father, and keep me close to you."

Looking up from my prayers, the pale and fearful expression on Lord Totmael's face alarmed me. I couldn't imagine what I had said in prayer that should disturb him. "Your god, your *father*, has spoken to you?" he finally asked. I nodded slowly and wiped the tears from my face. "On your feet, " he barked. "It's time for the burning! Now you will see how we honor our gods." I was nearly too exhausted to carry myself, but obediently I followed.

The ceremonial grounds were awash with people. Close to the wicker sculpture were the Druid priests in their white robes with colorfully painted borders. They all wore their distinguishing hairstyle, shaved over their crowns from ear to ear, giving their heads the appearance of being larger than normal. Their dancing and chanting added more pageantry to the exciting week. But I was numb to the festive atmosphere now, as were the three people I noticed within the circle of the dance, their chains barely visible in the torchlight. Lord Totmael, to my utter dismay, led me past all the merry and morbid folk, directly into the king's pavilion.

CHAPTER EIGHT
The Curse Causeless

King Milchu was holding court, resolving a dispute between two nobles over a cow. Seeing us approach Prince Lochru gasped, "There he is! Take him to the Druids!"

"My Lord?" Lord Totmael remarked incredulously.

"He's a threat to the prince, and he will burn!" Lochru shrieked.

Burn? Was this why Lord Totmael had brought me back, to burn?

"My Lord King," Lord Totmael saluted. King Milchu motioned Lord Totmael to silence. He quickly decided the previous case then turned his attention to us. "Prince Lochru, your Grievance!" King Milchu demanded.

"He tried to kill me!" Prince Lochru declared pointing a long finger at me. Turning to Lord Totmael he continued, "You were there. You didn't even try to stop him."

"Does that seem likely? I who have served and protected your father these many years?" Lord Totmael countered. "How much had you been drinking, My Lord?"

"No more than anyone else."

"Was *anyone else* present?"

"Yes."

"What did *anyone else* see?"

"They were sleeping."

"From too much drink?"

"How would I know?"

"Yes, My Lord, how would you?" Lord Totmael turned to King Milchu. "Is it possible, My Lord King, that this slave, who we know to be a powerful athlete, would have been unable to take Prince Lochru's life, had he wished to? Especially in light of Prince Lochru's drunkenness. Why is Prince Lochru not dead?"

"You make me out to be a fool," Prince Lochru snarled.

"You, Boy," King Milchu inquired worriedly, "Did you wish to take your master's life?" The blood drained from my face. My tongue became thick and dry. I couldn't speak; didn't know what to say if I could.

"What slave doesn't wish his master dead from time to time?" Lord Totmael humorously volunteered. King Milchu ignored him.

"Well?" King Milchu impatiently intoned.

"I... I," I swallowed hard then blurted, "God forgive me, but I hate him." I wiped the irritating tears from my eyes. King Milchu frowned darkly. He glanced around at the guests from many kingdoms who hung on every word.

"Your god may forgive you, but this court does not. Any breach of the peace during Beltane is punishable by death. It is appropriate that we prefer the word of the prince over the life of a slave. However, as Prince Lochru's perception may have been impaired, and as this boy has proven to be a valuable slave, we will be satisfied with public flagellation, severe enough to strike fear into the heart of any slave so ill disposed to his master's good health."

"Good King," Totmael suggested under his breath, "If it were a crime to hate Prince Lochru, half your kingdom..."

"SILENCE! I have passed judgement. Lord Totmael, you will personally see to his punishment. You, *personally*." King Milchu insisted.

"He's not well, My Lord. Might..."

"He has the strength to support his hate. Let him use it instead to endure the lash," King Milchu quipped irritably. Lochru sneered.

Lord Totmael growled between clenched teeth, "You little fool!" He jerked me roughly by the arm to the punishment yard. He stripped the shirt from me, then slowly and gently ran his powerful hands over my marred back. "I should have let him kill the bastard," he whispered angrily to no one. Lacing my wrists he ordered, "Pluck up your courage, lad. You can bear this." As his eyes met mine they mirrored the fear I felt in my own heart. Lord Totmael frowned and swallowed hard. "I won't have you dying of a faint heart, nor giving in to madness. You hear me? You've already been through worse than I'll be giving you."

Trying to still the almost convulsive shaking of my body, I clung to the pole, pressing my forehead hard against the leather ties. Lord Totmael wiped his nose and stepped away.

The yard quickly filled with spectators, all murmuring about the slave who had won the race and became so cocky, that he had tried to kill his master. My misery had become just another delightful event of the festival. Prince Lochru made a grand and self-glorifying speech. Slaves distributed sweet breads and filled empty mugs with Irish brew. All the while I trembled in absolute terror. Yet, it wasn't the lash I feared, but a petrifying fear that made the lash unbearable.

At Prince Lochru's signal the lash fell. The first six blows I took with surprising bravery, my groans barely audible above the gasps and exclamations of the onlookers. Lord Totmael skillfully avoided striking my wounds. But he lingered so long, snapping the lash, working it menacingly in his hands, that the anticipation was almost as terrifying as the blows. I wanted to shout, "Just finish it!" I can appreciate now that the crowd would not have been satisfied with a brief demonstration. Time had to be filled with either increased flagellation or Lord Totmael's dramatic posturing. The crowd was pleased with the show he gave them. Prince Lochru was not.

"Give me that lash! I haven't forgotten how to beat a man!" Prince Lochru ordered. He snatched the lash from Lord Totmael and flayed its straps across my back. I screamed and couldn't breathe. Lord Totmael's strokes were powerful, but controlled. Lochru's were rash, irregular, and violent, cutting to the bone and laying the flesh open as they ripped across the lacerations on my back. I shook with cold at the shock, yet my back was hot from the blood that flowed. The spectators, captivated by blood lust, watched with expectant eyes and gaping mouths.

"Three... Four... Five....," I counted the blows between my screams.

"He's to be beaten, not executed!" Lord Totmael demanded.

"Eight... Nine...," My knees buckled as I felt myself growing weak.

"You ungrateful bastard! He spared your life! Can't you have as much nobility?" Lord Totmael challenged.

The beating stopped.

"So, I wasn't as drunk as you made out!" Prince Lochru seethed. "You would have let him kill me."

"By all the gods of Ireland!" Lord Totmael swore as the lash cut into me again.

"Silence! You treasonous dog! He's mine, and he'll pay for his threat to the prince!"

"Eleven... Twelve... Father!... God!... Am I... to be crucified... too?" My strength fled. Only the leather ties held me as I slumped against the pole. My mind mercifully became dull to the pain. "Father stay close. Hold me close, Father," I called in grateful prayer. It suddenly seemed as if my spirit and my body were no longer one. I wasn't being beaten anymore, my body hanging there on the pole was. I hovered somewhere near. I could see all their faces, hear their voices sounding clearly, though far, far away.

"It's accursed you'll be, if you kill that boy!" Lord Totmael threatened as he blocked the next blow.

"What lie is this?"

"Hear him? Listen! He calls his father, Lord of the Otherworld. Where will you hide when he walks the earth next Samhain Eve?"

I could see as if through a mist Prince Lochru's eyes, wild with a terror he refused to admit. "Truly?" he whispered. Totmael nodded. 'Then *I* won't kill him," Lochru sneered. "*You* will." Lifting his voice to the watching crowd Prince Lochru proclaimed grandly, "If this worthless slave can survive three more strokes of the lash, I will spare him." He threw the bloody instrument at Lord Totmael.

Powerful, gruff, tormented Totmael, he didn't want to strike me. But three more blows by anyone else would surely be my end. He didn't know that I was gone already. Somewhere far away someone felt the sharp sting of the lash. It couldn't have been me. I was gently suspended, cushioned, in the dense, warm ecstasy of purest love, happier than I had ever been. Hate was gone. Pain was gone. All I felt was love, for myself, for God, for all of those sad, angry souls below.

The smell of singed hair and the terrifying screams of human victims forced my eyes open briefly. I was back within myself. The wicker man in the center of the ceremonial grounds had come alive. He was ablaze and rocked back and forth, peals of death coming from within. I imagined it was Old Father Molue come to haunt me. Suddenly I was ablaze too, so very hot, my back scorching with the heat, my tongue thick with thirst. Then chills and pain, unbearable pain. "Father!" I cried out. Within I fled, drifting first into blackest darkness, then rising out of myself once again, to the warm, pleasant comfort of love where I longed to remain forever.

"Shhh, I think he's coming around," a voice whispered through the heavy curtain of velvety darkness.

"Did you get any broth into him?"

"Maybe a swallow."

Sudden stabbing pain shot through me. I cried out, the sound of my voice reuniting me with my body's experience and shattering the darkness. Hot searing fever, throbbing pressure behind my dry eyes… oh, my eyes!"

"He's coming around. Call Lord Totmael."

The voice was nearer this time. A gentle hand wiped my feverish face. A cool wet cloth dispelled the heat of my blazing back. Through the narrow slits of my eyelids everything was formless, shapeless color. The velvety darkness once more closed around me. The warm light of love began to break and I rose to meet it.

Rough thumbs abruptly forced my eyes wide open; my head cradled between the large, weathered palms. "Holy Boy, wake up! Stay with us!" a gruff masculine voice commanded. My cheeks felt the smartness of a soft slap. My head hurt, my eyes wouldn't focus.

"Let me go! Please, let me go back," I begged, barely conscious that it was my voice that spoke.

"NO! You won't cross over during my watch! Get up, lad"

I was pulled up to a sitting position. The dullness fled my mind. The cloudiness left my eyes. Reality, along with its pain, came crashing into my consciousness. I was sitting on a cushioned bed in someone's hut. Meagan and Caitlin were there. Lord Totmael's two strong hands held me up by the shoulders. Bitter tears filled my eyes.

"It's been a long way back, Holy Boy, but you're coming out of this, whether you want to or not," Totmael calmly insisted. "Now you're to eat before you sleep again, or I'll come back, hang you up by the thumbs, and pour broth down you till it comes out the other end."

He motioned toward the women. Meagan sat to the left of me and Caitlin to the right, preventing my falling over. Caitlin lifted a mug of broth to my lips and I obediently choked it down, though I had no appetite to speak of. As soon as Lord Totmael was beyond earshot, and speaking as though I were no where present, Meagan clipped, "It's a cruel thing he's doing, snatching this boy from the Otherworld. And for what? More of the same from Lochru? It's the curse he's afraid of, not this boy he cares about."

"Maybe it's Prince Lochru who'll pass over. Then we'll all be free of him," Caitlin mumbled wistfully.

"Watch your mouth, child!" Meagan cautioned.

"Lochru?" I managed to sputter.

"Are you really back with us?" Caitlin breathed excitedly. "You've been out so long, weeks now. I thought sure you'd cross over."

"He may yet if you get him too stirred up," Meagan scolded.

"What's happened to Lochru?" I asked and swallowed another mouthful of broth.

Meagan studied me a moment, then her eyes grew wide and she whispered in superstitious awe. "Prince Lochru got drunk that last night of Beltane on some tainted brew. He danced madly round and round the burning sacrifice, until he fell unconscious among the ashes. In the night the charred bodies of the sacrifice rose up and attacked him, trying to eat his flesh so they could live again, or that's what he claimed.

"It was something terrible that happened. That's certain. He's been out of his head ever since, screaming in terror, scorching with fever, shackled to prevent him from harming himself and us who nurse him."

If he hadn't been ill he would have forbidden Lord Totmael's caring for you," Caitlin added.

"Totmael?" I puzzled.

"It's Lord Totmael who tended your wounds between his other duties. And it's his hut you've been laying in for weeks," Caitlin stated.

"He insists that you never be alone, so Caitlin and I take shifts caring for Prince Lochru and sleeping here with you. The two of you are more that a body ought to have to contend with," Meagan complained irritably.

The room began to move around me; slowly at first, then faster, until the little I had eaten threatened to come up.

"Here now," Meagan quickly ordered, "You've had enough. Lay yourself down and have a good sleep. But don't you cross over, or we'll be answering to Lord Totmael for it."

I gratefully felt the bed come up to meet me and lost myself in sleep.

On the morning of my seventeenth birthday I was finally strong enough to make the long walk up the mountain. Lord Totmael put me back to work, but I was ordered to rest whenever possible; no leaping sheep like hurdles or running footraces with the dogs. And I was instructed to lay bare backed in the sun for short intervals to toughen the tender new skin. Prince Lochru gradually improved as well, so I heard, though I never saw him. My duties were carefully arranged to prevent our paths ever crossing.

Caitlin's belly began to swell in the months that followed. She happily claimed the child was mine. But my incomplete penetration too many months ago was not sufficient to sire a child, and Prince Lochru's several efforts to bait me afterwards had been unsuccessful. Caitlin had to know. But I could scarcely imagine how difficult it would be to carry a child whose father was as detestable as Lochru. So I allowed her her fantasy, befriending her as much as was possible. The other slaves appreciated my indulgence of Caitlin. None were fooled, but all encouraged the masquerade. Of course Prince Lochru boasted of his virility, but he had nothing further to do with Caitlin.

The birthing was to be torturous. I would have been relieved to herd the sheep up the mountain and leave the ordeal to Meagan, but Caitlin begged so desperately for me to stay with her that Lord Totmael consented. For hours Caitlin lay in torment; sometimes trying hard to be brave; sometimes crying for her mother; and towards the end, screaming in agony.

She delivered on the Eve of Samhain. The child was born dead. Caitlin was inconsolable. Finally I suggested, "He's not gone, Caitlin, just crossed over. Our little son will never suffer slavery." As Caitlin's eyes met mine, her absolute faith in the words I spoke was clearly evident and somewhat unsettling, but I was glad for her to find peace in them. Caitlin laid her head against my chest and cried herself to sleep. I couldn't help but cry with her.

Prince Lochru became irrationally agitated over the stillbirth. As soon as the days of her bleeding were passed he had Caitlin sold to another clan. There was nothing I could do but pray.

The evening following Caitlin's departure, Meagan, Adomnan, and the others at the slave circle were laughing like conspirators of a well-executed plot. My grief over Caitlin's treatment made their good humor grossly irritating. "Look at his long face," Meagan urged. "Shall we tell him, or leave him to pine away?" the others said nothing but stared up at me with such sparkle in their eyes, that my curiosity was quickly becoming more of an irritation than their good humor.

"Out with it!" I ordered.

"Yes, your Holy Lordship, Prince Sucat," Meagan mocked. "Who was it Prince Lochru sold Caitlin to? Do you know?" I shook my head. "The fool," she whispered. "He didn't remember, or possibly he never knew, that she was from Ui Drona. He sold her into freedom, right back into her father's clan!"

The circle roared with the laughter that burst from every throat, mine the loudest of all. And in my heart I thanked God for answering my prayers and working everything out for Caitlin's good.

"That terrible sickness, then his mare threw her foal, now the bastard he sired is born dead. It's a curse Prince Lochru's under," Meagan professed with self-importance. "Just you mark my words."

That seemed to be the common assumption, as everyone nodded their heads knowingly and guardedly glanced at me. Unfortunately the curse, real or imagined, was believed to be my doing. With every mishap, disaster, accident, or illness that befell Lochru, tongues wagged and eyes darted to and fro, until, gradually, the casual camaraderie I had enjoyed with the other slaves was replaced by cautious avoidance. For the most part I was left to my work and to my only friend, my God.

If a captive survives his first year or two of slavery, successful adaptation to bondage becomes a possibility. By God's grace, I had survived.

The years followed one on the other. The demanding life of a slave remained my lot. I was frequently cold and hungry. But hard work kept me fit and avoiding trouble kept me humble. Periods of comparative contentment became longer (or I became content more easily).

Preferring life at the rath, Prince Lochru was seldom present at the settlement. Whenever he did visit, Lochru completely ignored me except on occasions of extreme drunkenness. Irritating humiliations and undeserved punishments always followed these bouts of intoxication, but these were infrequent and bearable. He never again abused me as he had that Beltane Festival. Nor were any of his perverse threats realized. My existence was almost tolerable. I had begun to believe that my life would never be anything more, until shortly before my twenty-second birthday.

CHAPTER NINE
A Voice in the Night

Idolized memories of the Roman world I had known played upon my imagination, unaware as I was that my sufferings mirrored all too accurately the fate of that world. In only six years Rome had been shaken to its core. In Anno Domini 406 Vandals, Alans, and Suebi had ravaged Gaul. Then they crossed the Pyrenees in 409 to raid and settle in Spain, establishing their own kingdoms in what was once a part of Rome. In Anno Domini 410 the unthinkable happened. Alaric the bold, Visigoth King and warrior, successfully sacked the Eternal City, Rome. Needless to say, General Stilicho never returned to enforce Roman civilization in Britannia, but remained occupied in Italy (until the emperor took his head). Grain by grain the world I had known was eroding away. I know that now, but in the isolation of Irish slavery none of this was known to me. It was just as well.

The predawn sky was black, the distant mountains a dark purple, as I knelt in the remains of a late spring snow. It had been a hard winter, following on the heels of a poor harvest. Hopes of an early planting season were gone, as the snow continued to fall.

I had grown several inches taller and my shoulders had broadened. My face was now host to a wiry beard and mustache. My Roman garments had been replaced by Irish trousers and a loose fitting shirt. Around my shoulders hung a great hooded cape pieced together over the years from rabbit pelts. Fur boots covered my feet.

Clutching my cape closely around me, I scrolled through the little book of verses. There was no moonlight to illuminate the words, but illumination was no longer necessary. Reviewing the verses in my mind, I confessed my failure in living up to them, prayed for grace to overcome my weaknesses, and thanked my Lord for all he had been and was to me.

The response was always the same (if I was humble and sincere). God rewarded me with an outpouring of love and forgiveness that saturated my mind, body, and soul like the joy of too much wine, but much, much more intoxicating, yet enhancing rather than dulling the senses. Not even the intimate and abiding love of a good woman was more profoundly satisfying and pleasurable.

For those who imagine me to be speaking in ignorance, I confess, I did come to experience that kind of love later in my life. Still, my intercourse with God in prayer has remained my ultimate satisfaction and pleasure. Perhaps this is not every man's experience, but God knew I was, and am, a passionate man, whose passions had been all but given up, save one consuming thirst for him. I say this to dispel any erroneous notion that I was a man of powerful discipline, rigorous and sober devotion, or piety. I did not beat myself to perform religious prayers. It was a delight, a joy; otherwise I might not have prayed at all.

The sound of approaching footsteps drew me out of my meditation. I was jealous of these moments of felicity and deeply resented the intrusion. Ignoring the interlopers, I remained in prayer as long as I could.

"On your feet, Holy Boy!" Lord Totmael's gruff bark commanded. I rose. My eyes fell instantly on Lucetmael, Chief Druid of all the North Country. He was leading a procession of Druids and their novices, one of whom was Prince Lochru. Their white robes and shaved heads, appearing and disappearing in the swinging light of the lanterns, gave them a mysterious aura in the predawn darkness.

In becoming a Druid, Lochru had found a respectable escape from his father's expectations. Druids were not typical candidates when the election of a new king was required. Besides, the whole idea of magical abilities, ultimate authority, and instant reverence was bound to appeal to Lochru. And his perverse blood lust could now find justifiable expression, as he offered sacrifices with unprecedented zeal.

Breathing heavily from the rugged climb, Lucetmael slowly approached me. I lowered my head. "I am Chief Druid Lucetmael, Master of Mystics. You will answer my questions," Lucetmael insisted with authority.

"Yes, sir," I answered without looking up.

"This is your holy place?" he began.

"All the earth is holy."

"Do you deceive by intent, or is it simply your nature to do so?"

"Forgive my insolence. This is, for me, a special place of prayer, but any other would serve as well." I watched the painted skirt of his robe as he slowly circled me; his hand as it glided over the altar stones; his feet as they stopped before me.

"The people here tell many fascinating stories about you."

"Your people have a gift for storytelling."

"Still evasive? Would you agree that every good story contains a kernel of truth?" He was baiting me but for what? Not knowing how to safely answer I remained silent.

"People say you died from the lash when a beardless boy. Yet you live. Wild animals freely offer themselves to you for food and clothing. You are never ill, though against all good reason you can be found here, praying, in wind, rain, sleet, and snow; before dawn and after sundown – the hours when men should fear the chance meeting of those crossing over. Can this be natural?"

He paused for several moments before his soft boots resumed treading the circular course. Snakes! There were shakes painted in knot-work on the skirt of his robe. I had never seen a snake in Ireland, not a live one, yet here they were twisting in and out, colorful images on the Druid's robe.

"They say you cast spells on children and simple people with the magic of your tales," he continued. "You take no pleasure with women… or men. Can this be natural?" He lifted my chin with the end of his staff. "By what unnatural magic were you formed? Look at me!" he demanded. I deliberately lifted my eyes to meet his penetrating gaze. Lucetmael nodded slowly. "The humble slave disappears. Who is this man with fire in his eyes? Where is the source of his power?"

"Hiee!" shrieked Lochru as he snatched the little book of verses from my fingers. A gasp escaped my lips. My face must have been a wealth of information to the searching eyes of Lucetmael.

"THIS gives you power! Your talisman," the Chief Druid pronounced.

"I have NO power."

"You cursed the harvest, brought the hard winter and the late spring snow," Lucetmael almost chanted. "You cursed with disaster my novice, Lochru."

"Lochru's a disaster without any help from me," I blurted stupidly.

"You don't deny the other?" Lucetmael glibly asked.

"Of course I deny it. I'm no wizard like you are. Would I be a miserable salve if I had the power to be otherwise?"

"I wonder?" Lucetmael waved the little book in my face. "What are these inscriptions?"

"My grandfather's words," I answered, then correcting myself, "The word of God."

Exclamations burst from the Druid's lips, as they immediately backed away. I stared at Lucetmael who grimaced uneasily. "You admit it?" he whispered cautiously. "Grandson of a god! Then why a slave indeed?"

Dear God in heaven, what had I said? I tried to speak but my tongue stuck to the roof of my mouth.

"He lies!" Lochru snarled with a superior air. "This pathetic slave only pretends to have power."

"You are a fool, Lochru," Lucetmael retorted. "He pretends he does not."

The Druids and their novices withdrew several feet away along with Lord Totmael. Lucetmael and his companions enjoyed an excited discourse. As I had no influence over the outcome of their discussion, I closed my ears to them. I prayed and kept on praying. Surprised by the warmth of the sun as it rose above the horizon, I stood warily to my feet. I was alone. I hadn't even heard their footsteps fade as they left me. I slung my cape over my shoulders and headed for the sheepfold. I had missed breakfast, but that was of no consequence. I had been fasting breakfast for several weeks, compelled to pray for vision in this stagnant existence.

I spent no time puzzling over the morning's events but went straight to my work. The sun lit up the sky, burning off the snow and providing my sheep with the tender shoots of new spring grass to feast upon. It was a crisp, but glorious day.

That evening I returned with the sheep as usual and secured them in the fold. The irritating squalling of an infant born to Lord Comnach several months ago, broke the harmony of the usual settlement noises. I deafened my ears to his crying and made my way to the fire pit where a kettle of stew hung over a moderate fire. The young woman stirring the stew smiled seductively and slowly looked me over. Her slender waist and ample breasts were appraised by me as well. (Every time the look in a woman's eye gives me such an invitation, my eyes absorb what can be seen, my mind imagines what cannot. I would prefer not to do so, but still I do. It isn't so much the looking that I repent of but the lusting.) She offered me a taste of the stew, which I took, and a taste of other delights, which I good-naturedly declined.

"Sucat! A story!" little voices suddenly clamored. Ciara, now nearly eight, and several other children flocked around me and began pulling on my shirt and trousers, shouting their favorite stories. From across the green Prince Gosacht came running along with several freemen's children, all determined not to miss the tale. I tossed the wee ones in the air and fought playfully with the older ones until Prince Gosacht and the others had reached us. Carrying the littlest child on my shoulders and with the others linked up behind me, we snaked our way, like a giant caterpillar, to a large rock which had been named "The Filid's Perch" in honor of all the stories that had been told there, Prince Gosacht's idea. The infant's continued bawling distracted me from my best telling, but the little ones were spellbound anyway.

"'Who are you? And what are you doing in my forest?' Roared the one-eyed giant.

'My name's Finn, and I've come to claim the golden apple tree,' retorted our hero.

'Well, I'm going to slice your head off, skin you like a pig, roast you on that pit and eat you for my dinner!' bellowed the angry giant.

A shrill scream jolted me to my feet. Lord Comnach burst through the doorway of his hut, gripping his infant by the ankles like a sack of turnips. His wife clung to him, screaming incoherently through her tears. Lord Comnach pushed her down and furiously dashed the baby's head against the wall.

Silence! Nothing moved but the splattered blood that trickled slowly down the wall and to the ground. Comnach threw the lifeless child at its mother and shouted with rage, "If you had kept better watch, the fairies would not have stolen my strong, healthy lad and left us their squalling brat. A fine mother you are!" He stormed off.

Cradling the little body against her breasts, the mother sat in the doorway, her eyes glazed, slowly rocking and humming a melancholy lullaby. The usual sounds of life returned to the settlement as everyone resumed their tasks or amusements. The children began, once again, tugging on my shirt, but I hadn't the heart for storytelling now. Gosacht took up the tale instead.

As familiar as the scene had been, the horror of such barbarity never lessened in my mind. In Britannia I knew that patricide was not uncommon when aging bodies imprisoned the elderly in their beds, but I had been too young then to consider the barbarity of my own people. Still, to murder an infant because he cries? It was no mystery that mothers frequently kept their children from their fathers' view until they were nearly grown.

From across the green my eye caught the sight of a woman making her way toward Lord Comnach's hut. She was a stranger, yet she looked familiar. Glancing at the freemen's gathering I saw, not only Prince Lochru and his Druid companions, but King Milchu. Their combined presence should have meant an evening of additional labor for me. Why had Lord Totmael not assigned extra duties tonight? King Milchu was sure to call for a story and music. Prince Lochru would be furious with jealousy and drink too much, then I... I sighed heavily and searched the other faces. The freemen and nobles were all known to me, but one. I couldn't be sure at this distance and after so many years, but he looked like the pirate captain himself, Sinell. Another swift appraisal of the woman confirmed my suspicions. It was Liddy.

Without a word, Liddy sat beside the grieving mother and, unconcerned with the blood and gore, placed her arm around the woman's shoulders. Together they rocked and quietly sang the baby to his rest.

"Holy Boy!" Lord Totmael's voice boomed across the green, "We'll hear a story!"

Obediently I made my way to the gathering of freemen, anticipating a long and difficult night, but determined at least to enjoy the music and storytelling while it lasted. I bowed respectfully to King Milchu, Prince Lochru, and the other nobles. Each man greeted me with such enthusiasm, that I might have been a peer rather than a slave. The women smiled sweetly, but that was not unusual. I was offered a seat and a mug of brew and asked to tell King Milchu's favorite tales. I was almost speechless with bewilderment at their uncharacteristic charity, but a swallow of brew loosened my tongue.

The telling was nearly the best I had ever done; tales of wars and lovers, violence and sex, with a few humorous farces sprinkled among them. I knew the Druids were watching to see by what magic I cast spells, but mystics are difficult to second guess. I didn't even try. I had fun, and so did everyone else in the company.

Prince Gosacht came running across the green and plopped himself on my knee. Prince Lochru laughed and joked openly, without the slightest indication of jealousy. Even Lord Totmael relaxed his stern façade and added his hearty laughter to the festive mood. I had never in six years seen him drink so much. Peculiarly, he drank, not like a man enjoying himself, but like a one trying to forget.

Liddy joined the circle, seating herself at Sinell's feet. The joy I felt when she came near is hard to describe. N, it was love I felt, and hope. Liddy made a difference in this world, even as a slave. Perhaps my life might count for something, too.

The pipes, cymbals, bodhrans, and bones came out, filling the air instantly with jigs and hornpipes, reels and airs. It was a night of dancing, singing, drinking, lovemaking, a classic Irish celebration, and the most fun I had had in Ireland for as long as I could remember. By early morning I welcomed the stillness of the starlit night; such a contrast to all that lively music and activity.

Prince Gosacht had fallen asleep in my lap long before the music stopped. Now I wrapped him in his cape and laid him beside the fire. Liddy, having loved her pirate captain into an exhausted sleep, walked over and sat beside me. She and I were the only revelers I knew to be awake and still sober. Lord Totmael's eyes stared into the embers of the dwindling fire, but he was motionless. How he had imbibed so much and still remained conscious was a mystery to me. I added several pieces of wood to the fire and stirred the embers to flame, then stared into the coals as I addressed Liddy.

"You rescued a girl from the Picts six years ago; a beautiful girl. And what you did was beautiful."

"I do what I can," Liddy remarked matter-of-factly.

"And that poor woman today... You're an inspiration, Liddy. I'll never forget you."

"Apparently I've forgotten you."

"There wasn't much to remember, a cowardly boy, full of vain pretensions. It was Scothie who was unforgettable."

"Scothie?' Liddy's face lit up with recognition. "Sinell's whipping boy! Son, you were no coward. Too spirited for a slave. Sinell respected you; wouldn't allow Lochru to break you. He said a noble Roman would prefer a hero's death to a life in slavery. That's why you were sold for the Beltane sacrifice. How did you manage not to burn?"

Beltane? Those Druids... then Lochru... The night had been too pleasant to ruin it with thoughts of fiery executions.

"Does Sinell have business with King Milchu?" I asked, trying to change the subject.

"Another raid. Only one ship this time," she answered.

"Whatever happened to her?"

"Scothie?" Liddy bent over to read my face. "You're still in love with her." She paused thoughtfully for a moment. "You'll be pleased. Sinell sold her as a British princess for a bride's price. Old Lord Gowan of Leinster wed her. She has been a good wife to him, and he worships her. Now she's a noble lady."

I *was* pleased. So pleased that I hugged Liddy like I hadn't hugged any woman in nearly six years. "Hey, there," Liddy cautioned, recoiling slightly from my embrace. "You're too fine a man to be throwing yourself at me. I might lose my head and forget I'm a good Christian woman and a pirate's whore." Her laughter was musical. "Any chance you'll lose yours?" she teased in mock hopefulness.

The merriest laughter I had ever known rolled out of me. "I do love you, Liddy," I chuckled, as I kissed her quickly on the cheek and turned back to the fire. Losing my head with a woman as handsome as Liddy was a possibility more immediate than she supposed. "Is there something in the air?" I asked playfully, sniffing like a hound. "Everyone was in such good spirits tonight."

Liddy became immediately sober. "The Druids prophesied that our troubles are at an end."

"I'm greatly relieved," I teased. "To what do we attribute this miracle of deliverance?"

Liddy frowned at my mockery. "They claim they have the powerful son of a god, whose sorcery is responsible for the bad harvest and the late winter. At Beltane, when he has burned for his crimes, his ashes sprinkled on the land will enrich the harvest four fold; his spirit in the air will insure temperate weather. Their abominable human sacrifices parade in the guise of justice."

After hours of merriment it was a bitter word to hear. My stomach churned. Now I understood the unprecedented charity of the nobles. I glanced at Lord Totmael. The gravity of his expression seemed to mirror mine. He struggled to his feet and unsteadily approached me. He said nothing, but thrust the little book of verses before my face. I couldn't believe he meant for me to take it, my "talisman". He nodded as I lifted my eyes to his. Immediately I clutched my treasure to my chest and stood to thank my peculiar friend, who still claimed to be no friend at all. He wore no mask now. All the grief that was in his heart was evident in the pools of his eyes. He placed his large hands on either side of my face and read my eyes, as if for the last time.

I love you, you old barbarian, I thought and thought hard, and I forgive all your harsh treatment of me. Lord Totmael leaned his forehead against mine, patted my face, then staggered off. I slowly sat beside Liddy.

"These men are all fond of you. You've done well," Liddy remarked.

"It isn't them I serve." Emotion choked my throat making speech difficult. "If they knew my heart..."

"What master knows a slave's heart?" Liddy interrupted, smiling sweetly, a puzzled look in her eyes. "Still, they all spoke kindly of 'Holy Boy' and of how much they will miss him while he's away. Where is it King Milchu sends you?"

"The Druids," I said woodenly. I rose and walked, as if in a dream, to my bed. Wrapping my blanket about me, I fell immediately into a fitful sleep.

"You have been right to fast and pray," a voice whispered in the night. "Soon you will return to your own country." I woke up irritated at the false hope my dream presented. I tried to sleep again. No sooner had I drifted off than the voice returned. "Look, your ship is ready."

I bolted upright. A chill swept over me. Collecting my blanket and walking stick, I started for my place of prayer. As I passed Lord Totmael, he raised up on one elbow, as he always had, and commanded, "Pray, Holy Boy. Pray for us all."

I swiftly crossed the creek and climbed in the darkness the familiar trail to my altar. Kneeling, I asked, almost fearful there would be no response, "What ship, Lord? Where?" Closing my eyes I clearly saw the whole of Ireland, as if it were small enough to fit on the palm of my hand. I was on the mountain near the forest of Voclut. The ship stood two hundred Roman miles to the southeast. Through Connachta to the sea. Two hundred miles! Was it possible? "All things are possible to them that believe." The verse from my little book rang in my memory.

Such was the faith God dropped into my heart, that I had no fear. I crossed the face of the mountain to the hollow tree and retrieved my knife, another pair of boots, two more pipes, and a large pouch. I then climbed the oak where sixteen strips of dried meat hung well above the ground. I collected them all. Water would not be a problem as springs, I had learned, were abundant in most of Ireland, and rain fell almost every day.

I started to look back at the settlement, but thought better of it. Amazingly surefooted in the darkness, I climbed without hesitation for about two hours. As I crested the mountain, the blackness of night had just begun to fade to purple. A new day was about to dawn.

"I, Patrick, a Sinner..."

BOOK TWO

FREEDOM AND FRUSTRATION

"I, Patrick, a Sinner..."

CHAPTER TEN
A Bitter Bargain

Salt! Teasing my nostrils, the faint smell of salt on a damp sea breeze. My footsteps quickened to match the beating of my racing heart. Boulders and shifting gravel flew by almost unnoticed, as I slipped and stumbled toward the crest of the mountain. Just three more bounds and there she was! The beautiful and glorious Irish Sea sparkled far in the distance. I wanted to embrace her like a babe his mother's breast and let her carry me home, gently rocking to the lullaby of surf and sea gull. Three, maybe four, more days at most.

After a brief rest, I began the long climb down, marveling with every step at all I had overcome; fog and forest, boar and bull, marsh and mountain, unseen by hostile clans and not pursued by Milchu's, or pursued too late. More than twenty-five days had passed since my dream had set me on this course. Would there be a ship? There had to be.

When at long last I reached the sea, a small sandy beach provided the massage my tired feet sorely needed. Alternately numb with disbelief, elated beyond words, or overcome with gratitude, I strolled up and down. Beyond the beach, both north and south, the sand gave way to a craggy coastline, far too treacherous for good harbors. My goal was yet to be realized, but it could wait just a bit longer. I stripped naked and plunged into the sea. Every little bit of freedom tasted unimaginably sweet. However, I didn't swim for long. Fugitive or freeman, I was still foreign, and that was all it took to end my freedom or my life in Ireland. The sun and a stiff breeze soon dried the sand and salt, allowing me to don my clothes.

South, there had to be a bay or at least a fair harbor in the south. The rocks along the shore quickly became unmanageable. I retreated to the woods above the coast, where ease of travel and protection from visibility accelerated my efforts appreciably. After a time a tree in the distance, leafless and limbless, caught my eye. Few trees are leafless in midsummer Ireland. Unable to conceal my zeal, I ran toward her and her sister masts, towering above a large curraugh.

"That's my ship!" I shouted to no one. Dropping to my knees I caught my breath and collected my thoughts. It was a pirate ship. It was the only ship. This had to be the one. I steeled my nerves and made for the dock.

The agitated barking of twelve Irish Wolfhounds and the angry obscenities from their handlers created such a din, that no one heard my footsteps on the dock, or even noticed as I stepped aboard the ship. The huge, shaggy hounds alternately whipped the pirates with their tails or raised up on two feet and bowled their handlers over. Those pirates not swearing were laughing boisterously. I couldn't help but laugh with them, alerting the first mate to my presence.

"I can help with those dogs, if you're headed for Britannia," I said still laughing. "I promise I'll earn my fare."

He sized me up skeptically, then motioned with his head toward the dogs. There was something familiar about him, or possibly all pirates looked pretty much alike. I carefully approached the handler most inept for his fury and gently embraced his two frantic dogs. The hounds calmed almost immediately and licked my face. One by one the other dogs quieted and nudged me affectionately for a pat on the head or a stroke of the fur. The skill I had gained as master of sheep and sheepdogs now served me well.

I glanced inquiringly at the first mate. He motioned for me to stay put, then approached a large man, bent well over the bow of the ship, who was inspecting for barnacles or damage, I supposed, and was too preoccupied to be distracted by the dogs.

"Captain," the mate yelled over the side, "this fellow who calms the dogs, he'll work for his fare to Britannia. Looks like a runaway."

Without raising up the captain yelled back, "Will he swear by Dagda that he will not betray us? Swear and suck our breasts to seal the oath?"

"No," I yelled in response, "but I will swear by God and Jesus Christ who made heaven and earth."

Visible ripples rolled across his back as the captain raised up and slowly turned. Sinell! Uncertainty, and more than a little fear, dominated my thoughts as our eyes met. Behind his eyes his quick mind seemed to turn over a number of possibilities, as he studied me in silence.

"Get – off – my – ship!" he commanded in penetrating monotone. Like ice against a bare back, the coldness of Sinell's voice sent shivers up my spine. I nodded, stepped back onto the dock, and returned to the shore – every step a prayer. I was discouraged, but I didn't despair. I had come too far. God had said my ship would be waiting. I simply mistook this one for mine. ...Perhaps further down the shore. There was a hut near the edge of the woods, just off the beach. If Liddy were here...

The howling and barking of the dogs resumed, intruding upon my contemplations. I closed my ears to the noise. At first I didn't hear the shouts behind me.

"Hey, you, fellow!" I turned. Sinell's first mate was running toward me. Now I remembered that face, the murderous fiend who had so ruthlessly ripped that infant from its mother's breast and defiled himself in her blood. I shuddered. Six years seemed like yesterday.

"Sinell says we'll take you on trust," he panted, finally reaching me. "Swear by whatever you like."

I was both relieved and fearfully apprehensive as together we raced for the ship, already moving out of its berth, and leapt aboard.

Except for giving some simple instructions to the dog handlers, I initiated no conversation with any member of the crew from the time we left Ireland, determined to call as little attention to myself as possible. I even prayed as unobtrusively and privately as I could, but God had so miraculously delivered me, how could I now refuse to praise him?

The wind was favorable and Sinell a skilled captain. We clipped along at amazing speed. Yet, it was the end of the third day before we landed, and nothing about this coastline looked familiar. After six years much could change, still, an uneasiness settled over me. Mot a tree was in sight, only rocky coasts as far as the eye could see. Sinell sailed us into a protected harbor and we disembarked, leaving just a few hands on board. We climbed the rocks, until, well above the level of the sea, we stared in disbelief at the devastation before us. Black, barren, deforested earth spread out for miles in every direction like an enormous funeral pyre, perhaps the terrible conclusion to a long drought, or a deliberate act of war. The smell of scorched earth and smoke filled our nostrils. Soot clung to our feet.

"Without the cover of forests we can't risk following the coast road," Sinell commanded. "Flynn, you will navigate our course overland."

Sinell drew a rude map with a piece of chalk rock, indicating our current position and our destination. I couldn't see well enough to determine where we were, but this was not Britannia, of that I was certain.

"We should move quickly, cross the open land, and get beyond those small mountains. Afterwards we're sure to find a river, or at least a stream," Sinell directed. "Peasant huts and small villages will keep us supplied until we sell the hounds. Let's go!"

We swiftly made our way over the low mountains only to find more charred desert beyond. One day ran into another as we hurried over hills, through valleys, and along the streams.

Except for an occasional vulture or raven, we saw no other signs of life. The blackened remains of several abandoned peasant huts excited such desperate fury among the pirates, that they began viciously fighting among themselves.

A thunderous crack split the air! Sinell had snapped his whip, then lashed it powerfully across the unruly pirates' backs. He held his whip in his right hand and a long bladed knife in his left. Steel cold eyes in his chiseled face glared murderously at his men.

"I'll kill every man of you if that's how you want to end this excursion," Sinell breathed icily, his voice just above a whisper. The men shook their heads slowly, one by one, then threw themselves down on the bank of the stream. "Fine. What you boys need is some rest and amusement. Holy Boy! Tell "The War of the Brown Bull" and play us a tune."

He couldn't have picked a longer story, from Queen Mauve of the friendly thighs, to Cuchulain, to the curse of the men of Connachta, war, sex, heroes, lovers, tragedy. It was a great tale. About fifteen minutes into the story the men had forgotten their troubles. Two hours later they had settled down, peacefully dreaming of heroes and home.

The men exhibited their discontent less obviously as we traveled on. Every evening they demanded another story to erase their terrible apprehension, and I obliged, mixing tales like David and Goliath and Noah and the Ark with their Irish tales. After two more weeks, our rations long since exhausted, the men were almost too hungry to listen, and I too hungry to tell. Men began falling by the way, too weak to persevere, until only three of us were left to manage the twelve wolfhounds, plus four other seamen and Sinell. The dogs were themselves so emaciated that their value in the market was highly suspect, but at least they offered no resistance to the leads.

At Sinell's signal we dropped limply to the ground for a welcome rest, every man and dog of us – all but Sinell, who turned viciously on Flynn. "Fine navigator! We've seen neither man nor beast for twenty-eight days! How much longer before we starve to death?"

"Is it my fault the land is waste?" snapped Flynn. "Why not eat those dogs?"

"I'd sooner kill you and feed the hounds," Sinell threatened coolly. "They have value."

Flynn frowned uneasily and carefully backed away. Sinell turned his gaze on the dogs; then his eyes met mine. "Had you landed in Britannia instead of Gaul," I quietly challenged, "we would not be so desperate."

Sinell grimaced. With determined and deliberate steps, he slowly approached, planting his feet next to my own. "A slight departure from our agreement," he admitted. "Still, what does it matter? You'll surely die with the rest of us, if not before." That was true enough. I nodded, obviously the wrong response. Sinell's eyes flashed and his voice boomed. "You say your god is great and mighty; why then pray for us! Can't you see we're all starving and not likely to meet another soul for days yet? Or is your god merely a pathetic dream, a foolish slave's fantasy?"

The others began to curse or laugh bitterly. I stood in amazement to face Sinell. Was it possible? Did Liddy's faith stir the tiniest bit in his ruthless breast? My heart was filled with hope, not for the food that I believed without a doubt my God would send (such absolute confidence was in itself a miracle), but hope that this bloody pirate might be turned.

"Then turn in faith with all your heart to the Lord, my God," I challenged. "Nothing is impossible to him, and his resources are abundant. Father God Almighty," I prayed boldly, "you who created all things, send across our path today food in abundance, that these pirates might know that you alone are God."

The wolfhounds unexpectedly leapt to their feet, barking excitedly and straining against their leads. Breaking free, they quickly disappeared over the hill. We all ran in pursuit. As we crested the rise, every pirate shouted deliriously at the sight of the twelve wolfhounds viciously containing an entire herd of wild pigs. Falling on our prey with all the savagery of starving men, we slew the greater number of pigs, fed the hounds, then glanced about for the means to cook the remainder. So focused had we been on the slaughter, that the dense forest standing before us had escaped our notice until now. In short time we had numerous fires blazing, a pig roasting above each one.

Everyone's spirits soared. The pirates thanked me one and all, and I directed them to thank God instead, fearful of receiving any glory that belonged to God. It amused me that the very food, which the Irish considered the finest fare, the food of kings and champions, was God's choice for our provision.

We feasted for two days. Those men who had fallen by the way were recovered, and hearing how God had provided, gave their most sincere thanks to him. Honey was found in the forest adding sweetness to our rich fare. After packing plenty of meat for our journey, we settled down for our last night at camp.

Flynn began carving a large section of thigh and rump, the portion that men fought and died over at major feasts, the champion's portion. So far the men had been more interested in replenishing their bodies than establishing their fame. Watching warily, I prayed that fighting would not ensue tonight. Flynn held the portion high above his head and shouted, "To Dagda!"

"To Dagda!" the others echoed.

Dagda? Grief constricted my throat. Would Dagda usurp the praises belonging to God?

To my absolute revulsion, Flynn proudly presented the champion's portion to me. How could I accept food offered to their god without offending the Lord who had so generously blessed us? How could I not accept without offending them?

"The Lord God Almighty sends us meat, and you praise Dagda?" I asked sadly. A deep frown settled across Flynn's puzzled face. I slowly shook my head, refusing the meat.

Flynn's eyes flashed with fury at the insult. Angry murmurs from the other men echoed his indignation. I retreated to the edge of camp, just outside the firelight, pelted occasionally by a well-aimed bone. I knelt to pray, then wrapped myself in my cloak and fell asleep.

Towards morning a crushing weight fell, immobilizing every part of me. I shall never forget as long as I live. Hardly able to breathe, I cried into the darkness, "Son of God!" Brilliant light burst upon me, the light of the rising sun, cresting the mountain and shining through the trees. The terrible weight immediately fled. I turned to see what the burden might have been. Nothing was there; nothing that I could see. Having no other explanation for the phenomenon, I believe it must have been the devil who restrained me and had to flee at the name of the Lord. The hushed voices of my companions whispered, "Did you hear? Did you see? He even commands the sun. What can we make of this fellow?"

For the next ten days my companions treated me with indifference. We had dry weather and food to eat. The day that saw the end of our supplies also brought the welcome sight of a Roman town. Most of the men remained in the forest, while Flynn, Sinell, the other handlers and I made our way to the marketplace. The hounds had recovered beautifully over the last twelve days, promising an ample reward.

While Sinell made inquires, we waited, hidden in a dark alcove beside the marketplace. In less than an hour Sinell returned with a small, round man and his three servants. They weren't dressed in Roman fashion or Irish or British either, and the language they spoke among themselves was unfamiliar.

The small man frowned. "I'm insulted," he proclaimed in Latin, a language I hadn't heard on anyone's lips but my own for so many years. "Will you presume to sell me broken down beasts, good for nothing but to be slaughtered and eaten? See how their legs bow, their backs sag, their noses are cold and wet with fever. If I weren't a fair man, I'd give you nothing for these hounds. As it is, I will give you something for your trouble, but I lose money in the bargain."

Sinell looked studiedly at the man then turned to me and asked in Latin, "What do you say?"

"I say, the man's a liar. These are fine animals. Their legs are sound; their backs strong; their eyes bright; and a healthy dog's nose is supposed to be cold and wet."

"Pay me the price you agreed to, or you'll be the one with bowed legs and a sagging back, you lying thief," demanded Sinell.

A thin smile pinched the merchant's face. He shrugged his shoulders. "Only business, nothing personal." He carefully deposited a fair amount of Roman coins into Sinell's palm. My services to this bloody pirate now completed, I sighed happily and handed the leads to the merchant's servants. Without warning Flynn seized both my arms in his vice-like grip, pinning them behind me.

"We had a bargain!" I shouted.

Sinell smiled wryly, his face only inches from my own. "That's right, Holy Boy, and I kept the bargain as honorably as any pirate captain would."

Flynn forced me across the square and onto the auction block. The slave trader, a dirty, obese man of questionable origin, began to haggle with Sinell over my worth.

"I'm a freeborn citizen of the Roman Empire. By law you are bound to…" Cut off in mid sentence by the force of Sinell's blow, I fell against Flynn.

"By your looks you are a runaway," the slave trader chided, "and I am too ignorant to know the law. Mind yourself," he continued threateningly, "or I'll have those idle thoughts beaten out of you."

The slave trader's assistant swiftly locked my ankles in leg irons and closed another around my neck. To feel again that cold metal against my skin; collared like and animal; deprived of the freedom I knew to be my right; betrayed by Sinell, the Roman trader, even God! I fought to control the rage and bitterness that boiled within me and poured venomously from my eyes into Sinell's.

Sinell's confident smirk dissolved into a cautious and doubtful frown as my eyes held him. The slave trader hastily thrust the money into Sinell's hand. Still in deep contemplation Sinell walked away, only once looking back.

The humiliation of the auction block was one aspect of slavery I hadn't experienced. The slave trader was appreciably annoyed when the scars on my back were exposed. A difficult slave never brought a premium price, and what else could such brutality indicate? I doubt I brought even as much as he had paid Sinell. The perverse pleasure I derived from that knowledge fended off my despair until nightfall.

It was nearly dark when our overseer, seven other newly purchased slaves and I arrived at a country villa. The shed where we were quartered was hardly large enough to sleep four adults, certainly not eight. The largest men sprawled themselves out on the floor. Arguments ensued, followed by lurid and violent tales of the abuse of men, women, and beasts who had had the miserable misfortune to be at their mercy. It was hard to understand how men who had been victimized themselves could so mercilessly victimize others.

I sat against one wall and rested my head on my knees, despairing my loss of freedom and my forced companionship with these men. Sleep finally overtook me. "Do not despair," that familiar voice spoke clearly in my dreams. "You will only be with them for two months."

Encouraged, I enthusiastically served my new master. Skills I had acquired as a shepherd translated easily to other animals, and within a week my assignment became the care of much of the livestock. Though hope was alive within me, homesickness was almost unbearable. Watching the master in his Roman robes, hearing his fluent Latin, impressed by his noble bearing, I saw my own father in him. Two months drug on like two years.

The sun had just risen one cool morning in late summer. Deafening myself to the loud chorus of snorts coming from the hogs, I carefully filled the trough with slop. As I reached down for another bucket, I felt a hand on my arm. The overseer, whose name I never learned, motioned with his head toward the villa.

"What have I done?" I inquired apprehensively, aware that the punishment yard lay just beyond.

"Lord Claudius wants to see you."

I followed him warily to the villa. He led me to a room, not unlike my father's study. Lord Claudius was seated at the desk and another man, dressed in coarse and simple garments, stood nearby. Lord Claudius shoved a letter across the desk and ordered curtly, "Read that."

Without picking it up, I read, "Augustus, decurion of the Roman Province of Gaul, to the household of Claudius, greetings and…"

"How is it you read Latin?" Lord Claudius interrupted.

"In the provinces of Britannia," I answered carefully, "all sons of Roman decurions and British nobles are educated, Lord Claudius."

"And in Rome *slaves* are often educated as well. If you presume to claim British nobility, how do you account for your slavery in Gaul?" I took a deep breath and opened my mouth to answer, but Claudius cut me off. "Never mind. Brother Iserninus has already explained all that." He glanced briefly at the man beside him. "But this is not just awkward. It's irritating and expensive. A Roman citizen among my slaves!" By now Lord Claudius was on his feet, pacing nervously.

"Not too expensive," volunteered the overseer. "He cost less than the price of two goats, and you got a full sixty days' work out of him."

"That's another thing!" Lord Claudius exclaimed cutting his eyes angrily at the overseer. He pulled a bag of money from his desk and counted out the Roman coins. "Do you swear that you are a Roman?"

My eyes met his. I swallowed hard. "I swear by God Almighty and by our Lord Jesus Christ that I am Patricius Magonus Sucatus, British noble and a citizen of Rome."

Lord Claudius sighed heavily. "Please forgive the disservice." He slid the coins into a small pouch and placed it in my hand. "Freeman's wages for sixty days. You are welcome to share our table tonight. A bath has been drawn and a room prepared for you."

Brother Iserninus handed me a complete set of Roman garments including a mantle and shoes. "Allow me to give you more appropriate clothing."

I could only manage to whisper, "Thanks be to God," before emotion made speech impossible. Brother Iserninus took me by the arm and led me in silence to the bath, where he left me alone to wash away nearly seven years of slavery and to shed so many tears of gratitude.

A slave or servant entered to add heated water to the bath. Then my beard was carefully shaved, my hair was cut, even my fingernails and toenails were cared for. At last I stood before a glass. My face was older, weathered, but the boy could still be seen in the man. I determined to put all those years of slavery behind me, pretend they never happened, leave all the pain, all the humiliations, locked away forever.

Lord Claudius and Brother Iserninus greeted me with surprised exclamations when I joined them long before dinner. "Can this be the same man, Iserninus? Master Patricius, why aren't you celebrating your freedom by indulging in an afternoon nap?"

"Thank you, no," I responded. "I'm anxious to know which is the best route to Britannia and what I must have for the journey."

"Which is the best route, Brother Iserninus?" Lord Claudius queried studying his wall charts.

"By way of the monastery in Lerins," Brother Iserninus suggested. The language was Latin, but his accent? "My brothers there share the same zeal for God that I see in you. Will you come, if only for a short time?"

"Do you know me?"

"As well as a man can be known by listening to his prayers every morning."

"You know Gaelic?" I asked uneasily.

Brother Iserninus laughed. "You look ill, brother," he said in Gaelic, like the native Irishman he was, "but be at peace. Yes, I understood every word. And I have wept with you, rejoiced with you, prayed for you, and admired you. What I have not done is judged you. You seem more than willing to do that yourself."

"Enough chatter in that detestable language. If you can't be civilized and speak in Latin, go elsewhere," Lord Claudius irritably chided. "It's bad enough that I'm forced to learn the grunting, garbled language of the Vandals!"

I had wanted to forget everything Irish, yet... "I would like to know your brothers, Iserninus," I strangely heard, amazed at the sound of my own voice.

CHAPTER ELEVEN
The Brothers of Gaul

Claudius offered a chariot and driver for our journey across Gaul, but Iserninus objected to the extravagance. Without the efficient services of the government of Rome, he explained, travelers were more vulnerable to attack by thieves and hooligans. A fine chariot would certainly attract unwanted attention more readily than a monk and a pilgrim on foot. I was appalled at the casual manner in which Brother Iserninus dismissed Rome as a failed empire. When I pressed him for more information, he admitted neither knowledge nor interest in the affairs of state. The Kingdom of God was his sole concern. Apart from this self-imposed ignorance, I found Brother Iserninus to be a clever man.

Iserninus was slightly younger than I and not nearly as austere as I had first imagined. We were almost the same height, but his frame was smaller and his muscles leaner, making him appear to be of less stature. Green hazel eyes, sandy red hair, and numerous freckles lent him a childlike aura, in spite of the self-inflicted baldness of his tonsure. He was a gentle man, never malicious, never unkind. And if he did unintentionally offend, which only happened after a few too many miles and a few too many drinks, he was quick to accept the fault and humbly beg forgiveness. I suspected he had as much pride as other men, but his determination to imitate Christ was greater than his pride. Like any good Irishman, he had a story for every leg of the journey. He had a quick wit and a delightful sense of humor. The only lack I saw in him was ambition.

At the end of a week of pleasant camaraderie our pace quickened and our good humor brightened at the sight of a sizable village. Since he hadn't volunteered the information, I finally asked, "How did an Irishman become a Christian monk?"

He frowned slightly as we continued to walk briskly down the road. "My parents were convinced by a merchant from Gaul, that I would have a better future if I were educated in Latin. They raised the money and sent me over. I worked for the merchant during the day and studied with the village priest in the evenings. I learned more skillfully than most, so the priest said. But his faith inspired my greatest interest and won my devotion."

"Still, as a Christian you needn't have given up everything and become a monk. I was *forced* to give up everything. Now, after so many years in slavery, I'm anxious to love a woman, to see her belly grow with my child, to gather my children on my knee and tell them all the stories I know, to have my own house, my own bed."

Brother Iserninus smiled sadly. "There was a girl," he began with a sigh, "radiant with faith. But her family forbade her marriage to a savage Irish Scot. A marriage was quickly arranged with a more suitable man, a Greek Roman, with no devotion for God at all. Rather than marry, outside the faith, a man she couldn't love, she accepted her parents' alternative and joined a sisterhood of Christian virgins."

"I'm sorry, Iserninus."

"Before she entered the community..." Iserninus stopped walking and turned to face me. "I might have been more chaste and sent her away, but I wanted to make her mine. She was mine. We have never been together, like that, again. She took her vows of celibacy and I took mine."

"I see," I muttered. We resumed walking together.

"If I never see her again, I will love her as long as I live," he concluded with the air of an heroic martyr. We walked in silence for a quarter of a mile. "In four years you are the only one I've ever confessed this to. Your silence tells me you don't approve."

"Then my silence lies," I quietly responded. "I have enough of my own sins to account for without judging yours."

"Sins?" he exploded stepping in front of me. "You believe that we sinned? That it wasn't love, but lust that I satisfied when she gave herself to me? That I selfishly destroyed her hopes for happiness in the arms of another man by taking her for myself, by not dissuading her from the course she took?"

His posture was so threatening I thought we might come to blows. Where was my gentle friend now?

"Brother Iserninus, I'm not a priest. I can't help you find your way."

"Well you should be!" he shouted angrily. "I mean to have your help, Patricius, to show me clearly where I'm off the mark, to help me find my way back. And don't just tell me to pray," he snapped. "I did pray and God sent you."

The discomfort I felt from his expectations made me long for the solitude of the mountain shepherd. I could imagine nothing so unforgivable as meddling irresponsibly with another man's soul.

"Iserninus, I do have one question. Did you enter the monastery out of love for God, love for your lady, or love for the fantasy of a noble martyr?" His green eyes darkened, and his freckles seemed to dance hotly on his reddened cheeks, but Brother Iserninus controlled his irritation.

"Helen – that's not her real name, but I will call her that for now – Helen and I... The vows we took were the resumption of courses formerly set. When we met we assumed that God had brought us together, that he intended we abandon our former plans and embrace a new one. 'Delight yourself in the Lord, and he will give you the desires of your heart,' the scriptures declare. She was my desire and God gave her to me."

I was dumbfounded. "God's a bit of a scoundrel then," I quipped, "to give her to you and take her away again! Or were you the scoundrel? Did your desires suddenly change, so the Lord had to put her away for your convenience? Or perhaps it wasn't the Lord you were delighting in at all. Perhaps God didn't *give* you the desire of your heart; you merely took her. That's a good verse though. I shall add it to my little book."

"You make me feel foul," Iserninus seethed glaring with wounded eyes into mine. "Why wouldn't God grant me the desires of my heart? I've been devoted to him since I was twelve years old."

"Even so, Iserninus, God doesn't pass out lovers or possessions, like trinkets, to self-righteous sinners who imagine their little devotions have earned them special favors. Recite that verse again."

"Delight yourself in the Lord, and he will give you the desires of your heart," he defensively pronounced.

"Exactly!" I concurred fixing my eyes penetratingly on his. "It is when *God* becomes the desire of your heart, Iserninus; when above all else you are desperate to know *him*, to love *him*. *Then* you are delighting in him. And it is *himself* he gives you. And that is enough."

Iserninus froze, ashen-faced, his hollow eyes unfocused. How fragile a man's faith! Had my unskilled tongue made a wreck of another poor struggling sinner? "I'm sorry. Let's find the church in this village. Speak to the priest, Iserninus. I'm no good to you."

When we had made our way to the church, I left Iserninus making his confession. I knelt at the altar, promising the Lord that I would never again meddle in the affairs of another man's soul.

The next morning we resumed our journey to Lerins. Just before passing through the gates of the walled village, Brother Iserninus turned into a large villa, knocked on the door, and passed a note to the woman who answered. I didn't ask what we were doing, but my curiosity was enormous. After a short time another woman stepped out, said a few hushed words to Brother Iserninus, and pointed to another structure within the courtyard.

I followed Brother Iserninus to the door and waited as he knocked. A woman, about twenty, shorter than average, but filled out and carrying herself with such assurance that she appeared taller, answered the door. Her hair, eyes, eyebrows, and skin tone were all varying shades of the same light brown hue, and left her strikingly colorless. But when her smile broke across her face like sunshine, her eyes twinkled like stars, and her laughter peeled like a thousand little bells stirring echoes of laughter from all those who heard her, then I fell in love with her, too.

"Patrick, this is…"

"The beautiful lady in the fairy tale," I interrupted.

Helen smiled sweetly. "So, he's been boring you with a hundred stories. Leave it to an Irishman," she chuckled. "Will you be staying long? I would like you to see my children."

"Children?" I queried. We entered the small building. There were seven village children of varying ages playing at a table or on the floor. Two were crippled. Another bore the intentional scars of abuse. Three were dim-witted. And one seemed bright enough, but had recently suffered severe starvation or illness.

"Aren't they beautiful?" Helen beamed.

Without a word Brother Iserninus and I took the children in our arms and began telling stories. The house rang with laughter. The love Helen had for Iserninus was as obvious as her love for all those children. But there was no lust or longing in her eyes, no pretense of noble sacrifice, just joy in sharing her work with him. Unlike Iserninus, she was at peace with herself, her God, and her vocation.

We enjoyed the noonday meal with them, then took once more to the road. The village wall was far behind us before Brother Iserninus asked, "What did you think of her?"

"I think everyone who knows that woman must love her. And I have seen few others as happy in their work. Her call to this life was surely genuine."

"And I was the rogue who corrupted her." Iserninus snipped threateningly. "Is that what you're saying?"

"She didn't appear too corrupt to me!" I bristled. "Just what drivel did you waste that priest's time with? You obviously haven't dealt with your problem."

"I confessed to being angry with you!"

"Fine! You want to be angry? You want to hear what I think? Well, I don't care what your sins are! There's nothing you have done that God hasn't forgiven men time and time again. The blood of our Lord Christ wipes the slate clean. But you want to dress up your sin, cherish it, weave it into a beautiful fairy tale, and revere it like a holy sacrament. You can't repent and be forgiven because you won't admit error. Your sins are clean sins; accidentally embraced because of the confusion of scripture; motivated by the purity of love not the carnal satisfaction of lust. But you miss the mark. Your sin, the one you must confess, is not the pleasure you took while your virgin lover suffered her violation. Your sin is pride, and it's tearing you apart, building a terrible wall between you and our Lord who wants so much to love you. God help you, Iserninus, because I can't!"

So much for my pledge never to meddle. We traveled in brisk silence for the remainder of the day. That night Iserninus prayed, not from a formula as he frequently did, but from his heart. And he didn't stop praying until, hours later, his tears had turned into laughter. Even after he had fallen asleep, laughter would roll out of him. Twice he startled himself awake. The next morning Iserninus slept until well after sunrise. When he finally rose, he greeted me with a kiss on each cheek and a warm embrace.

"I would tell you what happened last night, but since you only pretended to sleep it isn't necessary," Iserninus taunted.

"I meant well."

"I'm glad you were my witness. I'm glad God sent you to me. Freedom, that's what I found; freedom from illusion and fantasy; freedom to love without expectations; freedom to fail and try again."

"Freedom from your covenant with the monastery?" I interjected.

"No, but freedom to know and love the Master, who I had previously only served." he warmly declared.

The remainder of our journey was one of the most pleasant times I have ever spent in the company of men. By the time we climbed aboard the boat for the short sail to the island of Lerins, I had grown to love, respect, and appreciate Brother Iserninus more than any man I had ever known, apart from my grandfather, Potitus.

The monastery was a primitive settlement. A number of huts, even smaller than the slave huts in Ireland, were arranged to give each monk the most privacy possible and yet retain a sense of community. One larger structure must have been for dining. In the center stood a small sanctuary.

The atmosphere was strangely serene as Iserninus and I walked toward the chapel. The only sounds to be heard were the songs of surf and sea gull, the padding of our feet against the stones, and the muffled droning of someone reading aloud behind closed doors. It was near the end of the noon hour, and all the brothers were apparently gathered for their meal. Brother Iserninus, cautioning me not to speak, took me silently from dwelling to dwelling, grinning like a small boy displaying a clever model. We lingered in the chapel then made our way to a hut that served as a library.

Manuscripts were everywhere, but nothing out of order. Iserninus became absorbed as his eyes took in first one manuscript and then another. In his great love of scholarship, he reminded me of Amicus. Along one wall were copies of the sacred books of scripture. Hunger had made me slightly impatient with Iserninus' tour of Lerins. Now a new hunger displaced the cravings of my stomach. I lay the little book of verses on the reading table, then carefully removed a copy of the Gospel of John. I began to read, lingering longest on those passages, which contained the verses from my little book.

"Ninus!" A voice exclaimed from the doorway, interrupting our concentration.

"Brother Mathias!" Iserninus responded as he rose from his chair and greeted the older man's cheeks with kisses.

"How long have you been hiding in here?" Brother Mathias queried. A look out the window revealed the long hours, which seemed like only minutes, that had passed during our absorption. "Sir?" Brother Mathias said, calling my attention away from the window. His hand was extended, and I gripped it respectfully. "Brother Ninus seems to draw his nourishment from this library, but after an undoubtedly long trip, you might welcome some refreshment from our kitchen."

"Yes, thank you."

"I would have seen to it that he was fed," Brother Ninus protested.

Brother Mathias laughed, "Yes, Ninus, but men are easier to feed when they're still strong enough to walk to the table."

I liked Brother Mathias immediately. His raspy voice would have been unpleasant to listen to, had it not contained a warmth that delighted my ears. He was not at all a handsome man. His large nose was out of proportion with his face. A thick head of hair might have helped to balance its prominence, but the few gray hairs that circled his head only served to accentuate the obvious. He was about forty-seven, tall, with a waist so small, I marveled that he was able to support his unusually broad chest.

Ten men stood to their feet and immediately fell upon Iserninus with kisses and embraces when we entered the hall.

"Welcome home, Brother!"

"You're back for good?"

"The library hasn't been the same since you left."

"He's been hiding this good man in that library for hours now," Brother Mathias chided. "Exercise your Christian charity and take your places, so we can eat supper before he dies of hunger. Brother Ninus, introduce our guest." Humbled by the gentle rebuke, the men quietly took their places.

With the unmistakable air of a storyteller, Iserninus began, "I first saw this noble Briton slopping hogs for Lord Claudius. The story of his terrible fate and God's miraculous provision unraveled as I heard him at prayer every morn..."

"Iserninus," I interrupted, continuing in the language that only he and I would know, "had I wanted all men to know the contents of my prayers, I would not have spoken them in Gaelic."

Brother Iserninus nodded and began again. "This is my dear friend and brother, Patrick, a man whose tremendous love for our Lord has inspired and transformed me. Was that better?" he asked me privately in Gaelic.

"You might have stopped with 'Patrick'."

"I might have," he quipped.

"We all welcome you, Brother Patrick," Brother Mathias asserted motioning toward a place at the table. "And we are extremely grateful to find a man able to curb Brother Ninus's bent to make every statement an heroic saga. I do insist, however, that you two refrain from speaking privately in a language unknown to us when we are met collectively."

It was our turn to humbly take our seats.

"In our joy at seeing Brother Ninus, we were blind to anyone else," whispered the man on my left. "Forgive us. I am Brother Aurelius. This is Brother Bernicius." The introductions followed all around the table. Then we blessed the food and ate in silence, all except Brother Mathias, who read aloud during the meal.

"Lord, you have broken the chains that bound me... Let me praise you... Let this be the cry of my whole being: Lord, there is none like you... What kind of man am I? What evil have I not done? Or if there is evil that I have not done, what evil is there that I have not spoken? If there is any that I have not spoken, what evil is there that I have not willed to do?

"But you, O Lord, are good... merciful. You saw how deep I was sunk in death, and it was your power that drained dry the well of corruption in the depths of my heart. And all that you asked of me was to deny my own will and accept yours... You who are sweeter than all pleasure... O Lord my God, my Light, my Wealth, and my Salvation..."

"Whose words did we hear?" I asked at the close of the meal.

"The reading was from the <u>Confession</u> of Augustine of Hippo," Brother Mathias announced.

"Augustine?"

"Have you never heard of Bishop Augustine?" Brother Aurelius asked.

"No, or if I have, I've forgotten. But I should like to hear a great deal more. When did he live?"

"Bishop Augustine must be about fifty-five summers now and tough enough, they say, to live until Christ returns," responded Brother Mathias. "Perhaps you will travel to Africa one day and tell him what you find so fascinating in his <u>Confession</u>."

"He captures my own experience with the skill of his words," I quietly mused.

"Then we won't be alarmed if you become a bishop, too," Brother Mathias expressed pleasantly.

"You presume too much of a man you don't know," I suggested.

"You presume too little of the God we all serve. But let us neither accept too little nor expect too much." Brother Mathias rang the bell before him. All the men quietly cleared the table and left to their various occupations. Brother Mathias and Brother Iserninus led me in silence to a vacant cell, where I gladly retired for some much-needed rest.

Monastic life proved to be the perfect bridge from slavery to freedom. Many of our activities were strictly dictated for the service of the community, meal preparation and gardening, for example. Silence was imposed most of the day. Mandatory services of prayer and worship were scheduled at three-hour intervals, day and night, almost exactly the routine I had kept on the mountains of Ireland. Yet every day there were a goodly number of hours allotted for individual pursuits. During these hours I studied outside in the warmth of the sun, or in bad weather, in the library. I made it my goal to read and memorize as much scripture as I could master in a year.

I dared not remain much longer. But every day these brothers became dearer to me, especially Brother Mathias and Brother Iserninus. I can't remember ever having such feelings of ambiguity. Home tugged at my heart till I thought it would burst. Yet, when I determined to go, such grief wrenched my soul that I would delay my leaving another day... another week... another month.

As I looked through the window of my cell that last morning, the murky ocean stretched endlessly beneath a gray sky. Waves gently slapped against the rocky coast of the island. Continuously, a fine mist fell, distorting the sharp lines of the small boat that glided silently over the water. How heavy my heart as I set the monastic garments aside and donned my Roman tunic once again. It was nearly two years since I had sailed from Ireland. Further delay was unforgivable.

All the brothers accompanied me to the dock. Two dozen kisses and a dozen embraces later I placed my feet aboard the boat and watched my island home move away from me. Brother Ninus, as I had come to call him, shouted across the water, "Write to us when you've seen your father."

"I've lost the skill of writing," I yelled back.

"Then write without skill. We could use a laugh and you could use the humility," he teased.

I nodded. We were now too far out for my words to be clearly understood over the surf, even if I had been able to utter them. As the lines of the monastery gradually blurred in the mist, the disquieting certainty that I would never return settled heavily within my heart. I closed my hand over Grandfather's little book and turned my thoughts toward home.

CHAPTER TWELVE
Reunion and Remorse

"Your life will never be resolved until you make the full circle," Brother Mathias had counseled. "For you, monastic life is too comfortable. Even if you felt called to this life, which I know you do not, I would insist you return to your father's house and sort out the purpose of your past and future."

It was Brother Mathias who had rigidly enforced my departure, demanding that I stop hiding in the belly of the whale and discover God's will for my life. I was grateful to him, for I had lost the courage and the will to leave. Now, as my eyes feasted on the coast of Britannia, I marveled that I could have stayed away so long.

This part of my homeland looked like a foreign country to me. There seemed to be fewer people speaking Latin. Roman soldiers were sparse along the wharves, but gave the impression of Rome's continued involvement. It was deceptive but effective. I later learned that these soldiers were deserters who had refused to abandon their British homes and families when Stilicho pulled out. Now British merchants hired them to maintain an image of stability in a rapidly crumbling civilization.

I hired a chariot. The expense was much greater than I had remembered. I realized too late that I had gotten no bargain hiring the cheapest driver. He was the most unsociable, unpleasant, even offensive fellow I have ever encountered either before or after my years in slavery, though not during. My questions, comments, and observations were generally greeted with shrugs or grunts. What vocabulary he did manage was coarse and vulgar. He snored by night, belched by day, and scratched his groin with regularity. On the second evening of our journey he railed against me for my refusal to split the price of a prostitute's services.

"You're so cheap, you think you'll get your jollies free by watching!" he stormed, spewing spittle with every explosive consonant.

"Had I not been cheap, I wouldn't have hired you. And I would much prefer that you take your whore elsewhere. I can think of a great many things more pleasant than watching you, sweating and grunting like a dog with his bitch," I retorted hotly.

He grinned obnoxiously. "Well I guess you'll just have to watch, prayin' man. I won't be out the expense of another room."

The night was clear and the moon shone brilliantly, sufficiently lighting my way to the village church little more than a mile away. How sorely I missed my brothers from Gaul. I fell asleep at my prayers. Almost regrettably my driver located me early the next morning.

"How did you know where to find me?" I asked groggily.

"Where else would a prayin' man go who'd just turned down a good piece of ass? A shame too. No amount of prayin'll make you feel as good as I did last night. She even let me do her twice for the same money. Made me glad you left." At least he had demonstrated that he could put together more than one sentence at a time.

"Come on. We'd best leave the church before lightning strikes," I said, only half joking.

He guffawed crudely and slapped me on the back. "You're all right."

His improved good humor gave rise to almost incessant chatter. He answered all my questions from the previous days, impressing me with how little this man knew about anything but horses, whores, and ale. He knew the best stables, the best brothels, and the best taverns from one side of Britannia to the other. And he had absolutely no use for noble's-sons-turned-holy-men, who took aristocratic pride in their wealth, their title, and their privileged relationship with God.

"Pretending they love God and all his creatures while looking down their long noses at me! Humpf! Most of those men'll split the price, only insisting they have theirs first. Others pretend to be offended, while they watch with hungry eyes breathing heavily, like a man taking matters in his own hand, so to speak. But every now and then there comes a fellow who's a prayin' man from the inside out, not the other way around, if you know what I mean. Then I'm sorry I despise them all so much. Even one man like that in a hundred makes up for all the sorry pretenders. I apologize to you, sir, especially if I offended you in the church this morning. I wasn't sure you were a real one till then."

"I'll accept your apology if you'll accept mine. Sometimes my nose is just as long as any aristocrat's."

Another loud guffaw escaped him. "Maybe, but I gave you plenty of reason to look down yours. You can't look down it too often though, keeping your head bowed so low you look like you was beaten most of the time. What makes you do that?"

"Habit."

"Well, it's a habit a noble ought to let loose of, if you don't mind my presuming to correct my betters."

"Not at all."

His most revolting mannerisms disappeared, though his language remained punctuated with obscenities and spittle still rained whenever he spoke excitedly. A man decidedly immoral, but not evil, whose raw honesty was stimulating enough to win no small measure of admiration from me.

We arrived in Bannaventa Berniae shortly after dark. "What is your name," I asked my colorful companion as I paid for a room at the hostel.

"Well, that's a first," he marveled. "My name's Samson. My mother wanted to name me after a hero from scripture, and my father said, 'He's not going through life wearing the name of some pasty-faced holy man.' So Mother found the story of Samson, and my father liked it well enough. He just told me to stay out of places with pillars," Samson laughed loudly.

"He never warned you about Delilah?" I teased.

"Oh, now don't you get too preachy, holy man. I mean to find me another Delilah tonight, so you best run along to the church or wherever else you were going."

"It's been a real experience knowing you. Samson," I said smiling as I offered him my hand. He said nothing, just took my hand carefully, as though it were fragile, nodded soberly, and left for his room.

Unable to sleep and unwilling to awaken my father's household until morning, I walked the streets of Bannaventa Berniae for most of the night. The moon was not as bright as it had been the night before, but routes once familiar became quickly familiar again.

Coroticus's villa was still magnificent and only slightly smaller than I had remembered. I could imagine the loud laughter and music that rang through the night air when we had feasted together. I passed the village church, amazed at how beautiful it now appeared, when in my memory it had been drab and cold. Some of the stones were still streaked with the ashes from that fire ten years and a lifetime ago. The empty courtyard of the school echoed with my footsteps, recalling memories of dozens of little feet running through it after classes. For a long time I sat on the bench where so often I had told stories, remembering a multitude of things long forgotten until now.

Resuming my wanderings, I was impressed with how little everything had changed, as though I were out of time somehow and my long absence merely a dream. The seedlings in front of Ami's house were now large trees. That helped me to fix on reality in the surreal haze of the moonlight.

Amicus, my dearest friend, what kind of man had he become? What might he look like? What joys amused him now? And Audrey …Dear God! The joy of reminiscing crumbled. How was I to face her? And what of the child nearly ten years old, raised to hate the man who had made a bastard of him or her? Had Coroticus loved Audrey enough to take her to wife in spite of …everything? Could he have permitted her to keep the child another man had sired? Or had she married another, or never married at all? What contempt must Ami and Coroticus and all their families have for me – my own family as well – were they to know? Until now coming home had been a dream I didn't dare to believe. Now I was home and the dream had become a nightmare. But Brother Mathias was right, whatever lay ahead could not be apprehended until I had taken this hurdle.

The remainder of the night I wandered aimlessly, retracing every step I could remember. By dawn I was standing before the villa of Lord Calpornius, my home. I knocked softly on the door, my heart in my throat. No one answered. I knocked again, louder this time. Where could they have gone, I wondered? Had Father died? The family moved away? How was I to find them?

The door flew open, halting additional fruitless speculations. A tall, thin man with a pinched nose and an irritating air of superiority stared at me in silence.

"I would speak with Lord Calpornius," I ventured.

"Your letter of introduction, sir?" he said coolly, holding out his long fingers. I shook my head and he began to withdraw.

"Wait," I breathed excitedly, "My name is my reference, Patricius Magonus Sucatus."

"Another relative," he said, smiling as if his big toe were in a vice and he couldn't admit the pain. He nodded and closed the door.

At least I knew that Father was still alive. I paced like a caged animal, waiting for the door to open again. Judging by the sun an hour had already passed. Should I knock again? Perhaps Father was still sleeping and left orders not to be disturbed. Was I behaving like a peasant calling on him before breakfast?

Suddenly the door opened. Father glanced briefly at me, then looked back inside the house. "Victoricus! Who is this man left waiting in the street?"

He assured me you knew him, Lord Calpornius. I was equally certain you did not and assumed he would tire of waiting.

"Father," I said softly, unable to say more. Calpornius froze, as though his heart had stopped beating. "Father?" He haltingly turned his head until his eyes met mine then collapsed against the door facing. I lunged forward and caught him in my arms. "Get some water! No! Make it wine! I ordered Victoricus who hurried, ashen-faced toward the dining room. Two of our neighbors who had been watching me curiously from their windows ran to assist, as I helped Father into the sitting room and sat him on the couch. Victoricus brought water and wine.

After downing the wine in one long drink, Father carefully felt my face. "You're alive, Sucat? Real flesh and blood?" I nodded slowly. Throwing his arms about my neck, he wept unreservedly for several moments.

Victoricus swiftly escorted the excited neighbors to the door. Within minutes he was back with food and refreshments for all and Mother and Lupait with him. A better reunion I couldn't have imagined. Mother, her hair streaked with silver and so much frailer than I remembered, wept, "My poor, poor boy. How my heart has ached for you," as she continuously stroked or patted my hand. Surprisingly, Father didn't rebuke her tender show of affection or the multitude of her tears. Lupait, now a beautiful woman of eighteen, sat beside me. She giggled like a girl and teased me about the mischief I used to devise.

"Are you still so wicked, Sucat?" she whispered. "You're more handsome now than ever."

"Whether I am or not," I whispered back, "such a pretty angel ought not to be whispering to handsome, wicked men. Be sure you remember that little sister." Lupait blushed innocently. I kissed her on the forehead. "Does Grandfather still live?" I asked worriedly, suddenly aware of his absence.

"He's been ill, Sucat," Father said. "You'll need to see him, but I don't think he could bear the shock that I took."

"Victoricus," I called as I removed the ragged and worn book of verses from my neck. "Put this on his tray when you take Grandfather his breakfast."

"Yes, Lord Sucat, and may I apologize for leaving you in the street this morning?" he asked humbly.

"An apology won't be sufficient..." Father began to rail.

"A man can't be faulted for doing his best," I interrupted, "even if he does so in error. Your apology is accepted, Victoricus." Victoricus nodded and withdrew.

"You're beginning to sound like your grandfather," Father mumbled.

"If I don't get some sleep, I may be feeling like him as well. Is my old room still furnished with a bed?"

Mother stood immediately. "Yes, of course, Sucat. I'll have the servants draw you a bath and Lupait will see that you have everything you need. It's wonderful to have you home again."

It was well after dinner before I awoke, hungry and happy. I quickly donned the clean clothes that had been laid out for me and made for the kitchen. "Master Sucat! You needn't prowl around in the kitchen like a peasant. I'll set you a fine meal in the dining room. You're a real celebrity; a man come back from the dead is what they're saying. Go and prop your feet up. I'll be right along," chattered the head housekeeper.

She was kind and no doubt efficient, but she fell far short of the uncompromising quality of our former housekeeper. Julia... I hadn't thought about her for years. Now I remembered how warmly she had embraced me in the slave hut, whispering in that low velvety voice, "You've picked a hard place to find your heart." I grieved for Julia, Scothie, the little slave boy on the ship, Liddy, and others as I waited for my plate. How unsettling that when I had been in Ireland I had wept over memories from home, and once home I wept over those I had left in Ireland.

"Sucat, you're up!" Lupait exclaimed appearing in the doorway. "Grandfather is extremely annoyed. He keeps asking, "What is this?" and waving that dirty little scroll around.

"Tell the housekeeper to send my supper to Grandfather's room," I said, as I happily left the table.

"All this weeping and whispering is enough to drive a saint to swear! Will somebody please tell me where this came from?" Potitus's voice boomed through the door and into the hallway.

I knocked. Father opened the door. "Thank God you're awake," he sighed pulling me into the room.

"Are you taking God's name in vain? Here in my own room?" Grandfather roared irritably, unable to see beyond Mother who stood between us.

"MY grandfather could tell the difference between a man swearing and one praising God. I must be in the wrong house," I teased.

As his gaze met mine that twinkle that I had inherited lit up his eyes. "Sucat? What miracle is this?"

"One of many, Grandfather."

"You'll not leave my side until I've heard every one." He sat back in bed and hung the little book of verses around his neck. "The rest of you get out of here. I want to know what fruit nearly ten years of calloused knees could bear, and I want to hear it in private."

That night Grandfather and I laughed, cried, sorrowed, and rejoiced, until Grandfather fell asleep in the middle of a prayer just a few hours before dawn. There were things I didn't tell him; things too terrible for anyone but the man who suffered them to bear, and other things my shame made impossible to relate. And he knew, but he didn't pry. I covered him gently and returned to my room.

Just after sunrise I knelt to pray. A sharp gasp from behind propelled me to my feet. Mother slumped against the doorframe. Her shaking hands covered her mouth, and her eyes glistened with tears. "Mother? Is it Grandfather?" I asked hurrying to the door. She gently traced her finger over my scarred shoulder. "Oh, my poor... poor boy," she wept. "What have they done to you?"

I hadn't known a mother's love in so long. Her compassion bathed me with a joy and tenderness not comparable to others I had felt. "Sh, Mother, it's all right," I almost chuckled, holding her in my arms. "I can't see them, unless you force me to see them through your eyes."

A stone flew through the open bedroom window, striking the wall beside the bed. I just missed being pelted by a second as I glanced into the courtyard. "We've come to see the ghost!" The man in the courtyard hollered. He was a large man with a full beard and decked out in elaborate and expensive robes. Another man, more simply dressed and clean-shaven, stood beside him. Ami and Coroticus!

"Just a minute." I yelled back at them, slipping on my shirt. "Mother?"

"Go. Enjoy the day." I kissed her on the cheek, tossed on my tunic, laced my sandals, and raced to meet them.

"Amicus, my dearest friend!" I exclaimed exuberantly as we embraced. "Grandfather tells me that you have become a priest. And you, Coroticus," I continued turning to embrace him, "are you a peacock in your fancy clothes?"

"Don't you know who I am? Does your grandfather speak of nothing but priests?" he retorted playfully.

"When Rome pulled out, Coroticus' father assumed the throne in this province. Coroticus is prince and heir apparent," Ami related respectfully.

"Abandoned by Rome!" I shuddered.

"What could Rome do for us that we can't do better for ourselves?" bristled Coroticus.

"We'll soon see." My lack of enthusiasm obviously irritated Coroticus. "But if we can't have Rome," I cheerfully added, "we'll do well to have Coroticus." I bowed dramatically then slapped him on the back. His smile was somewhat ambiguous.

There was so much I wanted to know about each of them. How hard had rhetorical school been? What had occupied them for all these years? Were they married? Had they children... A cold, painful gnawing gripped the pit of my stomach. Pleasantries would have to wait. "What has become of Audrey after all these years?" I forced myself to ask.

Ami and Coroticus exchanged cautious glances. "We'll have breakfast at the tavern. Come. Let's eat and drink, then we'll tell you of all your old friends," Coroticus commanded. They moved toward the chariot. I couldn't follow. Whatever they had to say, I preferred to hear it in private.

"You know, don't you?" Ami queried as he turned around and read my face.

"Maybe something; not everything."

Coroticus sighed with pompous irritation, as Ami stepped back toward the courtyard and led me to one of the benches. We sat.

"The very night you were taken Audrey was due to return," Ami related sadly. "Her driver brought her to Bannaventa Berniae, but she never made it home. We thought perhaps she had gone with you to the coast and been captured, until we found her... at the foot of the great cliff."

My heart pounded. My breath came in shallow, rapid puffs. "Are you saying...?"

"She must have had a premonition," he interrupted, "a special sense that tragedy was to befall. How else could she have known that you were taken? The note we found next to her heart said she hadn't the courage to face the future without you, Sucat."

His words slammed against me like a wall of stone. I leapt to my feet yelling in anguish with every fiber of my being to avoid being crushed. I must have seemed a madman. "Take me there!" I demanded.

"I thought we'd get drunk or..." Coroticus began.

"Take me there! NOW!" I yelled.

During the long drive Ami and Coroticus made every effort to be lighthearted. I heard their voices but not their words. My own thoughts came in such rapid and confused succession that my head ached from trying to make sense of them. When my feet stood where Audrey's had on the high cliff overlooking the distant Irish Sea, anguish borne fury rose within me. "Why? Why, Audrey?" I railed incriminatingly. "Why couldn't you have waited?"

"What options have you left her?" Julia's voice wafted hauntingly in my memory. In the luminous haze of the distant sea I imagined I saw Audrey, her beautiful eyes full of despair and pleading desperately. She was the poor woman on the ship, dragging her abused body to the stern and plunging hopelessly into the sea. And I was there, standing aloof. I was the murderous villain. Guilt and sorrow compressed me as if in a vise. Great groans shuddered from the depths of my soul and passed my lips. I couldn't begin to pray. I could only wail and weep.

A hand lightly rested on my shoulder. I lifted my head. The sun was now low on the western horizon. For me time had stopped. It surprised me to see it had continued for everyone else.

"Sucat, Coroticus will be back shortly. Let it go. You've grieved enough. You must have loved Audrey more than we knew."

"Loved her? Dear God, if only I had!"

"Don't punish yourself, Sucat. Was it your fault pirates took you and Audrey lost hope?" Ami's compassion, like salt, stung the wound of my guilt.

"No, Ami. Audrey lost hope because..." I stood to face him. "...I'm sorry, Ami, so very sorry."

"I know, Sucat."

"No, you don't! But you've a right to. I've spent six long years in Hell, Ami! In Hell! Punished by God. I came to hate myself for my sins against Audrey, Father Molue, and especially our Lord. I prayed that somehow I could at least make it up to Audrey and to our... Only to find I'm a more contemptible, bloody bastard than I knew, with no hope for redeeming myself."

"Explain."

"Oh, God. Ami, I... Audrey lost hope because I... I pushed her away, called her a whore... and she with my child."

Ami was suddenly ashen-white, all but his eyes which blazed. "I don't believe it! Audrey consented to..."

"No!... no..." I interrupted brokenly, my humiliation almost as unbearable as my guilt. "She didn't consent."

"*YOU BASTARD!*" his voice boomed as tears poured from his eyes. "She was your *friend*! And *my* sister!" Ami backhanded me hard across the cheek." How do you dare to stand before me, to show your face among decent people?" His luminous eyes blazed with hate. My throat constricted. Knotted cramps gripped the pit of my stomach. "When? Where?" Ami demanded. "Where did you violate that sweet girl who adored you so much, she didn't even tell her own brother how vile you were?"

"The church; the night Father Molue died. He came upon us just after... I grabbed Audrey and ran, tripping over the candle stand. His robes caught fire. By the time I heard him scream there was nothing I could do. But... I might have done something for Audrey, given her hope."

"You bloody well might have!" he screamed and began beating me violently with his fists. I didn't fight back. This was one beating I deserved. But the blows didn't relieve my guilt. Justice demanded that my life be forfeit, not hers, not Audrey's, nor the unborn child's. I was the guilty one. Ami, exhausted from striking me, fell to the ground weeping.

Why hadn't I died in the pirate raid or under the lash or in the flames of Beltane? After all these years I was still no better than the lowest of all God's creations. My soul disfigured by the blood of three innocent people; my best friend broken and weeping at my feet; how hopelessly wretched I felt. Audrey's solution tempted me so seductively that I felt my feet moving slowly toward the edge. "God, help me!" I cried, fearful that I might lose control altogether. "What am I to do?" I planted my feet firmly.

Ami stood and turned away. I caught his arm. The murder in his eyes gave way to contempt. I dropped to my knees before him. "Ami, I couldn't possibly feel any greater sorrow for what I've done. God knows this is killing me. I don't ask you to forgive me or even pity me. Hate me if you must. But I beg you, as a priest, Ami, to assure me that it is possible for God to forgive me, to wash their innocent blood from my hands."

A long time passed. With every second I felt more vile and unredeemable. The faint rumble of Coroticus's approaching chariot wheels echoed the labored beating of my heart. Ami stiffly placed his hand on my head. "Of course I forgive you, Sucat," he pronounced without emotion, "even as Christ forgives the repentant sinner." He removed his hand.

"Come on!" Coroticus shouted from his chariot on the road below, "Night's falling!" I rose to my feet.

"Tell this to no one!" Ami demanded abruptly. "Why cheapen Audrey's memory?"

I nodded. "You're a good man, Ami, better than I'll ever be. You go on with Coroticus. I'm not through here."

Ami smartly stepped around me and joined Coroticus, leaving me to my sorrow.

There are sorrows that heal completely, given enough time for grieving, leaving only the greater depth of character that experience brings. Not so this sorrow. Though my long and intense mourning did minimize the crippling effects of grief, obvious scars, like those on my back, would forever mar the fabric of my soul.

CHAPTER THIRTEEN
Three Voices of God

"Sucat, have a seat," Father directed as I entered the room. His study smelled pleasantly of leather and parchment. It was our office now, but I still thought of it as his study. A second desk did little to change the atmosphere. I sat obediently and waited as Father carefully weighed his words.

"It's been nearly a year since you came home and time enough to modify your behavior. Your success in business depends on it." Father stood, walked around to the front of his desk, and tossed a handful of letters before me. "First of all your writing is worse than appalling. Victoricus writes better."

"Yes, sir, I know. I *have* tried…"

"Without success," Father interrupted. "You wrote better than this when you were fourteen. A man who sits on the town council must be able to communicate."

"Is there something more that I can do?" I asked. "For six months I have employed a tutor. I spend hours every week studying to regain what skill I had. I do fail but not from lack of effort, Father, from lack of capacity."

Father frowned doubtfully and sat on his desktop. "Very well. The trauma you've endured was bound to affect you. But there are other behaviors I can no longer tolerate: your infernal prayers every morning and afternoon taking you away from work for an hour at a time. You must appreciate that *I* never take off to pursue my own amusements during the business day. And more than that, explain why every conversation you engage in has to include a reference to God? Such juvenile, irksome, and unprofessional discourse has no place in business. Can't you see how uncomfortable our clients become?"

I slowly rose. "Am I guilty of preaching or lecturing?"

"No, but how many times a day do I hear an elated, 'Thanks be to God!' over someone's good fortune or, 'God bless you in all the good you do,' when they take their leave? And heaven help us all should a client ask anything about what happened in Ireland. Why, you and God were bosom buddies back then!"

I dropped my head, a habit I hadn't yet overcome. "Every man speaks out of his heart, Father. Would you change mine?"

"YES! I... No, I guess not." He ran his fingers distractedly through his hair.

"I am sorry, Father," I interjected solemnly. "I know I'm not the son you thought I was."

"You're right!" he exclaimed standing to his feet. "I don't know you, Sucat. You've been through more perils and adventures in ten years than I have in a lifetime. I admire you; deeply admire you. But you are a strange man. What are you fit for?"

"I... I don't know."

Father released me from my duties until he could find work more suitable to my talents and temperament. Demoralized by failure, I finally accepted Coroticus's challenge to a chariot race. Coroticus enjoyed racing almost as much as the Irish. I trained for three days, then drove my modified chariot to meet Coroticus on his course. The race was set for late afternoon. I arrived shortly after sun up to give my team most of the day to rest and to carefully examine the track. Coroticus arrived well after noon.

"Are you so anxious to lose?" Coroticus teased.

"Anxious for sport of any kind, winning or losing," I responded. "But it's a good thing for one of us that I arrived early. Look what I found." I held up a large, flat, brown rock, almost invisible against the dirt from the track. "There were three dangerous ridges on the course as well that I corrected. Come, walk the track with me. I may have missed a hazard or two."

Coroticus looked genuinely shocked and remained speechless for most of the lap. " These things happen when the track isn't used often. Don't be so appalled," I encouraged.

Convinced that the course was in good order, we set to work harnessing our teams. A few onlookers had gathered adding a little excitement to our friendly game. By the time we were mounted, however, it seemed the entire province had turned out.

"How many laps?" I yelled to Coroticus.

"Three!" he shouted back. "What kind of chariot is that?"

"The kind I drive best," I answered.

"Irish!" he sneered.

We positioned our chariots. Coroticus took the inside lane as I had expected. A flag bearer stepped forward. I planted my feet firmly on the thrace, elated with the surge of energy that pulsed through my veins. The flag dropped. My team bolted forward in perfect rhythm at the crack of my whip. Coroticus held back slightly, remaining at least a yard behind my lead. His horses were powerful but mine were swift. Certainly he was saving his steeds for an all-powerful rush to the finish. As we rounded the first lap something caught my attention moving across the track. I turned but saw nothing.

The break in my concentration gave Coroticus an edge. He surged ahead to the thunderous applause of the bystanders. Laughter rolled out of me. This was competition! I urged my team on until we were abreast of Coroticus. Glancing sideways at him I grinned and bowed my head slightly, then cracked the whip and bolted into the lead. I had raced often enough to know better, yet twice I had taken my eyes off the goal.

There was something ahead, an unevenness on the track. Jerking the leads dangerously to the left, I cut my chariot in front of Coroticus, narrowly avoiding a large stone. That's what I had seen before, someone purposely endangering horses and drivers alike. Had I been driving in Roman style, I could never have cut quickly enough to avoid disaster.

"Out of my way!" Coroticus bellowed, almost unheard above the thunder of the horses. Coroticus's steeds, fleeing the whip, collided with and climbed into the back of my chariot. I fell backwards against his lead horse, caught myself on the rim of the chariot, and barely managed to crack my whip. My horses and chariot lurched forward and out from under the hooves of Coroticus' team.

His stinging whip lashed my shoulder as Coroticus attempted to drive my team outside. The Irish were better sportsmen! I thought bitterly. At the crack of my whip my team flew well ahead of Coroticus and past the finish at the end of the third lap.

I swung into the outside lane and pulled my team down to a trot. Coroticus flew by. The crowd cheered. The flagman signaled his victory one quarter past the agreed upon finish. As my chariot circled the last leg, I stopped to collect two additional large stones and a small branch.

"Sucat, I never knew you to be a quitter," Coroticus taunted.

"I didn't quit until the race was won," I snapped, throwing the collection at his feet. "Before you race again, you had better secure your track. No game is worth risking a man's life or his horses."

"No one dies over a little stone or a stick, not usually."

"This has happened before?"

"Forget it! I won. You owe me a drink," Coroticus boasted.

"*You* won?"

"The race isn't over until the flag goes down," he insisted. "Stop parading your poor sportsmanship and treat me to a drink."

Though totally dissatisfying, the afternoon had certainly been illuminating. Without another word we mounted our chariots and drove to his favorite tavern. The tavern was dark and smelled of sweat, food, and ale. Coroticus led me to a table in an even darker corner of the room. "Sally! Maude!" he barked as we seated ourselves. Two women approached the table with mugs of ale and kegs of wine. Coroticus stood to kiss them both, then pulled Maude onto his lap. The women were both about twenty, of average height and weight. Maude had dark brown hair and sassy blue eyes. Sally was a curly-headed blond with large brown eyes that gave her a false appearance of innocence. Sally moved behind me running her hands across my shoulders, her fingers through my hair.

"My Lord, is this the man in the song?" Sally asked coyly.

Coroticus threw his head back and laughed, "The very same."

Sally slipped her arms around my neck. The impression of her firm breasts against my back spoke so loudly that I almost didn't hear her words. "Is it true you spent three days on the cliffs grieving the death of Audrey?" she whispered.

"What? How would you know that?" I demanded, startled from the enjoyment of lustful contemplations.

"You're famous," Maude retorted. "In every tavern they sing of you."

"More famous than your future king?" Coroticus chided playfully.

"Oh, no, my lord. I'm sure you're fame is *much bigger*," Maude teased seductively.

"What could they sing?" I asked.

Sally slipped onto my lap and sighed with an overly developed penchant for melodrama. "Oh, it's an old, old song about Audrey ending her life rather than live one moment without you. You must be a *rare* man." Her soft sensuous lips met and provoked caresses from my own. "I thought Audrey's brother was a treasure," Sally breathed heavily into my ear, "but you…"

"Besides," laughed Maude, "who wants a priest? hearing about GAWD all day."

I smiled at God's gentle reminder.

"You ladies don't believe in God?" I asked earning a pained scowl from Coroticus.

"I believe in *LOVE*!" Sally orated dramatically.

"Love? Same thing!" I teased playfully.

"Well, I guess I do believe in God," she proclaimed pressing her very fetching curves hard against me, her lips once more touching mine.

"No, pretty lady," I laughed looking merrily into her eyes, "you believe in *lust*. That's something else all together."

Sally's puzzled expression grew serious. She rose to her feet. "Then kiss me like you love me," she softly insisted, "so I'll know the difference."

"But I don't..." Sally stopped my lips with her fingers. Standing before her I worried that this might be the second race today that I would lose. "If I loved you..." I stroked her golden curls but remembered Scothie's auburn tresses. I kissed her forehead, the tip of her nose, then gently folded her in my arms and released through my lips the passion I'd reserved for so long; love that still burned for Scothie; desire that made me ache to take a wife. Sally's supple body seemed to melt into mine. I broke off the kiss, trembling as I held her close. Sally laid her head against my chest.

"You, sir, are a man worth dying for," she breathed softly. "Will you stay with me tonight?"

I stroked the top of her head with my cheek, unwilling to accept her invitation, unable to let her go, battling the two wills within me. It was a wife I wanted, not a romantic little tavern maid whose heart might easily hope for more than I would give.

"Maude," she said suddenly animated, "let's sing that song for him; the one about Audrey."

The spell was broken. "No, Sally, please..."

"*I* wish to hear it!" Coroticus demanded.

"NO!" I countered forcefully.

"No? No?" Coroticus challenged glaring angrily into my eyes. He slowly rose to his feet and assumed the threatening and arrogant posture of absolute authority. "It was ME, *COROTICUS*, that Audrey should have loved. She could have been my queen but for her misguided love for you. You can't imagine how completely devastated, how repulsive and wretched I felt, still feel, knowing that she chose death rather than settle for me. In four short months I lost the only man who ever loved me like a father and the only woman I ever hoped to love. I'll not love anybody or anything ever again! You weep for a few days then want to forget her. Well, it was *you* she died for. You owe it to Audrey to hear her song. Maude! Sally!"

Coroticus shoved me into my seat while Maude began playing a pipe and Sally began to sing.

> *'Twas out across the Irish Sea,*
> *Fair Audrey cast her eye.*
> *She wept and prayed so earnestly,*
> *To keep her love nearby.*
>
> *But Irish pirates have no heart*
> *For maidens fair and true.*
> *They stole her Sucat clean away*
> *Before the night was through.*
>
> *He'd fight, she knew, but could not win,*
> *Her bold young Briton boy.*
> *Doomed to a life of sorrow was she,*
> *Bereft of love and joy.*
>
> *She stood upon the highest cliff,*
> *And from there she did fly.*
> *She could not have her love in life,*
> *So, like him, she would die.*

The poetry was simplistic, the melody trite, the story a complete misrepresentation of truth, I judged critically in disquieting agitation. It was humiliating to hear myself portrayed as a player in a romantic tragedy and equally tormenting to reflect upon what I really was. But Coroticus was spellbound by the performance; his eyes alight with the kind of adoration and worship a man should reserve for God alone.

"I am sorry, Coroticus," I said worriedly. "But Audrey didn't die for me, only because of me. It wasn't you she was rejecting."

"Words! Just words!" Coroticus railed.

"Wouldn't her memory be better served by proving yourself to be the man she should have cared for? Not by cutting yourself off from love and worshiping Audrey as though she were a deity. If love is absent from your life then God is absent. It was Audrey who died that day, not Coroticus."

"GET OUT ! !" he roared, suddenly jumping to his feet and pointing at the door. Having failed miserably to help my friend, I stood to go.

"Thanks for the evening, Coroticus, ladies," I tossed enough coins on the table to keep Coroticus and the ladies amused for several hours, then bowed slightly and stepped to the door.

Sally hurriedly caught my arm. "Will you come back later?" she asked, her wide brown eyes as enticing as her kisses. As miserable as I felt the solace and comfort I could have enjoyed in Sally's arms was a compelling lure.

"No, Sally." I kissed her forehead then stepped through the door. "SING!" bellowed the voice of Coroticus as the door slowly closed behind me.

As I made my way to the stable, weariness wore on me, not form physical exertion, but from all my futile efforts to flee my past and find my way. I ached to feel a woman in my arms, to love her, to make her mine, to be comforted by her tenderness. But a man can't take a wife until he knows what he should become.

The stable boy saw me approaching and hurriedly began harnessing the horses. "What are you fit for?" rang in my ears, as if Father were speaking even now. What indeed? I paid the stable boy and mounted my chariot.

"Whoa! Who's that?" a coarse voice hollered from another chariot just pulling in. A muscular fellow grinning broadly jumped from his chariot and stood before me.

"Samson?" I queried.

"The same and proud you remembered after better than a year. It was sure a bit of good luck that I ran into you. You have a little time to spare on an old reprobate?"

"Right now, Samson, I have nothing but time, and no clear direction for using it."

"Well, climb out of that chariot, and I'll show you two of the prettiest tavern maids in Britannia. They're a mite particular who they get friendly with but awful pretty to look at. Then I'll chew your ear over a jug of ale."

"That might be more distraction than I can handle."

"The ale, the ear chewing, or the pretty maids?" he teasingly quipped. "Never mind. Wait for me. I'll grab some bread and a jug, then we'll go somewhere else."

Samson returned shortly and accompanied me to the stables and carriage house outside my villa. A servant unharnessed the horses and housed the chariots, while Samson and I walked by lantern light to a small pond in the nearby pasture.

"Are you idle by choice or circumstance?" Samson asked as he took a drink of ale.

"Not by choice," I grumbled. "It seems I'm not fit for anything but herding sheep."

"Herding what?" Samson remarked incredulously.

"Just imagine," I suggested, hurling two stones across the moonlit pond, "I could be the only British noble on the town council who was weathered like a peasant and smelled of sheep."

"Sure might shorten the meetings," Samson laughed boisterously.

"Shepherding is not an acceptable option, of course, nor one I would care to resume," I continued unable to share his good humor. "But I've seen nearly twenty-seven summers, and I still don't know what I'm to become."

"Now you've just confused the hell out of me. What's wrong with being what you are?" Samson asked, seating himself on a large rock.

"What I am?" I challenged, tossing another stone. "What am I, Samson?"

"Well, I'll tell you. When I want to buy a horse or just get some good advice on mine, I go over to Whitby's up north a ways. He's the best man with horses and he won't try to cheat you. When I need a smith, I can depend on Old Will down by the coast road for the best work at an honest price. If I want a good whore... well never mind that. The point is, now I need a priest and it was you I came to find, not knowing if you'd be where I left you, but there you were. Now, I don't know anything about sheep herding..."

"Samson, I'm not a priest. If I led you to think..."

"The hell you aren't. You're a prayin' man, a real one. Folks like me who stay too busy or mostly too ashamed to talk to God, we depend on praying men like you. I'm sure sorry you're so confused. Plain as day to me.

"Now that's sorted out, sit down and I'll tell you what I need your thoughts on. It's the wife. Now don't you go hanging your head down. I know you thought I didn't have a wife the way I go whoring all the time. Well I do. She was just my woman before, nothing special, the only difference being she was the whore I lived with. I don't know if she had other men. Wouldn't fault her if she had. Whatever babes she bore I raised same as if they were mine, just like someone else is raising all the bastards I sired.

"The point is, recently she's got to praying and going to church. She's not just religious. It's real with her like it is with you. She's changed, like a beautiful angel or something, always kind, always smiling, loving me with her eyes. I don't guess I ever really loved her before." Samson stood and turned away from me for a long silent minute, then cleared his throat. "The thing is, when she's lying there next to me, and I'm aching all over just to touch her, then all the whores I've been with come to mind. Well, I feel so dirty, I can't... Father, what am I to do?"

Father! I shuddered. No point arguing with him. "What is it you want to do?" I asked, standing to face him.

"I don't want to go back like it was. I guess I want to clean myself up, stop all the swearing and whoring and drinking. But, God knows a mongrel can't make himself a purebred. If I try reforming myself and fail, I'll be more miserable than I am now. Maybe it would be best to walk away from that angel," he suggested, his voice breaking. "I don't deserve her anyway."

"That angel who used to be a mongrel?"

"No, I think she must have been a purebred all along." Samson turned away again, this time for several minutes. "You're sure not saying much," he finally grumbled.

"Only death can completely change a man, Samson."

"What kind of solution is that?" he bellowed.

"An impossible solution. But with God nothing is impossible. You can be born again. But you have to want *God* more than you want the body of your angel. I think perhaps you do."

"Even if I do," he said somewhat embarrassed, "why would God want me?"

"Why would God want any of us? Maybe he sees the germ of a purebred in every mongrel. But know that he does want you, Samson. He's been drawing you to himself. It's time you told God all the things you told me."

"I can't pray! I'd be too ashamed to..."

"Tell him. Tell him you're ashamed. Tell him you feel dirty and hopeless and desperate. Tell him again and again until you know he's heard you. What do you have to lose but your pride? And don't let your tears shame you, Samson. Tears are the herald of every death and birth."

Samson fearfully knelt with me and together we prayed and wept and persevered until Samson, bold and full of faith, aggressively embraced the transforming love of God and claimed for himself the innocence and peace of a brand new life. I arranged for him to make his confession to Amicus, a real priest, and for him to remain a guest in our villa for a few days, an unnecessary precaution. Samson was amazingly untroubled by doubts. His refreshing simplicity and honesty left me as much in debt to him as he felt he was to me.

"A bee has no choice but to make honey. You have no choice but to give hope to rascals like me," Samson surmised. "Think on it. Priest, shepherd, maybe the only difference is the size of the lambs."

Like a slave I had expected to be told what to do, what I should become. I was comfortable with Father making my choices for me. Comfortable but not content. "You must sort out the purpose of your past and future," Brother Mathias had counseled. What did my past have to do with now, a past best forgotten? But if all things do work together for good then Brother Mathias was right. I had received without doubt at least one clear direction. For the next three weeks I fasted and prayed and meticulously retraced all the events of my life. A pattern emerged. Like that lump of clay on the potter's wheel, I saw myself taking shape. I still couldn't see myself a priest, not a good one, not like Grandfather. Yet, the potter had the power to make of the clay anything he chose. I decided to remain in prayer another week before requesting counsel from the bishop.

Before the week had ended I was disturbed by a dream. My desk, the one in Father's study, was standing on a sizable rock overlooking the sea. I sat at the desk watching a small boat rowing silently to shore. Victoricus stepped off the boat with a large number of letters in his arms. "Your correspondence, my lord," he said, as he did every morning. I took the letters and opened one. "The Cry of the Irish" was its title. I began to read the text and, as I did, other voices could be heard reading with me:

"Holy Boy," Totmael's gruff voice called. "We're asking you to come," Liddy continued. "Walk among us again," Gosacht added. "Holy boy, we're asking you to come, walk among us again," they repeated over and over.

My chair crashed to the ground as I leapt to my feet. The multitude of letters scattered like leaves across the rocky shore. No! I couldn't, wouldn't read anymore.

On my feet, stark naked and shaking with fear like a willow in the wind, I awoke. It wasn't just a dream. I knew that voice behind the voices. I fell to my knees. "Father God, why command what I could never obey? Please, please don't ask this of me. I can only refuse you. I can only fail."

I had been willing to become a priest; even knowing that my father would be furious and without his support my poverty would scarcely support a wife and family. Wasn't that enough? Why hadn't God left me a slave in Ireland rather than teasing me with the taste of freedom only to throw me back?

Avoiding prayer, I joined the family at breakfast that morning for the first time in four weeks. Father was pleased and asked me to meet with him afterwards in his study.

"Sucat, good news. I've found a place for you. After studying all our accounts I was amazed at the increased production of our laborers on both estates. You have a remarkable gift for managing people, especially as you have accomplished this without threat of force, so I am told. What cleverness makes them work so hard for you?"

"They don't work for me, Father. I promised each man the opportunity to buy his own freedom once he had produced enough to match the price of his purchase and the cost of his upkeep. Those who voluntarily stay on as freemen may work to purchase a piece of our land in the same manner. Any slave who had the capacity but lacked the ambition to work for his freedom, I sold."

"That's outrageous!'

"No, that's justice, Father. And I want your word that you will honor my contracts with those men."

"You put it in writing?"

"Certainly! Could I expect a slave with any intelligence to take the word of his master?"

"You insult us all, Sucat!"

"Yes, sir, I suppose I do."

Father fidgeted nervously, "I can't argue with your results. And, of course, I'll honor any contracts you have written. But you can honor them yourself. You still have a place in our office." Father picked up the ledgers. "Apparently you have kept our expenses well below the average of our last three years. Yet you have purchased properties, maintained livestock and equipment, made major repairs to the villa, and still paid ten percent of our profits to your grandfather's church. I need those talents working for me. Sucat, please look at me."

"Yes, sir."

"I want to apologize for having criticized you. With your exceptional head for finance your writing skills, or lack of them, are certainly negligible. And it wasn't our clients who became irritated and uncomfortable with your religious zeal, not entirely. It was I. Instead of making you less zealous my actions have only made you more so with your fasting and praying. Let me be the one to answer your prayers, Sucat. You are an asset to this family. Be as holy as you need to be, just promise you will never leave us."

"Even if I become a priest?" I asked apprehensively.

"A priest!! What does God expect from me? Isn't it enough to have one holy man in this family, giving our resources to the poor, entertaining every sort of low class scum? like that obnoxious simpleton you hosted last month. I had grand hopes for you, Sucat, hopes that died ten years ago. I dared to dig them up again and for what?"

"Bury them again, Father. The Sucat you built those hopes around died in Ireland."

Father was sullen the remainder of the day. My attitude was hardly better. Grandfather, now in good health, prayed for us both.

With every day that passed I was more convinced that my call to the priesthood was genuine, but I deafened my ears to the voice of the Irish. God had to be merely testing me. He couldn't justifiably require that. Not of me, not of anyone, I asserted, until my sleep was troubled by two more dreams.

In the first my eyes, looking into my soul, saw a man within me praying. His language was beautiful though foreign to me, and his prayers intense and powerful. "Who is this praying?" I asked. The man continued praying as though I hadn't spoken, until his prayers were finished. Then he spoke in a language I could understand. "He who gave his life for you, he is the one who prays for you, prays that you might love and serve your Lord and Master willingly as shepherd to my sheep in Ireland."

The second dream was similar, but only a voice prayed within. I saw no man. The voice prayed in a heavenly language also outside my understanding with groans and deep sighing. When I asked, "Whose voice is this?" The word came to me, "You do not know how to pray in this matter. The Holy Spirit himself makes intercession for you."

Nearly numb with awe and reverence I surrendered. The whole person of the Trinity had spoken, God the Father, God the son, and God the Holy Spirit. What could I say but, "Here am I, Lord. Send me."?

The following two weeks I was sicker than I had ever been. Mother thought it was food poisoning. The housekeeper thought it was a summer fever. Father thought it was irritating. And Grandfather said nothing, but he seemed to recognize the havoc was a battle of wills. It wasn't just a battle. It was a war. The best I could come up with was a kind of truce.

"Father God," I prayed, "I will devote all my energy, all my talents, all my time to pursuing this course. If I have mistaken your direction, as I desperately hope I have, tell me. If I am too deaf to hear you unstop my ears. But if this is the course you maintain for me, if I must yield my neck to the Irish yoke again, please, please give me the courage I lack to follow where you lead."

CHAPTER FOURTEEN
The Improbable Priest

"Amicus," I yelled as he mounted the steps to the church, "Wait." Ami stood with obvious impatience as I ran across the street and bounded up the stairs. "Ami, I need to speak to you. I've had some dreams."

"Sexual fantasies?" he asked.

"No, it isn't confession I need. Well, of course, I need confession, but not about these dreams. It's direction I hope to get."

"Fine, I can direct you to the bishop."

"No. Help me to see the possibilities first."

"Sucat, I'm very busy! Oh, don't look so tormented. All right. I am a priest after all. Come in and expose your great dilemma." We entered the church, knelt briefly to pray for wisdom, than sat in a small alcove.

"I believe God calls me to be a priest," I blurted out nervously.

"You? What makes you think you have the character, the moral fiber, the integrity to represent God as his priest?"

"Nothing. I'm not at all comfortable with the whole idea, but the direction is unmistakable, Ami."

"Your bishop will determine that. But seriously, Sucat, what training have you had? Most priests spend a year or two in a monastery learning discipline and studying the scriptures."

"I spent nearly two years studying in the monastery at Lerins before I returned to Britannia," I replied.

"You never told me."

"We haven't spent one whole afternoon together since I returned. When was there opportunity to tell you?"

"I can't show favoritism, Sucat. I've explained that. As a priest I must treat everyone equally."

"Yes, I admire your convictions, Ami. I'm grateful that you still see me at all. But I treasure your friendship, Ami, and I miss it."

"This isn't about me. Tell me, what is the unmistakable direction you have received?"

Ami listened intently as I related the three dreams. Then I explained the several times previously that God had directed me in the same way. He stared at me oddly for a time, then smiled a half smile and nodded his head.

"So, you are being called to Ireland. Well, brother, I'll do everything in my power to see that you get there."

"You believe my understanding is right?"

"Dead right. But there are some obstacles you'll have to overcome. First, you'll have to be a priest, but even a priest can't operate without a bishop. What bishop wants to extend his responsibilities to shepherd the savages in Ireland? I'm not sure how we'll get around that one."

"Can't a bishop be appointed for Ireland?"

"It's not done that way. Christians living in an area not served by a bishop petition the church to ordain a bishop for them. Bishops aren't ordained where no Christian community exists."

"But how can there be a Christian community in Ireland if there are no priests or bishops willing to build one? How can they hear without a preacher?" I asked impatiently.

"That is the paradox, Sucat. No current bishop is shepherd of Ireland. Even if you went to Ireland as a priest you would have no authority to baptize converts or administer the sacraments. Only a bishop has that authority. Without a Christian community in place you could never petition to be made a bishop. And it is highly unlikely that you would be acceptable as a candidate at any rate."

"With God nothing is impossible," I retorted, trying to suppress the smart of his last remark. "If God wants me in Ireland he will overcome every hindrance. If he doesn't, and I am just deluded, then thanks be to God. The prospect of returning terrifies me."

For a moment Ami's face was starkly severe as we both seriously considered the doubtful success of such a mission. "Let's at least get you an appointment with Bishop Eusibus," Ami suggested. "No, on second thought... Have you been baptized, Sucat?"

"No, I thought..."

"...that if you waited until you got all your major sins behind you, you could wash them all away in baptism and be responsible for far less when you stand before the judgement seat of Christ. How many times have I heard that? But, if you would become a priest, the time is now. Let me hear your confession, Sucat, and see you baptized. Your sins can be erased and no other living soul ever need hear of them. I would not want your chances compromised by past errors."

Ami's determination and cunning were inspirational. Like any good competition the challenge now excited me, but only as long as I looked at the challenge, not at the ultimate goal.

Confession took several months and brought a release that I desperately needed. Ami was thorough, but listened with great difficulty. Often I felt guilty for putting such a heavy burden on his shoulders. As a result, we covered very little at each confession.

"Sucat, I had no idea how very much you have suffered, and what you may face when you return," Ami remarked at my final confession. "Let us pray that your wickedness doesn't run so deep that God will be forced to take similar measures in the future." Ami had a deft skill for beating me as surely with his words as Totmael had with the lash. "All candidates for baptism are required to fast for forty days prior to being presented before the assembly," he continued. "The fast requires that you eat nothing during the daylight hours while you pray and memorize the rule of faith. Considering the magnitude of your sins, I prescribe that in addition you limit what you eat in the evenings to bread and water as a sign of true repentance. Come to me on the last day of your fast, and I will present you to Bishop Eusibus to be scheduled for examination and baptism."

"Thank you, Ami."

"Father Amicus."

"Of course, Father Amicus," I said, sadly bewildered at his lack of warmth.

At the end of my fast I was examined, along with every other candidate, before the whole assembly of the church to determine if I truly understood what I professed to believe. Baptism followed. Only those of the assembly who were baptized Christians were allowed to witness this mystery of the faith. The children were first to be baptized. They entered the baptismal fountain, the womb of the church, like newborn babes. As the initiates professed again the creed, the consecrated water was poured over them three times by Bishop Eusibus in the name of each person of the Trinity. The bishop pronounced their sins forgiven, their old life washed away, and a new one begun. Ascending from the fountain they were clothed in pure white robes and a cross of olive oil marked on their foreheads. The attending priest, Father Amicus, placed his hands upon each of their heads and prayed for them to receive the seal of their faith, the Holy Spirit of God, as an indwelling presence.

I watched with great exuberance, like the joy I had felt in Ireland when Liddy came to Milchu's settlement and I knew there was another who shared my faith. Or the joy I had felt in Lerins with so many Christian brothers. All these people knew and loved the same God that I loved and served, and I was one with them.

The men were baptized next, four others and myself. It takes a good measure of humility for a man to openly reject his life and, like a baby, enter a new one, especially in the face of so many witnesses. That's as it should be. "God resists the proud and gives grace to the humble," the scriptures say. I reminded myself of that as I stood with all the ugly scars of my past exposed, scars only seen by Mother until now. Would that those also could be washed away.

"By what Christian name do you wish to be known?" Bishop Eusibus inquired.

"Patrick," I said without a thought, surprised by my own voice. Patrick, the name Iserninus and my brothers in Lerins had presumed to call me, and which I never challenged. Sucat had surely died and now I would see him buried.

"Patrick, do you believe in God the Father Almighty?" Bishop Eusibus asked, and I forgot about everything but the beautiful symbolism of baptism; the washing away of all my sin and guilt; the burial of my former life and resurrection to a new one; the outward expression of that exam Christ had mercifully altered in my vision so many years ago.

"I believe in God..." I professed in the words of the rule as I followed the rite to its conclusion.

Clothed in my white robe I knelt before Amicus. He wept as he prayed for me. I'll never know what was in his heart, but his tears blessed me. My dearest, dearest friend, who knew every terrible deed I had ever done, spoken, or thought in so far as I could remember, yet forgave them all and buried them forever.

The women were baptized last. There is nothing more radiantly beautiful than a woman in love with her Lord. Like Iserninus' Helen, these women glowed. But even in this sacred setting I found it impossible to watch the virgin baptisms without considering whether their naked attributes might satisfy my desire in a wife. Fresh washed yet spotted already. God had a long way to go before he could make a decent priest out of me.

Anno Domini 419

"To the honorable Patricius Magonus Sucatus, from Brother Mathias and all your brothers and devoted friends at Lerins, greetings and most sincere congratulations upon your recent baptism and your delinquent submission to God's call to the priesthood. How fervently we have all prayed that you might finally see what has been so obvious. Iserninus nearly had to be muzzled to prevent his insisting that you become a priest while at Lerins. But I feared you might find another whale's belly to craw into if confronted too soon. God be praised. His time is always best.

"It is my hope that this letter will confirm to you the correctness of your decision and help your bishop to pursue your ordination without delay. Many men from Lerins have entered the priesthood, but none I would more readily recommend.

"May our Lord continue to bless and direct you. You are always in our prayers, beloved brother. Will you take a new name as some do, or shall we continue to address you as Brother Patrick? Remember us to the Lord."

Brother Mathias

Father Amicus' glowing recommendation and Brother Mathias' letter provided Bishop Eusibus with the necessary evidence of my suitability for the office of priest. But correspondence and bureaucracy being what it is, more than a year had passed since I first told Amicus of my dreams. Now I sat before Bishop Eusibus, along with two younger men, Malach and Auxilius, also candidates for ordination, answering questions regarding my call.

"I'm prepared to accept your call to the priesthood, but this desire to work in Ireland concerns me. Why do you wish to go among barbarians? You can only suffer the fate of every other man who has attempted what you suggest. Martyrs are to be admired but only true martyrs, not those who would throw their lives away. Perhaps you have mistaken the meaning of your dreams. Do you have these dreams or visions often?" he queried.

"No, sir. Seldom in fact."

"Just because you seldom dream, you can't simply assume that when you do it is the voice of God. Your unusual experiences could well trigger any manner of dreams."

"Yes, sir. Bloody, chilling nightmares still haunt me from time to time. Fortunately, I seldom suffer those anymore either. But why would I suddenly dream differently, hear voices calling me? One voice I know to be the Lord's."

"You know? How would you know for certain? You were asleep. I believe you feel guilt for having left behind so many others who remain in slavery while you enjoy freedom. I believe your difficulty assimilating into a society nearly foreign to you after so many brutal years has made you anxious to quit this world altogether, to long for a kind of success in death that you know you will never have in life."

"I am not without success, Bishop Eusibus."

"You certainly had no success as a slave. The stripes on your back attest to that. And your own father has expressed no end of exasperation at your lack of learning and your apparent inability to make up for those lost years. He even relieved you of your job as his secretary, if I'm not mistaken."

"That was over a year ago," I protested. "Father found my talents were better suited to…"

"Come now, don't get so offended," he interrupted. "Our responsibility is to find the truth. If your pride suffers, so much the better. It is perfectly obvious to me that you have every reason to wish to terminate your life in a blaze of glory. I won't have it. As long as I am your bishop I will prohibit you from ever returning to Ireland. What is your response?"

"I pray that you are right," I answered," and that you will not be setting us both against the will of God."

Before the sun had set, the call, which I had confided to Amicus over a year ago and which he had kept in strictest confidence, had flown from my interview with Bishop Eusibus to Father's ears; whether by the bishop or by the two younger priests, Malach and Auxilius, I'll never know.

"What nonsense is this?" Father yelled as he burst into Grandfather's room and confronted me. "It isn't enough that you repudiate my direction by becoming a priest? Now you make me a laughing stock with all this idiocy about returning, of all places, to Ireland? You make yourself a fool and me the father of a fool!" His anger dissolved. "Sucat, tell me I'm mistaken."

An uncomfortable silence followed, then Grandfather cleared his throat. Turning on him Father lashed out, "You encourage him!"

"Please, Father, Grandfather is no more at ease with this than you are."

"At ease?! Appalled, aghast, angry but never at ease! Sucat, you were dead to us once. Never, never again!"

The silence weighed heavily as I considered how best to answer his challenge. His eyes bore into mine demanding a response.

"Was it Calpornius who brought me back from the dead?" I asked respectfully. Father and Grandfather exchanged troubled glances. "This life I have, God gave me. If he requires it again, how can I say no?" Father turned away, whether from grief or pity I couldn't tell. But Grandfather stared sadly as one might look with pity on someone whose senses had fled. "I won't be leaving tomorrow at any rate. I will have to be a bishop if I'm to have the authority I need."

"A bishop?" Father gasped. "Then I have nothing to worry me but an addled son. A man of your limited education, Sucat, could never be a bishop."

"Just like a man of your limited faith could never be a deacon?" Grandfather countered.

"Will you delude him with impossible expectations?" Father snapped.

"Nothing is entirely impossible," I replied. "I admit it appears to be. Even if I can manage it, I expect it will take years. And at present, I see no reason why I can't follow your direction, Father, *and* the Lord's. Managing your finances takes far less time than managing your correspondence. May I suggest a truce on the subject for the time being?"

"For the time being," Father agreed and grudgingly shook my hand.

"The time being" stretched on for seven years without even the glimmer of an end to my waiting, and without any indication from God that my course was to change. On the contrary every prayer affirmed my call, while every door slammed in my face. I stood precariously on the edge of life, the past eroding under my feet, the future beyond my reach.

During those long years the face of Britannia decayed with alarming speed. It became readily apparent that Roman law, not Christian virtue, had inspired the nobility of public service. Lust for power and wealth available for the taking slowly turned former statesmen into selfish potentates. Private armies were recruited to provide protection against Saxon invaders and Irish pirates. Being comprised in large measure of former Roman soldiers, the armies were fairly successful. But I wondered how long their efficiency would last without the continued discipline that had inspired the fame of the Roman Legions. As for civil law, each province took care of its own.

In Bannaventa Berniae my father and the other men on the town council tried hard to maintain the court, school, park, and public bath. Coroticus had assumed the throne and was sympathetic to their efforts. However, clever men facing the justice of the court learned quickly how to influence King Coroticus, until the court became a sham, unable to guarantee justice or enforce its judgements. Security soon became an incredible expense for every landowner and merchant. Inevitably there was little capital to invest in the public services. Even the public school was finally forced to close. Young men were now referred to the monastery for their education.

In spite of all this men carried on as though the current troubles were a passing irritation. As soon as Rome had eliminated her adversaries, she would again embrace her beloved Britannia. We were, after all, still citizens of Rome!

My sister, Lupait, was married to a young noble of Father's acquaintance shortly after I had taken my vows as a priest, changing the complexion of our household. Hers was the first marriage I assisted in administering.

Lupait seemed to be reasonably happy and bore her husband two children over the next three years. The boys were a delight for Mother and Grandfather, worrisome for Father, and a pleasant distraction for me.

The year I turned thirty-three a terrible fever swept every village along the coast. Grandfather and I worked tirelessly in our efforts to comfort the sick and dying. Many people survived. Mother was fifty-four when the fever struck her. She never recovered.

Mother was an unobtrusive person, modest, quiet; whose presence was never noticed so much as her absence. As though a bright candle had gone out and could never be rekindled, our home felt darker, less vibrant without her. Believing that she now lived with our Lord, still prayed for me, still shared – though more unobtrusively than ever - all that I did, kept my heart from accepting that darkness.

Grandfather was miraculously untouched by the fever. However, at seventy-eight the long hours and enormous energy he had expended took their toll. He suffered terrible pains in his chest and his legs, and spent most of his time in bed or in prayer.

"Patrick," he said months later as I visited with him in his room, "I've prayed as hard as I know how. I've fought this Ireland thing as long as I can. But all I hear from the Lord is, 'My ways are not your ways, nor my thoughts your thoughts.' Clearly the Lord wants you in Ireland. I'm convinced of it. Before I get any weaker, I want to give you my blessing. But don't let your father hear of it. I don't enjoy our rows like I used to."

I knelt. Grandfather placed his hands on my head. He prayed and prayed. Sometimes I understood him, sometimes not, but the overall meaning was clear. God would open the door to Ireland, and I would enter, and the blessings of God would follow.

Two days later Grandfather died. I tremulously removed the little book of verses from his neck and replaced it on mine. I knelt beside his bed, as I had so many times before, and thanked God through my tears for every prayer my beloved grandfather had prayed on my behalf and every moment we had shared together. I felt as if a vital part of my own body had died, leaving a raw, open wound that constantly ached.

Fleeing the pain I plunged more fervently into my work. My success as a priest impressed me with the Potter's skill. How many rascals had joined the flock in those seven years! And how many little ones enjoyed the services so much better, knowing that I would treat them to a story in the courtyard after every one.

The bulk of a British bishop's workload, effective correspondence, still remained outside the scope of my talents - so Eusibus discovered, as had my father before him. My acceptability as a candidate for any bishopric looked increasingly less likely. When fatal illness overcame a local bishop I was never considered as a replacement. Father Amicus' talents, however, propelled him into that office, making Ami, at thirty-three, the youngest bishop in Britannia as far as I knew. I didn't begrudge him the position. Still, I despaired. Year after year, all my efforts toward Ireland produced nothing more than fodder for the good humored jests of those who ridiculed my vision.

"Anno Domini 426

"To Patricius Magonus Sucatus, brother in Christ of all true believers, from your faithful friend and brother, Iserninus, greetings. Do not be discouraged or doubtful, Patrick, as I know from your letter you are. God will work everything out, if you but stay to the course. Let me assure you from personal revelation that your vision is true. When you return to Ireland, God has called me to go with you. Stay fluent in Gaelic, brother, or is that still the language you speak in prayer? We all pray for you daily. Remember us before the Lord.

"Your beloved brother, Iserninus"

Exuberant after receiving that encouraging letter and another from Bishop Eusibus finally releasing me from his service, I determined to see Amicus. Unable to locate him, I sought out Coroticus, who might have known of Ami's whereabouts. It was late evening, not the best time to discuss major issues, but my enthusiasm would not be deferred.

And what can we say to all these things? If God be for us, who can be against us? All things work together for good to those who love God and keep his commandments. For God so loved the world that he gave his only begotten son, that who believes in him should not perish but

CHAPTER FIFTEEN
An Open Door

The tavern was darker than I remembered, suffused thinly with smoke from a partially obstructed chimney. A young tavern maid approached. "I haven't seen your handsome face in here before. Are you a stranger or a hermit?' she laughed coyly. I was fully twice her age, but I was captivated none the less.

"I make it a habit to stay out of dangerous places," I teased.

"We entertain only the best clientele. I'm sure you'll be perfectly safe. Besides, you look like a man who can take care of himself."

"Maybe so, but it isn't the clientele I fear," I whispered. "Would you know where I might find King Coroticus? It's important that I see him."

"He's in his private room through that door at the back of the tavern. The bishop is with him. But, unless you're a close friend, I wouldn't risk disturbing him."

I nodded and slipped a tip into her palm. "Now that I've come to your place, drop by the church sometime and visit me at mine."

"You're that handsome priest! The one in the song! Lord Calpornius' son!" she giggled, impressing me once again with her tender years. "I only work nights. The other maids said we'd never see you in here past the noon hour. Won't they be surprised?"

"I'll take their interest in my affairs as fine compliment and pray that I haven't made a mistake in coming tonight."

"If you have, I hope it's one you'll make again." She winked then turned to another customer.

I walked to the back room. Coroticus' loud laughter and Maude's titters could be heard through the door as I loudly knocked.

"Come in," bellowed Coroticus, "and bring plenty of ale." I stepped through the doorway. Maude straddled Coroticus' lap and Sally, Ami's, as they sat at the table. Both women were bare breasted, their bodices fully unlaced, their hair disheveled. Neither man noticed me. Embarrassed for both of them I dropped my head and turned to go.

"Father Patrick!" Ami exclaimed as he leapt to his feet. "I…"

"Peace, Ami," I spoke over my shoulder and stepped to the doorway.

Sally hurried across the room and threw her arms around my neck. "Stay," she enticed, her lips meeting mine.

"He's not staying," Ami called sharply.

"Please, stay," she entreated again. How many years had it been? I carefully removed her arms from my neck. She was as alluring as ever, and her bare skin drew me to caress the gentle curves of her breasts. By God's grace, only my eyes succumbed to that pleasure.

"Can you fetch me a mug, Sally? I asked.

"I'll fetch whatever your heart desires," she crooned seductively, then hurried from the room.

A glance at Coroticus confirmed that he was far too full of ale and too engaged with his lady to be distracted by the business I had with Ami.

"Ami, I..."

"Is this about Ireland?" he cut me off sharply.

"Yes."

"Forget Ireland!"

"Could we go somewhere else to talk?"

"No! I can't think of a thing I have to say to you, Father Patrick, that I haven't said already."

I had come to see my friend only to be silenced by my superior. "I'm sorry, Bishop Amicus," I said sadly, "I shouldn't have interrupted your... leisure. I'll see you at the church tomorrow." I turned to go.

"Wait, Patrick," Ami sighed frowning, "Stop looking like someone just killed your favorite puppy. I'll hear what you have to say. My *leisure* needs interrupting."

The crescendo of passionate titters and groans from the king and his lady in their rhythmic recreation had become an uncomfortable distraction.

"Can we get a table in the front?" I begged. "A man who fasts should never linger where dessert is being served."

Ami's hearty laughter broke the tension. "If you could but write with the same wit," he remarked. "That's a proverb I would do well to remember. Come." We made our way to the main room.

"Father?" a gruff voice called.

"Samson! What a delight to see you! You remember Bishop Amicus?"

"Yes, sir, I do. You fellows want to join me?"

"Be glad to." I noticed the surprise on Ami's face as we sat at the table, but I felt he was sure to find Samson as pleasant as I did. "What are you doing here, Samson?"

"Filling my eyes and my belly with good things! But don't you go to worrying. I may be looking, but I'm stopping short of lusting."

"Then you're a better man than I am, Samson," I laughed.

"Aw, I don't need that anymore, not with the angel I've got. You shouldn't either. Haven't you taken a wife yet?"

"I've abandoned that hope."

"Then I say you're just a mite too particular," Samson continued. "From what I hear any number of maids would like your feather in their cap. Imagine my surprise when I realized the praying man I'd carried to Bannaventa Berniae was the same romantic devil in all them tavern songs."

"Don't believe everything you hear, Samson."

Sally arrived with my mug of ale and slipped herself disconcertingly onto my lap. I attempted to discretely slide her onto the seat beside me. Sally didn't budge.

"I can believe my eyes, can't I?" Samson chortled. "If you're too timid let me..."

"No, Samson, I appreciate your good intentions. But I can't ask a British woman to risk her life among the Irish Scots. I'll not marry." Sally teasingly nibbled on my ear.

"If the bishop in Rome prevails none of our priests will marry." Ami expounded irritably.

I laughed, not quite sure if he were serious, and took Sally's pretty face between my palms. "I haven't seen the women of Rome, but in Britannia that won't be popular." Sally's eyes danced. "Now, be as kind as I know you to be, Sally, and leave me," I requested fondly.

"Oh, kiss me first. Make me melt in your arms like you did the last time," she entreated.

"That was a long time ago, Sally. I wasn't a priest then."

"So?"

"I'm sorry, Sally."

"So am I," she sighed dramatically, "So am I."

Sally kissed the top of my head, ran her hands across Ami's shoulders, winked at Samson, and left the room. We drank our ale in silence for a few moments.

"I didn't know you knew Sally," Ami grumbled into his mug.

"Not nearly so well as you know her, or were about to know her," I quietly challenged.

"So, all those crazy stories are true?" Samson suddenly inquired. "You really plan to go back to those head hunting barbarians?"

"A bee has no choice but to make honey," I reminded him.

"What has Ireland got to do with bees?! " Ami lashed out. "A man with any sense would have given up that foolish notion long ago. Can't you hear the people laughing behind your back, Patrick? Priests, artisans, merchants, even bishops. Everyone ridicules your supposed visions and mocks your effrontery in promoting yourself, unqualified as you are, as a candidate for bishop. Arrogant dreamer they call you! Irish ignoramus! Suicidal simpleton! Have you the faintest understanding of the humiliation you have caused your father? People point and make jokes in the marketplace. 'The hopeless father of a fool,' they say. Even I have endured the snide wit of your accusers. Do you suppose your..."

"Here now," Samson challenged, "aren't you being a bit hard on him?"

"Who are you to correct me?"

"Someone who respects this praying man. And who are you to belittle him?"

"Samson!" I interjected, "Bishop Amicus is my oldest and dearest friend."

"Then you'd best be working on getting' some new ones," Samson countered. "But back to the subject at hand, I may disagree with his meanness, but he could be right about this Ireland business. Do you imagine Britannia is just boiling over with praying men, so as we can afford to lose one?"

I sighed heavily, irritated at the inquisition. "Perhaps not. But I know the Irish have even less."

"And whose fault is that?" Samson exploded raining spittle. "If they didn't go killing every one that stepped off the boat they might have a few. What makes you think the same thing won't happen to you?"

"I expect that, at some time, it will, Samson," I admitted uneasily.

"Well that the dam... most outrageous thing I ever heard! What good is a praying man to any of us if he's dead?!" Samson railed. "I DON'T KNOW!" I shouted. "I don't know. I only know that God led me out of Ireland and now he leads me back. What else can I do but press forward? Ami, I thought you of all people supported me in this."

"That was when I dared to believe it might be possible. You said it yourself, 'If God wants me in Ireland, he will see to it that I get there.' Well, you're not there, are you?"

"But I can be," I calmly stated. "That's what I came to see you about. Bishop Eusibus has released me, Ami, to serve you." I handed him the notice from Bishop Eusibus.

"I have evidence that in the south of Ireland a community of Christians exists without benefit of clergy of any kind. Isn't that justification enough to send me, now that you are my bishop?" Ami stared skeptically. "Read this letter from my brother in Lerins if you still doubt whether my call is genuine." I produced Iserninus' letter. Ami carefully read both letters several times.

"If I accept the responsibility for sending you," Ami mused, "your work must be limited to only what the Christian community requires. I presume a great deal allowing what my senior bishop forbade. Your untimely death would be the end of my career. Until you are Bishop of Ireland and your life is on your own head, you will be forbidden to freely evangelize pagans. Can you work within these boundaries?"

"Yes," I barely whispered. The goal was won.

"Very well, leave as soon as your brother from Lerins can join you. I'll begin arranging for funds to support your mission tomorrow. Come see me in the afternoon." Ami stood to leave. "Samson, it was good to see you again," he said smiling officiously. He motioned with his head toward the door. I stood and walked with him.

"Sucat, I've know Sally for a long time," Ami anxiously volunteered. "When I meet here with Coroticus she tends to get a little too familiar. But I've never... not since I became a priest, though... What you saw here tonight..."

"Ami," I interrupted, "could *I* judge you? God keep you, dear friend." We embraced and Ami left. I returned to Samson at the table.

"Samson, I need to send a letter to the island of Lerins off the coast of Gaul. Would you take it as far as the coast for me? I pay better than I used to."

"Sure, I'll take it clear to Lerins. And I won't charge you a penny more than I would anybody else."

"Done. Now come on home with me. I won't have you wasting your money on a room when we have plenty of spare beds at the house."

"Priest or prayin' man, I still feel a mite uncomfortable socializing with nobles. If you won't be too offended, I'll pass. ...Aw, there you go hanging your head again. Haven't you gotten over that? I don't mean to be ungrateful but... Well didn't you see how that Bishop smiled like he had a poker up his ass? And your father's the same. I know *you* think a lot of me, and that means something, makes me feel real pleasant, but..."

"It's all right, Samson, I understand. I'll meet you here for breakfast tomorrow with the letter and the fee in hand. Thanks for doing this."

"Any time. And if you ever find yourself short of *real* friends, count me one."

"I already do."

I knocked quietly on the study door.

"Come in," Father's voice rang out.

"Father," I said carefully as I entered and stood before his desk, "I've been granted permission to minister in Ireland."

Father's face grew ashen as he slowly stood. He walked to the window and said nothing, but stared in disbelief as if the whole idea were foreign to him. Gazing glassy-eyed out the window he began to expound, "Sucat, you have responsibilities, to me, to your sister, to your church. These cannot be ignored. If you want to enlarge your ministry here, I can arrange it. I'll fund any kind of project you wish. I've been unforgivably tight-fisted in the past, but..."

"No, Father."

"Think how productive your work could be. All the proceeds from the lands you are due to inherit can be yours now, today!"

"Father..."

"Tell me what it will take to make you stay and it's yours," he insisted turning to face me.

"Father, you knew this day would come."

"NO! I never believed my son would be fool enough to actually go through with such an ill-fated enterprise!" he snapped. "Now what will it take?"

"I'm not for sale," I answered.

"NOT YET, anyway!" he snidely quipped.

From that day until the day I sailed for Ireland, Father scarcely spoke to me. Over the next two weeks Lupait offered me her share of the inheritance, Bishop Eusibus asked me to be his minister of finance, and equally tempting offers came from most of the people I knew. Even those who had ridiculed me before now begged me to stay. All the fuss and attention was wearisome. I can only imagine the pressure put on Amicus to rescind his approval and support of this mission. A letter finally lifted my spirits.

"Anno Domini 426

"To Father Patrick, greetings from Brother Iserninus and your friend Samson. We leave as soon as the weather will permit and should arrive within two weeks. I am most anxious to begin our adventure together. God be praised!

"Your beloved Brother Iserninus"

Adventure or disaster? Whatever the case, now it was about to begin.

CHAPTER SIXTEEN
To Ireland

Gold sparkled on the face of the water in hundreds of miniature reflections of the brilliant sun. The breeze scarcely stirred. Cries of sea birds seemed to echo in the stillness, as I loaded my travel bags onto the boat. We would sail with the tide. By then a good breeze was sure to fill our sails.

My emotions swung like a carpenter's plumb; bursting with excitement and enthusiasm; overwhelmed by apprehension and fear. Brother Ninus, as I now called Iserninus, was a great encouragement. He had arrived full of expectations, and eager to carry his faith back home to Ireland, as he had longed to do for several years. He had patiently followed the Lord's leading in waiting for me. When Samson had deposited him at the villa three weeks earlier, the years we had been apart seemed to disappear. Like childhood friends, we swapped stories and histories, then shared all our dreams for Ireland. His vision was far greater than mine, as a dreamer's is likely to be. Mine was more practical and meticulously thought out. How wise was God in putting the two of us together.

When I needed the solace of silence, as I did now, Brother Ninus seemed instinctively to know. He said nothing as I carefully scanned the coast, trying to memorize every detail of my homeland. But visions of that terrifying night long ago, when first I sailed for Ireland, disturbingly filled my mind instead. The weathered gray buildings along the wharf were suddenly ablaze in my mind. The sea birds' cries repeatedly echoed the screams of terrified captives. The wooden sailing vessels became Irish curraughs, with their naked masts piercing the sky. My heart began to race.

"Patrick? Are you all right?" Brother Ninus asked worriedly, jolting me back to the present.

"Yes. I will be. Let's go ashore until the tide turns," I suggested.

Brother Ninus secured his bag with mine on the ship, then walked with me back onto the shore. The wind came up. The tide would soon change.

"Father Patrick!" A child's voice called. "Father Patrick, Father Patrick," a chorus of children's voices chimed in. At the crest of the hill and running down the road towards us were most of the little children from my village church.

"What is this?" I asked, as they flocked around me, pulling on my arms and hanging onto my legs.

"We wanted you to remember us in Ireland," Jonathan, the oldest boy, explained. He nodded to Serena, a girl nearly his own age. She handed me a leather pouch slung by a long leather strap. On it the children, or some of them, had painted a man sitting. His mouth was open. Seated and surrounding him were six little, eager-faced listeners, all painted as colorfully as the man.

"Do you like it, Father Patrick?" Jonathan asked. "The man is you and the children are all of us."

The children waited with expectant eyes for my response. "Yes! It's a fine, a grand, gift. You have all done well," I finally managed to say. "Every day I promise to carry it. Only I will think the man is Christ, and the children are all of you, who continue to listen to his stories." I knelt and individually embraced each child, determined not to mar my thanks by tears. How I loved these little ones. More footsteps alerted me to the presence of others.

Father approached with Lupait and my two little nephews. Friends and neighbors, even Victoricus and our household staff followed. Beyond them the parents of these children, fellow Christians from the church I had served, Coroticus, Bishop Amicus, Samson, and a few other colorful characters, including Sally and Maude.

"I'll wait for you on the boat." Brother Ninus whispered then walked back down the dock.

Accusingly, Father inquired, "Sucat, will I ever see you again?"

"If God wills. Will you pray for me?"

"Pray? Praying was your grandfather's business, not mine!"

I nodded sadly. "I'm sorry I have to leave you, Father"

Father gripped me firmly. "I promise every morning," he whispered rebelliously into my ear, "To pray, that God will send you back. A great piece of me goes with you to Ireland." We embraced for as long as convention would deem appropriate and just a bit longer, then Father wiped his eyes and nose, slapped me affectionately on the back, and turned aside. Lupait swept between us.

"Write to me, Sucat. I won't let Father see your letters, so it won't matter how awful they are." I smiled and kissed her, then each of my nephews. Lupait and the boys joined my father, as I received well wishing from all the others, along with numerous gifts and tokens. Coroticus' gift was an expensive and ornate set of mugs, much too precious for my use in Ireland. Most of the gifts were of little practical use, but I could only graciously receive them. As Coroticus made a pompous farewell speech, an excellent use did occur to me.

"When, in the future, I have need for a fool in my court, I can always send away to Ireland," Coroticus concluded in jest. He laughed at his own good humor, along with everyone else and slapped me soundly on the back.

Ami was the last to address me. "God speed, Father Patrick," he said with unexpected formality. "Father Malach and Father Auxilius will accompany you to Ireland and manage the church's funds, as well as assist you and Brother Iserninus in whatever way you deem best. I have sent them on to the ship."

Malach and Auxilius? In Ireland? "Bishop Amicus," I countered, adopting his official tone, "they would serve me best to remain here. Would you put two more lives at risk?"

"Serving the Christian community? How threatening could that be?"

"Even the Christians are ruled by pagan kings."

"Enough, Patrick. This is my decision as your bishop, and you will honor it," Ami demanded. "God go with you." He made the sign of the cross and turned away. Emotional moments were awkward for Ami, I told myself, excusing his abruptness.

"Patrick!" a voice yelled from the ship. "Hurry!" The ship was moving out of its berth. I turned to my Father.

"Pray for me...every day," I yelled. "You promised!" Father frowned and nodded determinedly. I ran for the ship, tossed the bag of gifts to Brother Ninus, and leapt aboard just as she cleared the dock. Before we were fifty yards out all my well-wishers had gone. Part of me stayed behind, disappearing over the hill with them, leaving an emptiness that was quickly filled with old, familiar, and haunting voices. "Holy Boy, we are asking you to come. Walk among us again." I set my face toward Ireland and, from that moment, I never looked back.

The sail to Ireland could have been a pleasant time of relaxation and meditation. The weather was mild, the sea smooth. But the addition of Father Malach and Father Auxilius to our ranks generated some genuinely unChristian attitudes within me that were not easily overcome.

Father Auxilius was taller than I, excessively slender, with a constant hunger in his eyes. In previous assignments, I had found him more prudish than truly pious. He invariably had a number of reasons why any undertaking was bound to fail, but had no initiative of his own. Argument with him had proved pointless. Instead I had forged ahead without responding to his numerous complaints, and he invariably followed, grumbling all the while.

Father Malach was a short and zealous fellow, with a good head for figures. His absolute confidence and unlimited energy made him seem formidably powerful in spite of his small stature. These qualities might have served him well, but for his self-righteous attitude. He was sharply and unmercifully critical of anything he considered inappropriate or questionable, and was resolutely unshakable in his opinions. Neither man had spent any appreciable time outside the company of British nobles, a poor background for work among savages.

Did Ami intend to rid himself of two troublesome priests? I wondered. Or did he presume to set upon me two critical spies? I repented of these malicious thoughts immediately. Certainly my bishop had felt there was safety in numbers. My success was his one concern.

"Father Patrick, quit sulking in your corner and rescue me from those vultures," Brother Ninus laughed, as he approached me. "There isn't a thing I can do that doesn't provoke a nibble from one or the other."

"So you've uncovered their special talents?" I responded.

He began to elaborate, but I interrupted, "Whatever jests you need to make at their expense had best be made now, Brother Ninus. Once we are in Ireland, I won't permit any one of us to speak ill of the other."

"You won't permit?! Will you presume to dictate to me?" Brother Ninus protested.

"I will."

"And if I don't agree?"

"Then, Ninus, I must assume, God has different roads for us to travel. You know I value your opinions. But on the whole, anyone who travels with me must follow or get out of the way. I can't risk petty contentions. The dangers are too great."

"Well, thanks be to God!" Brother Ninus quipped merrily. "A man, who can take the bull by the horns, is the only sort I would join in a cattle raid. But you might enlighten your astute colleges. They suffer from the delusion that the mission is theirs, and you and I are only along as interpreters."

A heavy sigh escaped as I pondered whether my greatest challenge would be the Irish, or these two fine examples of nobles'-sons-turned-holy-men.

After almost twenty-two hours at sea a brilliantly green island glistened through the mist. It delighted me to see the awe on the faces of Father Malach and Father Auxilius, and the sheer joy in Brother Ninus's eyes. Even as a captive, I had thrilled at the beauty and majesty of Ireland, like an enchanted dream or a magical fairyland. The enchantment hadn't faded.

The bay we entered hosted a sandy beach and a dense forest beyond. A wharf with two parallel docks attached stood near the rocky reef at one end of the shore. A ship was secured to the moorings. A half mile down, near the curve of the bay, another dock hosted one more ship. There were a few additional curraughs in various stages of repair or construction on the beach. Near the forest several huts could be seen, some large enough to warehouse cargo, others individual dwellings. There were a few animal and slave pens near a raised platform that served as an auction block. This was, without doubt, the very same harbor, where a cargo of Irish wolfhounds had once promoted my passage from slavery to freedom. Our ship docked and the crew began unloading cargo.

"Let's go. We're only in the way here." Father Malach ordered. "Don't carry those bags like that, Father Auxilius. There's a proper way to do everything. Father Patrick, Brother Iserninus, did you hear? We need to be going ashore."

"I don't see anything that looks like a hostel." complained Father Auxilius as he followed Father Malach down the dock.

Brother Ninus laughed, grabbed his travel bags, and handed me mine. "Come on, Patrick, before our two eager friends begin to irritate the natives." Brother Ninus leapt eagerly off the ship.

Ireland! I had thought I was prepared. I could only stare, motionless, at the coarse and weathered men on the shore. My feet were like lead, every step an enormous effort. At first I felt numb, then visions of blazing wicker and screaming victims, decapitations and shriveled heads, bestiality and bloody lashings exploded in my mind. My heart began to race. My skin felt cold and clammy, yet perspiration trickled down my forehead. I dropped my bags, and leaning against a post, vomited into the water. "That courage I've been asking for," I prayed, "This might be the time, Father. Don't bring me this far and let me down."

"Patrick!" Ninus' concerned voice shouted. I heard his footsteps on the dock, then felt his hands on my shoulders.

"Just give me a minute, Ninus," I said.

Gradually the trembling left my body. Strength rose powerfully within me. I breathed heavily two or three times then raised up, confident once more that God would give me the grace to endure whatever lay ahead.

"This is deplorable!" Father Malach scolded, having rejoined us on the dock. "Parading your weakness before these people. We have to set a standard here."

"Father Malach," I insisted quietly but firmly, "that will be the last time you criticize me in public, or Brother Iserninus, or Father Auxilius either for that matter. Nor will you say anything disparaging in private except to the person you decry."

"I don't have to accept direction from you!" Father Malach interjected. "Who..."

"Yes, you do!" I interrupted. "You have two choices. You can get back aboard that ship and return to Britannia, or you can swallow your pride and accept that this arrogant ignoramus, as you so fondly call me, is the man that God has charged with this mission. Now make up your mind. You have until the tide turns." I walked past him onto the shore.

Followed by Brother Ninus and Father Auxilius, I approached several men at work on a beached curraugh. "I'm in the market for information," I announced in Gaelic. The men stopped working and looked suspiciously from one to the other. I withdrew from my gift bag a beautifully enameled hand mirror. "Would anyone know where I might find Captain Sinell?"

"Sinell?" spoke the man obviously in charge. He gestured toward the curraugh docked at the far pier. "He's aboard his ship. But I can't say as he'd want to be found by the likes of you." The other men laughed rudely as the informant reached for the mirror.

"It's his woman, Liddy, I need to see. Which is his hut?" The man's face drained of color. He tipped his head and cut his eyes in the direction of one of the huts. "Thank you," I said, releasing the mirror. I picked up my bags and crossed the beach with Brother Ninus, Father Auxilius, and now Father Malach, following.

"Liddy," I called, as we reached the hut. I peered within. "Liddy?" We wandered around to the back of the hut. Liddy stood, spoon in hand, over a nicely boiling kettle of stew. She had to be in her early fifties now, slender, though not quite as lean as she used to be, a bit more silver in her hair, and still a handsome woman.

"Good day to you, Liddy," I greeted.

"What stranger speaks in Gaelic?" she challenged.

"Milchu's Holy Boy, twenty years gone," I answered.

Liddy left her pot and approached me, intensely studying my face, especially my eyes. She nodded smiling, then a dark frown swept the smile away. "You left this God forsaken place. What foolishness brings you back?"

"God has not forsaken the Irish, Liddy. We've come to..."

"Priests! You are all Christian priests!" She threw her arms around me and sang happily, "God be praised! And welcome back!"

"Foreign Dog!" Sinell's voice boomed as he rushed toward us. He easily tossed Father Malach and Father Auxilius like rags to the ground, and made for me. "You dare to touch my woman?" he yelled, backhanding me across the face.

"Sinell! Please!" Liddy interceded, stepping between us. She took the blow Sinell meant for me and collapsed to the ground.

"Liddy!" Sinell breathed worriedly. Ninus swiftly helped Liddy to her feet and away from the two of us.

"You Bastard!" I roared, knocking him off balance with the force of my fist. Hate, that I thought was conquered long ago, transformed me. Having caught him off guard, I struck Sinell again and again and again. Not for Liddy, not entirely, but for every day I had been forced to spend in slavery, and every abuse I had had to endure.

"Patrick! For God's sake! Stop!" Ninus screamed roughly. I struck again. His back against the hut, Sinell pulled his knife.

"Holy Boy!" Liddy shouted angrily, stepping between us once more, "Remember who you are!"

My raised arm froze. I considered Sinell's bruised cheek and bloody lip. Who was the Christian and who was the barbarian now? Sinell deliberately sheathed his knife, his eyes never leaving mine. I stepped away from the hut, picked up a large stone, and hurled it, with all the force of my anger and frustration, towards the sea. "God, this is too hard for me!" I protested through clenched teeth. "You should have picked a better man."

Sinell began laughing. "'A better man,' he says. Who is he, Liddy?"

"You know this man, Sinell," Liddy responded.

Sinell approached, rolling his head and working his injured jaw. Like facing a wild boar, I watched every movement cautiously. "You're the first man to get the better of me in thirty years," he said. "It won't happen again. Still, I can't afford you as an enemy." He extended his hand in a gesture of friendship. I looked warily from his hand to his eyes.

"Do you presume to be my friend...or my master?" I challenged, my determined gaze matching his.

Sinell frowned and slowly lowered his hand. His eyes searched mine. "What was it Liddy called you?" Recognition cast a dark shadow across his face. "Holy Boy! Can friendship be possible?"

"All things are possible," I muttered, as though the words tasted bitter in my mouth. He frowned doubtfully and extended his hand again. I received his gesture, like a man accepting an uneasy truce rather than birthing a friendship.

"Let's drink to our health," Sinell suggested. "Liddy see to this man's companions, while I get some ale from the ship."

"Don't trouble yourself, Sinell. You might forget the ale and bring shackles instead. We'll be going as soon as I've had a word with Liddy."

"You're a careless man to hurl insults at me!" he retorted hotly.

"I was careless to think you honorable once. Only a fool fails to learn from his mistakes."

"Fair enough," Sinell grumbled uneasily, "but I'd like the chance to learn from mine. Stay until we've had a talk, then you can speak with Liddy. Send your brothers back to their ship if that makes you feel more comfortable. I still need some ale." Sinell made for his ship.

Father Auxilius, hampered by his ignorance of Gaelic, inquired in Latin, "Who is that vicious brute?"

"Sinell's a pirate captain, a slave trader," I responded. "And Liddy, now she's a true Irish saint."

"A slave trader's whore?" Father Malach exclaimed contemptuously. "It takes precious little to be a saint in Ireland!"

The pain I saw on Liddy's face matched the grief and anger in my own heart. "Father Malach!" I seethed. "Do you never..."

"Be at peace, Holy Boy," Liddy chirped bravely in Latin, approaching us from her kettle, "I'm not easily offended, especially after your generous compliment. And as for you, Father Malach, you may call me 'whore' if you like. God is my judge, not self-righteous British priests. But be *very* careful. Don't think Sinell won't understand your insults. Now, if you will rest in the shade of that large oak, I'll call you when the stew is ready."

"You both speak Latin?!" Father Malach remarked incredulously.

"Yes," Liddy responded, "but you won't have to speak a word in any language for Sinell to read what's in your hearts." Father Malach and Father Auxilius humbly retreated to the shade of a large oak by the forest's edge.

"Liddy, you're always an inspiration!" I sighed smiling. "Tell me. Is Sinell to be trusted?"

"What a foolish question! Of course not! If it isn't God you're trusting, you'd best get on that ship and sail out of here!" I felt like a schoolboy duly reprimanded. Liddy returned to her kettle.

"Brother Ninus, keep those two out of trouble," I said as I stepped toward the hut. "And a prayer or two couldn't hurt."

"Are you sure you'll be all right with that pirate?"

"There's only one thing I'm sure of, Ninus."

Inside the hut, the cool, musty pleasantness of the damp earthen floor, and the tidiness of the simple furnishings created a feeling of well being. This was Liddy's home, not just the house she served. On one wall there was even a cross hanging. Sinell had mellowed considerably in twenty years.

Sinell stepped through the doorway. On one shoulder he carried a barrel of ale, and in his free hand several mugs. Liddy entered behind him, filled three mugs, then hurried through the doorway without a word.

Sinell's hair was mostly gray now, his hairline slightly higher on his forehead, his beard copper, but with strands of gray showing through. For all that he was still powerfully muscular and trim. His whip still hung from one hip, his flexible paddle from the other. I shuddered.

Sinell and I filled our mugs and sat drinking for some time in uneasy silence. "My nights were tormented after I betrayed you in Gaul," he finally spoke. "I want to know why. A pirate isn't troubled by such things," he said flatly. I made no response. He drained his mug and filled it again. "Why do I feel that I owe you?" he growled, glaring at me.

"God knows, but I'll gladly collect on the debt. Can you arrange a meeting with the king of Leinster, and find me a pair of good Irish trousers?"

Sinell, speechless, stared in disbelief for several moments. "The meeting I can arrange," he stated contemplatively, "but the trousers?" We broke into simultaneous laughter at what seemed an absurd request in light of the first. Liddy stepped into the hut, smiled, grabbed a few pinches of dried herbs, and left. Our eyes followed her.

"Do you know what she did, when I bragged of my treachery against you?" Sinell asked soberly. "She wept. I don't know who she prayed for more, me or you. A peculiar woman, Liddy."

"Sinell, will you give Liddy her freedom?" I asked.

Sinell bolted to his feet. "I can't! And that's not part of the deal!"

"Then sell her to me, and I'll free her!"

"NO!!"

His obstinacy angered me. "If you care for her, why can't you at least make her your wife, instead of your whore?" I demanded, standing to face him.

"Because then she would be free!" Sinell shouted, slamming his fists on the table, a tremor in his voice. He sank back into his chair. "SIT DOWN!" he ordered. I sat facing him, anxious to study and understand his uncharacteristic emotion.

Sinell took a long drink, a distant look in his eyes. "Liddy was always incomparably beautiful, intelligent, graceful. From the moment I captured her I prized her, wanted her, not just her body, but all of her. Still, business is business. A group of Picts paid a handsome price for Liddy. Made me a rich young man. That night, as I miserably counted my earnings, I heard her pleading and screaming. I tried to deafen my ears, but still I heard."

I glanced beyond Sinell and saw Liddy, a silent silhouette in the doorway.

"When I found them, the Picts were drunk and savage. They had... the vicious bastards! What fool would take a prize mare and ride her so mercilessly that she could never foal, then injure her so completely that her life was spent in a single night?" Sinell swallowed hard. "Liddy was nearly gone. Death would have been a mercy. I drove those bloodthirsty sons-of-bitches back with my whip! Threw some Roman coins in their faces! And carried Liddy, bruised and bleeding, to my hut. I thought she would die. She cried out over and over in the night. By morning the bed was soaked with her blood and her tears." Sinell cleared his throat. "Can you understand now... whatever your name is?"

"Patrick."

"Patrick. A good name, Patrick. You wear it well. I'll never forget that night, Patrick. Do you imagine she can?" I glanced quickly again at Liddy. Silent tears glistened on her face. "Why do I tell you this?" Sinell asked irritably. He took a long drink. Liddy turned to go, but stopped as Sinell set down his mug and continued his hushed confession.

"I swear to you, Patrick, before all the gods of Ireland, I didn't touch her, beautiful as she was, not for a long, long time. When I did, I was so careful not to hurt her. Now she gives herself to me willingly enough, but if she were free, what would compel her to stay? Maybe I'm a fool, but I'd be lost without her."

"You're lost even with me, you bloody pagan, unless you give your life to the Lord," Liddy quietly scolded wiping the tears from her cheeks.

Sinell sprang to his feet. "Liddy! You're a troublesome woman."

"Why have you never told me what you fear, Sinell?" she asked.

"I fear nothing," he retorted in chilling monotone.

"Of course," she replied submissively. Liddy turned to me. "Listen to me, Patrick. You come to Ireland risking your own freedom for love of the Irish. Well, Sinell is *my* Ireland. I no longer wish to be free."

"Liddy," Sinell breathed, as he gently took her face between his callused palms. Without taking his eyes from hers, Sinell ordered, "The stew is ready, Patrick. Go and eat."

CHAPTER SEVENTEEN
His Severed Head

That evening, Sinell was in exceptional good humor. He sent word to every man and woman along the beach to join us around the fire circle, and most of them did. Our first night to serve God in Ireland and we were surrounded by some of the fiercest, most barbarous men on the island apart from the Picts. Father Malach and Father Auxilius sat like two frightened old women throughout the evening, wisely remaining silent. Even Brother Ninus was uncomfortable with the crude and brutal humor, vulgar gestures, and raw sensuality. It was a long way from British nobility and the brothers of Lerins to the cut-throats of Ireland.

I was introduced as an old acquaintance, a bard from Britannia. As I recounted many of their favorite stories, all of them pagan, and most of them violent and vulgar in one way or another, Brother Ninus stared open-mouthed. Perhaps I should have refused to tell those tales, or some of them. But keeping these people in good humor seemed to be a wise course. Besides, they were good stories, if a bit too colorful. It was a blessing that Father Malach and Father Auxilius knew nothing of Gaelic.

Before the night ended, Sinell had arranged for two chariots and a driver to carry us to King Diarmuid's Rath, and several shirts and trousers to replace our Roman robes. Liddy had provided information about clusters of Christians who lived in this southern kingdom. I was elated with our progress and thankful for the day. My brothers, on the other hand, were only thankful that the day would end.

A few hours before daylight, the lovers and lingerers had finally retired or fallen asleep where they lay. Father Malach, Father Auxilius, Brother Ninus, and I stretched out next to the fire and fell asleep.

"Patrick, wake up!" Sinell commanded the next morning, nudging my shoulder with the toe of his boot. I sprang to my feet, my mind fuzzy with sleep, but keen enough to be cautious. "I haven't much time," he barked. "We sail with the tide." We? I thought worriedly. A wiry young man, not more than nineteen stood nearby. Perhaps he meant...

"You look better with whiskers," Sinell remarked, observing my unshaven stubble.

"Liddy has your clothes. Conleng here will take you to King Diarmuid. I assume you can still drive an Irish chariot?" I nodded, relieved. "Diarmuid's a ruthless man," Sinell cautioned, "but known to be reasonable if the proper respect is shown."

"How much proper respect do you suggest I take?"

Sinell smiled slyly, "As much as you can carry. Here." Sinell handed me a cloth bearing his emblem, a red boar. "Diarmuid knows me. I just hope I'm still on good terms with him."

"I share your hope!" I remarked doubtfully.

"Conleng, leave us," Sinell ordered, then he led me a few paces away from those who still slept. "Patrick, you see me as a beast who shredded your life once and can be expected to do so again, an accurate assessment," he stated flatly. "Were I in your shoes, the hate that I see behind your eyes would surely be in mine. It may be unreasonable to expect any other relationship between us."

"I admit my heart is slow to follow my head, but I have renounced my hate for you, Sinell."

"Have you?" His voice was chilling, his eyes piercing. "Then swear an oath that makes us brothers, and I won't be forced to kill you where you stand." He drew his long knife. "I'm not so foolish, that I would let you live as my enemy."

"My only enemies are the enemies of my God, Sinell. He requires that I love even them. An oath won't be necessary."

Sinell grumbled, "But for Liddy's fondness for you, and this irritating debt I feel, I'd lay you open and be done with it!" Grabbing my hand he sliced my palm with the point of his blade. "Maybe an oath isn't necessary for you," he snapped, drawing the blade across his own palm, "but it is for me."

He laid his bloody palm against mine, gripped it firmly and swore with absolute conviction, "Your blood is now my blood, your family, my family, your friends, my friends, your enemies, my enemies. I am bound by this oath as long as there is blood in my body. And may your God strike me dead, if ever I betray you again."

"Your blood is now my blood," I repeated with equal conviction, but admittedly ambiguous suspicion, "your family, my family, your friends my friends, your enemies... my enemies. But, Sinell, I will show your innocent victims mercy, and I will not be a party to their abuse. I am bound by this oath as long as there is blood in my body. So I swear in the strong name of the Trinity, God the Father, God the Son, and God the Holy Spirit."

"Fair enough!" Sinell agreed. "Liddy, bring some bandages!" he yelled loudly.

"Sinell!" Liddy gasped, as she saw our hands.

"Hush woman," Sinell barked. "And make haste, the tide's about to turn." Liddy dressed and bandaged Sinell's wound with the skill that comes from much practice.

"Patrick, I'll look you up when I'm back in port," Sinell said, gripping my uninjured hand.

"God go with you, Sinell," I replied.

"Better keep him with you," Sinell sternly cautioned, then walked away.

"Let's get you washed up, then you can change your clothes," Liddy said flatly, walking toward the hut.

When I emerged from the hut, Father Malach and Father Auxilius were staring at the dying coals of the fire. Father Malach was the first to notice me.

"Would you like to trade those Roman robes for some good Irish trousers?" I inquired.

"You'd have us all become barbarians?"

"If you can alter a man's heart by changing his garments, our work in Ireland will be simple," I teased.

"But you don't look anything like a priest!"

"Most of Ireland has never seen one."

"We haven't been sent to *most* of Ireland, only to the Christian community," Father Malach officiously argued.

"Thank you, Father Malach, for reminding me of my mission! And let me remind you both, that not all bishops agree that clergy should dress differently than the people they serve. Some even forbid it. Your fine robes or Ninus' monastic habits do not make you holy, any more than these trousers make me a barbarian."

I left them and joined Brother Ninus and Conleng who were readying the chariots and horses for the journey. By the time we had the horses in harness Father Malach and Father Auxilius had joined us, still in their Roman attire.

"Brother Ninus," Liddy called, as she approached, "I've packed some dried fish, winkles, blood pudding, bread, and here's a keg of ale to suit the British palates." Liddy handed Brother Ninus a basket, while one of Sinell's pirates, left behind as her bodyguard, loaded the keg onto the chariot.

"Father Patrick, you'll find the Druids in Leinster more moderate than those in the north, but just as jealous of their power. If you get into any trouble, Conleng will get word to me. God keep you," Liddy expounded.

"And you as well," I responded, kissing her gently on both cheeks under the cold eye of her bodyguard. I mounted my chariot with Brother Ninus behind me, while Father Malach and Father Auxilius joined Conleng.

"Lead on," I commanded Conleng, who was staring at me with an amused twinkle in his eye. He whipped his horses and bolted westward. I followed at his heels. The pace he set was swift, not so fast as to endanger life and limb, but enough to tax the endurance of a man almost twice his age. Brother Ninus enjoyed a good laugh at my expense, as I tossed him my cloak and wriggled out of my shirt. "I don't hear you offering to drive," I shouted, as we sped over the narrow forest road. He only laughed the merrier. By the time we burst out of the woods and into open meadows and rolling hills, I was wet with perspiration and ached in every joint. We came upon a fresh water spring near a large thicket and slowed to refresh the horses. Brother Ninus, Father Malach, and Father Auxilius dismounted and drank heartily, while Conleng and I waited with the horses. I tried to work the tightness out of my shoulders by rotating them.

"What's the matter, *old* man?" Conleng laughed.

"Nothing a little shower couldn't fix," I chuckled and, as the other three stepped away, I splashed my young upstart with the ice cold water. Like all good fellows he splashed me back several times, giving me the shower I required and a good laugh as well. We let our thirsty horses drink, but carefully gauged the speed and quantity consumed.

"You drive pretty well for an old foreigner," Conleng allowed.

"I drive pretty well for an Irishman, young or old," I retorted, "But you're driving is exceptional. Do you race often?"

"Every festival!"

"I thought as much."

As we got back to work silently tending the horses, the hushed conversation between Father Auxilius, Father Malach, and Brother Ninus was easily overheard.

"We should be meeting with the Irish Christians, not racing chariots and playing water games like adolescents," Father Malach asserted.

"And this meeting with the king, what purpose can it serve, but to bring *him* personal glory," Father Auxilius added.

"We need land if we are to build a church, or even have a place to live." Brother Ninus explained patiently. "For that we need the king's favor."

"What's wrong with open land, like this?" Father Auxilius asked.

"All land in Ireland is claimed by one clan or another," Brother Ninus explained.

"Then lets find the owner and..."

"I think we're about to meet them," I said, startling my critics. They all looked at me, then followed my eyes to the crest of the hill, where eight painted Scots, swords and shields in hand, descended toward us at a run. Conleng swiftly disappeared behind the horses and into the thicket. Seven of the warriors surrounded Brother Ninus, Father Malach, and Father Auxilius. One stood guard over me.

"Are these women or men that they have no beards and wear dresses?" the largest warrior queried. Two Scots attempted to peer under Brother Ninus's and Father Auxilius's robes, while another pulled Father Malach's head back by the hair and kissed him on the mouth.

"Not a woman!" the warrior declared, spitting in revulsion, and eliciting loud laughter from his fellows. The warrior pushed Father Malach to the ground.

"Too little hair to hang," another warrior complained, pulling on Brother Ninus' tonsured hair.

"Who wants a beardless trophy anyway?" the big man questioned. "Their horses and chariots are enough. Just kill them and let's be off."

"We are men of peace bringing gifts to King Diarmuid," I quickly announced.

"Ahh, you speak Gaelic," the big man, obviously the leader, stated as he approached. One side of his face was painted blue, the other hosted blond hair and eyebrows, a carrot red beard, and intelligent blue eyes. "Your speech and clothes are Irish," he observed, "but your head is foreign. I'll remove it for you." He grinned wickedly and raised his sword.

"It's a brave warrior who will take my head and steal the king's tribute," I challenged without flinching, though inside my heart was racing.

"Under whose banner do you bring tribute?" He queried arrogantly. I lifted the sign of the red boar.

"Sinell!" He remarked with noticeable respect, lowering his sword. "How unfortunate for you. King Diarmuid threatened to hang him by the thumbs and roast him slowly over a hot fire the next time he set eyes on Sinell. It's doubtful either you or the tribute will be missed."

As he drew his sword again, such fury swelled within me, that I felt a full two feet taller.

"Hang our heads from your belts!!" I roared, hardly recognizing the booming resonance of my own voice, "and with my lifeless mouth I will shout your thieving treachery! Until Diarmuid and Sinell hear of it! Then *your* heads will be the trophies they bear to their huts!!" The sky darkened, and a strong wind began to blow. "The voices of my dead brothers will cry out the offense!" I continued to rage, "Until every bard in Ireland will sing how shamefully you betrayed your king! And your families, in dishonor, are cut off from your kindred forever!" A flash of light split the sky. I thrust my hands toward heaven. "STRIKE ME DOWN!!!" my voice echoed in the thunder. "Or by God's fury I may call down fire from heaven and consume your miserable souls!!!"

Wind suddenly screamed through the trees. Lightening struck, once, twice, three times, setting ablaze a scraggled oak to the left of us, not unusual for a sudden summer storm, but certainly timely. My eyes bore like fire into those of the warrior captain. He began to lower his sword. For some incomprehensible reason this fueled my anger. Slowly the warrior leader dropped to his knees before me. My eyes moved appraisingly from one warrior to another, each kneeling in turn. Only Brother Ninus, Father Malach, and Father Auxilius met my gaze, but even their eyes were filled with fear. How peculiar.

Peculiar or not, I was now in control, and I had better make the most of it. Conleng remained hidden, and I thought it best not to expose him, though I wondered at his motive. I mounted my chariot and donned my shirt and cloak. Rain began to fall and a stout wind whipped mane and tail.

"Who will drive my brothers?" I demanded of the bewildered warriors. The leader stepped forward without a word and took the reins in hand. Brother Ninus, Father Malach, and Father Auxilius mounted behind us, and we proceeded through the driving rain to Diarmuid's Rath.

King Diarmuid's Rath was considerably larger than King Milchu's Rath had been. There were just as few buildings, but each was substantially larger. The feast hall could certainly seat well over five hundred. The rain-washed, shriveled heads that adorned its exterior walls drew wide-eyed stares of horror from Father Malach and Father Auxilius. Even Brother Ninus stared sadly at the evidence of primitive barbarism. It had never occurred to me that, having left Ireland when he was barely ten, this land was more foreign to Brother Ninus than it was to me.

The rain had stopped, leaving the fresh aroma of an Irish spring. The herdsmen, craftsmen, brehons, warriors, and slaves all watched curiously as we slogged our way through the mud to the feast hall. Two slaves hurried to tend our horses. Another brought us refreshment. The warrior leader, along with three other warriors, entered the feast hall, taking Sinell's favor and the bag of gifts with them. We waited outside for some time. Muffled voices could be heard within, speaking rapidly and excitedly. The voices became silent as three men stepped through the doors followed by the warriors.

The seven colors worn by the leader of the three marked him as the king. He was a big man with a round bulbous nose, dark hair, and a red curly beard. He had thin lips and deep set, dark eyes, the kind that would make a man look angry even when he was laughing. With him was a white headed Chief Druid, who looked so like my own grandfather, that I had difficulty taking my eyes from him, and a third man, slight and slender with dark hair and blue eyes, who wore six colors making him the king's bard or filid. I dropped respectfully to my knee and bowed my head. Brother Ninus and the others followed suit.

"So you bring gifts!" King Diarmuid stated flatly. "You are fools! I can have you killed or sold as slaves. Your gifts, your horses, your chariots will all be mine. What do you have to say?" he queried.

"You are a noble man, King Diarmuid," I responded without raising my head. "We have heard stories of your justice and wisdom. Your judgement is certain to be fair."

"Stories? From Sinell? That prince of liars?" Diarmuid retorted. "On your feet."

We stood and collected our travel bags. Brother Ninus glanced worriedly at me. I had no assurance to give him. Fortunately, Father Malach and Father Auxilius were blissfully ignorant of King Diarmuid's threats.

The warriors escorted us as we followed King Diarmuid into the feast hall. We were ushered to the head of the table near King Diarmuid's throne. Chairs were appointed for us, and servants quickly placed sweet breads and drinks on the table as we took our seats. I glanced across at Father Malach and Father Auxilius. Their expressions were grim, as they slowly observed in the ghostly light of the torches and candles, the many shields and heads that decorated the interior of this hall. Brother Ninus was carefully observing the bard and the Druid, who stood on either side of the throne.

"Sinell!" King Diarmuid began, "How is that old pirate?"

"Well enough," I responded, avoiding his gaze. "Not as hard as he used to be."

"A pity," King Diarmuid sighed. "That woman of his would make a Christian of him!"

I ventured a quick glance from the Druid to King Diarmuid. Neither looked hostile. "Do you oppose Christians?" I asked as casually as I could manage.

"What's another god? Christians are no harder to rule than any other people. But it's a bad choice for a pirate," King Diarmuid expostulated.

He was a reasonable man, then. My expectations began to rise. King Diarmuid lifted his mug and began to drink. We did likewise. The bard took his cue and started playing his pipe. King Diarmuid said nothing more, just ate and drank while the music filled the hall. Fifteen minutes passed. The idleness wore on me like a bed full of fleas.

An old Irish tune that I had once played with considerable skill was now sounding from the pipe. Feeling a bit too confident and anxious to be active, I asked, "With your permission, King Diarmuid, might I accompany your bard?"

"Fiacc?" Diarmuid called.

"Delighted to hear him, King Diarmuid," Fiacc said. He curiously handed me a wooden pipe. I played a few warm-up notes, nodded, and then began piping a lively jig. That done, I played a favorite air from the north, one Fiacc had evidently never heard. He listened eagerly like a musician who truly loved his craft, then we launched into another jig that got progressively faster and faster until my fingers could no longer match the notes. It was exhilarating. Laughing, I handed Fiacc the pipe, bowed in deference to the superior player, and returned to my seat.

"A fine bit of playing," King Diarmuid remarked, his eyes meeting mine for the first time. "But why does Sinell send me a bard...?" He broke off, leaving his question unasked. I was captivated by his gaze, and terrified. Like Sinell's, his were the eyes of an intelligent man, but absolutely ruthless; principled, yet devoid of conscience. King Diarmuid stood threateningly to his feet. The wildness that marks a boar's eyes, when he finds himself cornered by a powerful opponent now flashed in his, sending a chill through me.

"You are no bard, but a wizard!" King Diarmuid accused. "Will you presume to curse me, as you did my men, with the fire that dances in your eyes?!" He turned sharply away and toward the Druid.

"Who are you?" the Druid then demanded taking the cue. "What is your business with King Diarmuid?"

I stood respectfully to face them. "We are all priests, who have come to serve the Christians in Ireland."

King Diarmuid and the Druid exchanged surprised glances. "Why come here? I am not a Christian," King Diarmuid asked.

"You well know there is no law in Ireland to protect foreigners, no land we can buy. Families will not sell outside their clans without the approval of the king and the nobles." King Diarmuid began scowling. "We humbly ask for your protection, and that you might inquire whether the clan will part with a small piece of land, where we can live and work."

"Charity?" King Diarmuid sneered. "I would not have taken you for beggars!" He lifted the bag of gifts and slammed it angrily on the table, provoking gasps from Father Malach and Father Auxilius. "Did you think me so cheap I could be bought for a bag of trinkets? or charmed by a simple melody?" he bellowed.

"No, King Diarmuid. We thought you so great, that you might have a heart of mercy for strangers."

"Ono MacOengusa," King Diarmuid called. The Druid immediately followed him to a corner of the hall. So low were their voices that I scarcely made out a word of their discussion. Ono frowned doubtfully, then deliberately nodded his head. With a flash of his eye and a flick of King Diarmuid's wrist, the attending warriors jerked Malach, Auxilius, and Ninus to their feet, pinning their arms behind them, and laying their swords across each throat. The warrior captain behind me carefully drew his sword.

"A heart of mercy you expected?" King Diarmuid stated flatly, returning to the table. "First we'll see of what mettle Christian priests are made. You told my men that if they severed your head, your lifeless mouth would shout the injustice. Is that right?"

My heart skipped a beat. Our eyes met as I reluctantly confessed, "Those words did come out of my mouth."

King Diarmuid nodded. "Then we will sever one of your heads. If the mouth speaks, the others will have the land and protection you request. If not, we will take another and another, until we know whether all Christian priests are liars." King Diarmuid sat, took a drink, and ate another bite of sweet bread, while I prayed silently for some kind of direction.

"Will you gather your nobles to witness the miracle... or misfortune?" I asked.

"A public trial? Yes," he agreed warily, glancing once toward Ono MacOengusa, "a trial should have its witnesses. A feast! Tomorrow night!"

Another wave of his hand signaled the warriors to release my brothers. Poor Father Malach and Father Auxilius hadn't understood anything but the sword at their throats. They both looked exhausted with fear. Brother Ninus was harder to read. The warriors shoved the three roughly to the door. Their captain gently indicated for me to follow, but I hung back until the door was shut, then turned to haggle, if possible, with King Diarmuid.

Our accommodations for the night were no worse than any slave's. A small turf and wattle hut with a thatched roof, a tiny window, and one guarded doorway, was our protection from the elements. The only furnishing was a covered bucket for urination and defecation. The straw covered dirt floor was to be our bed.

By the time I had joined them in the hut, Brother Ninus had translated the events of the day for Father Malach and Father Auxilius. I was greeted with a hostile silence, for which I was extremely grateful. I needed time to think, to pray. I sat against the wall and began slowly tracing my finger over the storyteller's picture on my little leather pouch, reviewing in my mind the possibilities for tomorrow's trial.

"I don't understand you," Father Malach burst out accusingly. "You go to your death like it's..."

"We have to accept what we can't change, Father Malach," I counseled.

"I accept that you've made a mess of this whole thing!" Father Malach snapped. "Bishop Amicus knew you couldn't be trusted to stay out of trouble. But what could I do, with you barking orders like some potentate? Now we'll all pay for your error with our lives!"

My heart sank. "I always expected to give my life in Ireland," I solemnly admitted.

"To give it! Not waste it!" Brother Ninus barked irritably.

"Well, I didn't expect it!" Father Auxilius fearfully interjected. "I'm not ready to die. Have you no fear at all?"

Fear, like a grasping relative, had greeted me the moment we came ashore, and had remained distressingly close at hand ever since. I thought they knew. "When I think what they may do to me, Auxilius," I anxiously confessed, "I'm sick with fear. ...So, instead, I think what I might do... to make these moments worth the life I give. - Ninus," I continued turning toward him, "my life, death, will not be a waste."

"What about ours?" Father Malach grumbled to no one.

Looking away, I slowly removed Grandfather's little book of verses from my neck and lovingly ran my fingers over its well-worn binding. "Ninus," I beckoned. He crossed the hut and squatted in front of me. Speaking privately in Gaelic I asked, "if King Diarmuid honors his word and you and the others live, will you see that my father gets this?"

Brother Ninus frowned. "You made a deal with King Diarmuid?" I nodded. Brother Ninus carefully took the little book, dropped his head, and wept. "Could we have both missed God so dismally, Patrick, that our adventure ends before it has begun?" he finally asked. I couldn't answer. "I suppose one day, when I reach heaven's gates, I shall find you one of the white-robed martyrs."

"If I were dying for my faith, and not for stupidly shooting my mouth off, I might be more inclined to believe that," I responded defeatedly. "But I'll be with our Lord, whatever I'm wearing."

Father Auxilius began pacing nervously, his fingers anxiously twisting the fabric of his robe. "Shouldn't you tell..." Brother Ninus began.

"No," I interrupted. "It may be a false hope. Better for all of us to prepare to meet our God." I began reciting in Latin a Psalm of penitence: "Have mercy on me, O God, according to your loving-kindness; in your great compassion blot out my offenses." Brother Ninus joined with me, "Wash me through and through from my wickedness and cleanse me from my sin." Fathers Malach and Auxilius added their voices, "For I know my transgressions, and my sin is ever before me...."

"I, Patrick, a Sinner..."

Sinell

CHAPTER EIGHTEEN
Will You Hear A Story?

Like a festival day, the rath was buzzing with activity the following morning. My brothers and I should have been exhausted. We had prayed, worshiped, sung hymns of praise, shared our fears and weaknesses, even laughed together for most of the night. Yet none of us was the least bit tired. We aggressively ate the breakfast of bread and mutton that was served, while, like boys on holiday, we swapped stories about our past adventures, past loves, and past dreams that never came true.

"I feel like a child again," Father Malach mused. "I've never been this honest with anyone."

"I've never been this scared," Father Auxilius allowed, forcing our fears once more into the light.

The long, long day finally faded into twilight. The large frame of the warrior captain stepped through the doorway and over to me. Without the paint he looked less fierce, and a great deal more intelligent. I stood.

"My name is Sechnall. It is my sword that will take your head. I have worked long and hard to make it sharp, strong." He held up the sword for my examination. Was this courtesy extended to all victims? I wondered. Feeling faint, I obligingly studied the weapon. "Your death," he quietly assured, "will be swift and painless." A faint smile turned the corners of my mouth. This wasn't a custom, but a kindness. Sechnall extended his hand in a gesture of friendship, and I received it. He frowned as our palms met, then carefully unwrapped Liddy's bandage, and examined my wound. "Whose blood do you share?" he asked worriedly.

"Sinell's."

"Sinell!" He breathed a heavy sigh. "In taking your head, I lose my own. Come!" he ordered. We reluctantly followed.

The hill leading up to the feast hall was teeming with people, like so many ants hurrying up and down. Nobles and their ladies, dressed in colorful clothing and decked in ornate jewelry, entered the hall, while servants and slaves, busy with their labors, came and went, and common folk clustered around the doorway to peer within. All heads turned as we were ushered to a bench along one wall and seated. Whispers and snickers rose like a wave, then subsided.

The multitude of candles, rich food, and warm bodies in the crowded hall contributed to both the stifling heat and the smell of grease and sweat, possibly accounting for my nausea. Or perhaps it was the din of constant chatter, laughter, orders being shouted, and music faintly played that made me so uncomfortable. A quick glance at Father Malach and Father Auxilius revealed the struggle with fear and faith evident in their faces. Brother Ninus stared calmly and sadly at the floor.

Someone passing stopped before me. I looked up to see Fiacc, holding out a pipe, not the rude little pipe he had allowed me the day before, but a finely crafted instrument, beautifully finished and painted. King Diarmuid caught my eye and grinned snidely. That sly fox would get as much amusement from this head as was possible, I thought. Before him the ornate mugs, given me by Coroticus, decorated his table.

I stood to my feet and played a few warm-up notes, which could scarcely be heard above the gaiety. Imagining myself to be alone on some solitary mountaintop, I closed my eyes, and poured my whole soul into the beautifully melancholy and haunting tunes that found birth in the heart of a homesick shepherd boy so many years ago. I must have played for twenty minutes. When I opened my eyes, the hall was silent, and every eye was on me.

"You have been called to witness a trial," King Diarmuid announced immediately, his voice booming against the stillness. "This Christian claims his mouth will speak even without his body attached." A number of disbelieving gasps and chuckles rippled among the revelers. "Does he lie?" King Diarmuid asked sarcastically. "Or will we see a miracle?" Loud laughter wafted throughout the hall, as King Diarmuid mockingly opened and closed his hands, like puppets, pretending they spoke to one another. "If we are disappointed, and his mouth remains silent," King Diarmuid continued, "we will know what liars all Christians are. Then, though I have agreed to spare his brothers, I will throw them out of Ireland. And I will drive every Irish Christian from the Kingdom of Leinster as well."

Murmurs filled the hall, as the nobles looked me over, some laughing, others concerned. Father Malach and Father Auxilius listened eagerly to Brother Ninus' translation of King Diarmuid's terms. That terrible fear left their eyes. Free from the responsibility of their deaths, my own was now more bearable.

"Nobles of Leinster," King Diarmuid resumed, "The man wishes to speak even before we take his head. Will you hear him?"

A gray-haired old noble, slightly stooped, stood to his feet. He bowed low before me in mock reverence and pronounced, "Speak, oh foolish one! We will hear you!" The entire assembly erupted into laughter. I was amazed to feel the curl of a smile on my own lips.

"Will you hear a story?" I asked.

The nobles and their ladies sat forward expectantly, like the eager children painted on my pouch. Tremendous love, that had no origin within me, now filled my being, allowing me to experience what the heart of God must have felt for these people.

"Not too very long ago," my tale began, "God wanted to speak to men, but human ears could not hear the voice of God. 'I will become a man, then they will hear me,' God said. So he found a good woman, planted his seed in her, and grew himself a man's body."

"Like Cuchulain! Son of Lugh and Dichtre!" the old noble interjected.

"Yes!" I eagerly confirmed, "like Cuchulain, only this God-man didn't become a mighty warrior with spear and sword. He became a filid."

Nods and sighs from my enrapt audience indicated their pleasure at this new twist to the old tale.

"Everywhere the God-man went he told stories... of how much God loves all people and wants them to love one another. But this was too hard for men. They had evil in them, murder, hate, treachery, lies, taking pleasure in the injuries of others. Even those who wanted to love couldn't. The sweet fruit of love can't grow in a heart already sown with the thorns and thistles of evil.

"So, God took the evil into his own man's body and struck it down, killing the God-man and the evil with him. His blood became a poison to evil, and the drink of love. Now any seeds of evil that take root in men can be destroyed by that blood. And all men and women, who drink of it, can be *free*... to love."

"Tell us, which god is this?" the old noble insisted.

"There is only one God," I answered.

"Are you mad and a fool?" The old noble chided. Murmurs and debates instantly filled the hall.

"I am the filid!" I proclaimed with passion. "This is *my* story! In it there is only one God! ...He loves every one of you. He died to give you this freedom, and yet he lives. All he wants in return is for you to love him and to love each other, in this life and in the Otherworld... *He sent me*," I insisted, struggling with emotion, "...to tell you this before I die."

Judging by the many luminous eyes and studied countenances the message had moved them. So great was the silence, I could hear the beating of my own heart.

"My... severed head... may not speak to you," I continued with some difficulty, "but I pray these words will speak, again and again, until you know and believe, how very precious you are to Him."

In the silent moments that followed, I prayed desperately that they might read in the transparency of my face, the love of God that burned for them in my heart.

"Are you finished?" King Diarmuid asked irritably.

I might have said more. At least I had accomplished what I came to do. If only one were to seek God and find him, my death would have purpose. I took a deep breath and looked squarely at King Diarmuid. "I am ...ready to die," I stated reluctantly.

King Diarmuid avoided my gaze, but signaled to Sechnall. *Sechnall*, my new friend. I had to smile at the absurdity, but only a little. He approached, his sharp sword glistening. "Perfect love casts out fear," I quoted unconvincingly to myself. "Dear God, I'm not perfected yet. You'll have to take me fear and all."

Sechnall stopped before me with troubled eyes. "When it's my time to die," his voice resounded throughout the hall, "I want to be where you are, with this God who loves you."

"He loves you, too, Sechnall," I encouraged, wishing for time to tell him more. "After this bloody business is over, please, go and speak to my brothers."

"What is his name, this god you speak of?" voices approaching from behind me asked. Before I could turn to answer someone pulled me by the arm. "Did you say you are Christian?" "Where do you get this God's-blood?" another noble stood and inquired.

"ENOUGH! Sechnall, take the sword!" King Diarmuid roared.

"My brothers will tell you all you wish to know," I said, pointing to Ninus, Malach, and Auxilius. The men nodded and soberly moved away. Reluctantly Sechnall raised his sword with a trembling arm.

"Wait! Please!" I breathed fearfully, "Sechnall, have arms of iron, swift and sure." Sechnall nodded his head, took a deep breath, set his jaw, and raised his sword again, this time steady as a rock. I swallowed hard, took a deep breath, and closed my eyes.

"Hold!" a woman's commanding voice insisted, "I would hear more."

"I would hear more," the old noble chimed in.

"Yes, let us hear him again," a young voice concurred. Other voices joined in agreement. I opened my eyes, frustrated at the postponement of the inevitable.

"But the *trial*," King Diarmuid countered.

"Our Good King Diarmuid," the woman saluted, rising to her feet. It was a low velvety, voice. "Surely the stranger has passed the trial." Sechnall lowered his sword. Excited chatter filled the hall. I strained to see the face of my defender.

"How could that be possible, Lady Gowan?" King Diarmuid crooned, as if speaking to a child. "We can all see that he still wears his head. The trial has not begun."

"A filid's words continue long after him, without benefit of body or head," Lady Gowan responded with irresistible charm. "Must we kill the bard to prove the obvious, my lord?" I could see the fascination and irritation in King Diarmuid's eyes as he stared unflinchingly at her.

"She's right, King Diarmuid," the old noble agreed laughing. "So say I," said another. Others indicated their similar feelings with shouts, clapping, or pounding on the table.

King Diarmuid rose to his feet, scowling. "I pledged these strangers land and protection should he pass this trial," his voice boomed. "Are you still so eager to let him live? Who will part with his land?"

The nobles glanced nervously from one to the other, while the lady looked contemplatively around at me. "Scothie!" I whispered. She turned back to King Diarmuid. "I might have a hill or two I could spare," she offered.

"So be it!" Diarmuid capitulated, throwing his arms up in frustration.

Sechnall embraced me. Others patted me on the back, drank to my health, or just smiled. I could only nod weakly as the culmination of thirty-two hours without sleep and intense emotional stress sent waves of exhaustion sweeping over me. Sechnall led me through the crowd and out the door. Leaning against the nearest wall, I closed my eyes and slid to the ground.

"You're a fool, but a brave fool," said an angel, who floated to her knees before me. It *was* Scothie, still beautiful, her crystal blue eyes peering into my soul. She stroked my face gently with her fingers, provoking a decidedly carnal response from every nerve in my body. Had I the strength I could have... I closed my eyes and thanked God for my weakness.

"Sechnall," she commanded in that soothing, rich voice, "in the morning, take them to Twin Hills."

"It will be my pleasure, Lady Gowan."

Rising gradually from a large plain were two perfectly matched hills, or small mountains. In the valley between them flowed a stream fed both from rain and snow that ran off the mountains and from an underground spring. The spring was surrounded by lush vegetation and flowering trees that made the spot resemble a man's vision of the Garden of Eden. The rest of the valley was only sparsely wooded, leaving plenty of good land to pasture cows, the most common medium of exchange in this world without currency.

Unlike the valley, both mountains were covered by forests, though not densely covered. Their most remarkable twin features were oak groves that at one time had been meticulously groomed. Several trees still bore monstrous, but artistically carved, figures on their trunks. Why these groves were no longer sacred or accessible to the Druids was not apparent from anything I could see, but the well-beaten paths indicated their continued visitation by the common people.

"Father Patrick," Father Auxilius called breathlessly, "Lady Gowan is in the valley and asks to see you."

In my fantasy I imagined myself, still just under sixteen, running down the mountain, sweeping her into my arms, and plunging into a passionate affair that never ended. But more than thirty years had passed. She was no longer Scothie, but Lady Gowan, and I was no longer Sucat.

When we reached the valley, Lady Gowan approached, smartly dressed and bearing herself like a woman in charge. I smiled as the memory of the ever-efficient Julia came to mind. Seen in the light of day her signs of ageing were more apparent, but so minimal that I marveled even more at her beauty. Her expressive eyes were a bit deeper set, and fine wrinkles lined the corners. Her lips were less full, her skin slightly less radiant. But not one of her auburn tresses had grayed. Even her figure remained trim, her breasts firm, or well supported by her garments.

"A hundred thousand welcomes, Father Patrick! Isn't that what they call you?" she began.

"Yes, Lady Gowan, it is," I assured her, "and may I offer you my profound gratitude for your brilliant intervention on my behalf last evening."

"You must extend your gratitude to Sinell's woman, Liddy. She exhausted herself to get word to me of your plight."

"It's good to know that she has influence with a noble woman of your stature, and that you are so kindly disposed to a slave."

She studied me bewilderedly. "As you are the man in charge of this enterprise, I want to make my position clear," she continued. "You are free to use this property in whatever manner suits you, as long as you and I are at peace. Let me show you the boundaries of your influence."

"Lady Gowan, your offer is generous. However, we do not ask for charity, nor will we accept any. We have the means to buy this property, or if that is not acceptable, to buy a long-term agreement that will ensure our use, whether you and I are at peace or not. I can't build a church on..."

"...on the whims of a woman?" she interrupted.

"On a questionable foundation," I concluded, beginning to enjoy our repartee.

"You anticipate difficulties in working with me?" she challenged. I dropped my head, trying to suppress my amusement. Difficulties hardly described the conflict I anticipated. Lady Gowan lifted my chin with her fingertips, and captured my eyes with hers. "Your eyes twinkle when your thoughts are wicked," she teased.

"Or when I'm amused," I added defensively.

"Do I amuse you then?" she breathed seductively.

Dear God, how I still loved her. "No, beautiful lady," I softly spoke from my heart, "you inspire me."

She blushed and glanced nervously away. "I will consider your terms," she said irritably, "though I think you impossibly arrogant to refuse my generosity."

"One of my many short comings, Lady Gowan," I concurred.

"Yes, it is," she retorted. "Sechnall can show you the boundaries. I'm sure you are anxious to begin work on a shelter. Good day to you, Father Patrick."

"God go with you, Lady Gowan." I replied.

My skills at building shelters of turf and wattle were a bit rusty. The first attempt was judged sufficient only for a storage hut, but those that followed were sound and secure. Father Malach was a zealous builder, Brother Ninus meticulous, and Father Auxilius artistic. We built our dwellings in the valley, but placed them carefully so as not to be seen from the spring, our garden made sacred by its own beauty. Our shelters built, we were ready to begin work on the first Irish church.

"Where will the church stand?" Father Malach eagerly asked.

"At the heart of the oak grove," I replied.

"A center for pagan worship? Impossible! I feel cold and clammy every time I go near that place," he protested.

"He's right, Father Patrick. I think it should be burned to the ground and left barren forever," Brother Ninus proposed.

"And what do you say, Father Auxilius?" I asked.

"It would be a shame to burn all those beautiful trees," he responded. "I find the grove calm and serene." The one man I could usually count on to disparage any project was now my only supporter.

"Brothers, if the grove is evil, isn't our God more powerful than any evil?" I asked. "Should we allow these people to think our faith isn't great enough to replace their old beliefs? Our sanctuary too feeble to reclaim the Druid groves?"

"I see your point, Father Patrick, but we'll have to spend a night in prayer over that place before I'd be willing to lay a foundation," Father Malach asserted.

"What better foundation could be laid?" Brother Ninus speculated.

Blessed unity, so rare that I value every instance. We spent a glorious night in prayer and fasting. It wasn't as intense as the night at King Diarmuid's Rath, yet increased the bonds that melded us together. The following morning Lady Gowan loaned us several slaves to help with the project and tools as well. Within two weeks we were celebrating Christian worship in our own sanctuary.

The building was modest, holding not more than thirty people standing comfortably. There were two rude benches on opposite walls for the elderly or the very young or infirm. On the altar table were candles in candle holders, the scriptures, and containers for the bread and wine of communion, though these would remain unused until a bishop were present. Behind and above the altar, hung a crucifix. There was nothing more.

Christians from all Leinster began to hear of the church. By the third Sunday, our fifth week at Twin Hills, the church was full. I had discovered in Britannia that every lesson of scripture could be taught through a story, indeed many scriptures were already stories. How eagerly the Irish embraced this storyteller and his tales. But might people come to be entertained, rather than to worship? The usual applause and shouts that followed every especially good delivery did concern me. Still eleven adults had asked for instruction in the Christian faith following the first two services, so, doubts not withstanding, I continued to be the filid priest.

This third service, Liddy stood near the altar, and to my astonishment, Sinell was with her. Liddy was radiant; Sinell skeptical. Lady Gowan made her first appearance at church, beautiful, but cold as a snowflake on an iceberg. Sechnall and several nobles I remembered from King Diarmuid's Rath were present, including a young couple, Maciul, Diarmuid's younger son, and his wife Lallocc. There were several common folk and slaves I had met the previous weeks and others I had yet to know. All listened with attentive ears and curious eyes, as I translated the Latin scriptures into Gaelic.

"For God says, *'Those who were not my people, and the unloved nation, I will call my beloved. They shall become sons of the living God.'*"

My attention was drawn away from the readings when a delegation of Druids entered the sanctuary with Ono MacOengusa in the lead. I nodded respectfully then continued another reading.

"*And what can separate us from the love of Christ? Affliction, hardship, hunger, nakedness, peril, or the sword? NO! Nothing, nothing at all.*" I elaborated the scripture lessons with a variation of an Irish tale similar to the prodigal son, and as usual, received the same unsettling but enthusiastic response. As I had expected, Sinell whisked Liddy away before the benediction, appearing a bit less skeptical, but certainly not convinced. At the close of worship I referred a good many more people to Father Malach and Brother Ninus for answers to their questions or confession, then stepped outside. Lady Gowan, whom I had had no private conversation with since our first day at Twin Hills, was talking and smiling almost flirtatiously with Father Auxilius. She cast a cold glance toward me. Feeling rebuffed, I turned to reenter the sanctuary and was intercepted by Chief Druid Ono MacOengusa.

"Will you walk with me young prophet?" Ono inquired with such authority, that the answer was assured before the question was asked. I felt I was neither young, nor a prophet, but I was curious.

"If you would walk with a Christian, then I would walk with a Druid," I answered.

As we proceeded in silence along the side of the church, I noticed some untidy sprigs of grass that had sprouted on the turf roof. I pulled them off and gently twirled their stems one at a time between my thumb and forefinger. It was a harmless activity that helped alleviate my apprehension. Was this man seeking information or a victim for ritual sacrifice?

"Since your illuminating performance at King Diarmuid's Rath, I have endeavored to know all that Christians believe," he stated simply. "I find much that agrees with our most ancient teachings."

"How can that be?" I asked incredulously.

"You teach, for instance, that God is distinctly three, yet one sole God. Am I right?" he asked.

"Yes, the Father, Son, and Holy Spirit, co-equal, co-eternal, one in substance, majesty, and purpose," I responded.

He took from my hand a twirling clover and pointed to each of its three leaves and its stem.

"Three, yet one. We Druids have always believed in the sacred oneness of the three," he explained.

"But what of the nature of God? I have seen Druid abuses and sacrifices," I said accusingly. "Twice I was chosen to burn."

Ono stopped walking and eyed me curiously, slowly nodding his head. "It was not always so. Few remain who know what the Druids once believed. ...Certainly not those who follow Lucetmael in the north."

Perceptive old wizard. How swiftly he had deduced my nemesis, Lucetmael, and my sojourn in the north. My life was forfeit should anyone know me for a runaway slave.

"Your deliverance from Lucetmael's devices speaks well of your god. Be at peace, Patrick. I only wish to gather information about this god," he continued, his absolute sincerity assuaging my fears. "Not to discover the secrets of his very remarkable priest."

"Perhaps you could tell me what the Druids once believed," I suggested, keenly interested in the roots of his faith.

"No, our time is passed," he said tiredly. He peered intently into my eyes. "You have kindled a flame, Christian. This fire you have begun, no man can extinguish. It will consume all Ireland. But remember the Druids," he cautioned soberly. "Religion always becomes corrupt, when men of faith become instead, men of power. I pray this will not happen to yours."

This man was no evil wizard. The power and wisdom of his words generated such awe, that I strangely felt him to be a prophet of God.

Over the months that followed Ono MacOengusa and those Druids who followed him took instruction in the Christian faith. There was little we taught him that he didn't already believe. The gospel of Christ he readily embraced, along with most of his disciples. Following their conversions the Christian population in Leinster grew steadily.

CHAPTER NINETEEN
Bishop Palladius

As priests we were authorized to hear confessions and assure those who truly repented that they were forgiven, to preach and teach God's Word, to feed widows and orphans, to care for the sick, and to visit those in prison or enslaved. These things we did. We even set aside one large hut to shelter little ones who had been abandoned as fairies' brats and rescued from streams and crossroads. Maciul and his wife, Lallocc had embraced the faith and joined our settlement, assuming the difficult task of caring for those little ones. Sechnall had joined us as well and enlisted men to care for the livestock, hunt game, and provide for our security. Because these three and a good many others were determined to learn to read and speak Latin, tutoring took up what free time we may have enjoyed. Our multiplicity of tasks was challenging, thrilling, and exhausting. It was also expensive, so Father Malach frequently argued. Funds were tight, but the cows we had purchased would calve in the spring, and the seed we had sown would yield a winter harvest, if we could just get by until summer.

The temptation to reach into those funds set aside for the purchase of Twin Hills was often overpowering. We had built our compound on faith, believing God would make it ours. But Lady Gowan had avoided Twin Hills after our first day, and her attendance at services was infrequent. I finally sent Father Malach to her home.

"Lady Gowan stubbornly refused any payment," Father Malach said in exasperation upon his return. "She was so charming I didn't trust myself to haggle with her for too long."

"Did she give a reason for her refusal?" I asked.

"Not exactly. She asked why you hadn't come, and I explained that I handle the finances. She wanted to know what you thought of her. I told her you were not in the habit of talking about anyone in their absence. 'He's said nothing?' she asked. She acted like a woman scorned, Father Patrick. Can you think of anything you have done to offend her?"

"No, but who knows what might offend a woman?" I suggested.

"Patrick, *you* will have to go speak to her," Brother Ninus insisted.

"No, that could be disastrous, Ninus," I responded without explanation, and let the whole matter rest.

Our hard work bore fruit, in the church at any rate. Because of the distances traveled, most Christians only came to services once every month or two, yet there were so many that, by the end of the first year, four services were held every Sunday, in addition to services twice daily during the week. By the end of our second year more than three hundred people were requesting baptism, eighteen felt called to become priests, Sechnall among them, and eleven men and women wished to pursue a celibate life of service and meditation. It was time to petition for a bishop. Father Auxilius crafted the petition and Brother Ninus secured the signatures of the baptismal candidates, which consisted of marks or pictures of their family crests, with their names written by Brother Ninus alongside. Father Auxilius and Father Malach excitedly made ready for their journey home.

"Be sure to give my letter to Bishop Amicus. I want him to know of the success we've seen here," I instructed Father Malach.

"Perhaps it will encourage him to cut loose with more funds," Father Malach responded practically.

"Once I'm ordained as bishop, Father Malach," I reminded him, "we can't expect the continued support from Britannia. We'll be on our own."

"All the more reason to get what we can now," Father Malach pronounced flatly.

"Father Auxilius, be sure the letter I gave you goes to my father, Calpornius, and find out whether that petition can be presented to Bishop Amicus or must go to Bishop Eusibus."

"What if no one knows?" he asked defeatedly.

"Then give it to Bishop Amicus," I said simply. "God bless you both."

We saw Father Auxilius and Father Malach board the ship and cast off. I was greatly tempted to go with them. If the bishops agreed that I was to be ordained Bishop of Ireland, I would have to be present for the ordination, but to leave these sheep without a shepherd for even a month concerned me. I was the one who assuaged irate masters when their slaves became Christians, and angry parents when their children accepted the faith. I paid off crooked brehons when one of my flock came under judgement, and my monthly visits with King Diarmuid kept him assured of our good will in spite of many and varied rumors to the contrary. My brothers were certainly competent to run the church and our compound, but these other problems required an advocate with intimate knowledge of the culture. To be offensive, even in ignorance, was answerable by blood. Until I knew for sure about my appointment, I would remain in Ireland.

We had all come to depend heavily on one another, but we did manage during Father Malach's and Father Auxilius's absence. I began to feel guilty for not having encouraged Brother Ninus to seek out his family sooner. If we could manage with two of our numbers absent, surely we could have functioned for a short time without Brother Ninus. While harvesting turnips and onions one afternoon I informed Brother Ninus of his opportunity. "As soon as Father Malach and Father Auxilius return, Sechnall has agreed to help you locate your family, Brother Ninus. Forgive me for not sending you sooner."

"To be honest, I've been hesitant to return. When they sent me to Gaul, it was to become a prosperous merchant, not a poor monk," he confided.

"Nevertheless, you're to go," I insisted. "Will you be telling the little ones stories this evening, or is it my turn?"

"Yours, but try not to scare the wee ones like you did the last time. I don't care how good the story is."

"Ah, but those older lads loved it," I laughed.

"Look! Isn't that Lady Gowan's chariot?"

It was.

"Whatever she wants, I'm sure you can see to it. I'll be at my prayers." I picked up my basket of turnips and onions and turned to go.

"This is the fourth time you've hidden in your prayers. What is the mystery between you and this lady?" he called after me. "You don't answer, Patrick. I shall be forced to entertain the speculations of Father Malach and Father Auxilius." His good humored jesting irritated like pumice stone against a bare foot. "Why did she shun you for nearly two years? Why do you now avoid her?" he shouted. "You've seen that face. Do you imagine I am made of steel?"

I placed the basket at the door of the storage hut and walked swiftly into the shelter of the woods.

Lady Gowan's sudden interest in me had been much harder to bear than her indifference, though secretly it delighted me. I'm unsure what precipitated the change. One Sunday her superior air disappeared. Her eyes followed me throughout the service. For the first time she appeared to seriously consider the text and the homily. Some kind of healing must have taken place within her. The following Sunday I was especially pleased to see her again, and for the first time in two years she smiled, beautifully and honestly, as she greeted me. I wasn't troubled that she could read in my eyes the love I felt for her. It is a Christian's responsibility to cultivate love for all people. But the blush of her cheeks made me ashamed that love was not all that she had read. At that moment I knew I could never trust myself to be her priest and confidant.

Her visits to our compound were frequent after that. Fortunately, our work was so demanding that I seldom had to make excuses for the brevity of our exchanges. But occasionally, I did retreat to pray. It was the coward's way out, I knew, but avoiding conflict seemed preferable to confrontation. As soon as my appointment as bishop was confirmed, I could baptize all the new Christians, ordain the men I was training as priests, and Ninus and I would be off to other corners of Ireland to spread the faith, removing me permanently from the discomfort of the situation. Until then, I could only pray and pray some more.

Brother Ninus and I, anxious to meet Father Auxilius and Father Malach, made for the coast a day early, along with Sechnall who drove the extra chariot. We left Sechnall to tend the horses near Liddy's empty hut, then walked down to the wharf to find Sinell. Sinell was sitting against a beached curragh, a jug in one hand and his long knife in the other.

"So, Patrick," Sinell slurred hospitably without getting up, "you've left your holy hill to visit the bloodiest damned raider on the coast of Ireland. How condescending of you. Or was it Liddy you came to see? Must have been Liddy. You know what a scoundrel I am."

"I know you're drunk," I laughed.

"You ever get drunk?" he asked.

"I can't afford to."

"Too many enemies? That's why I don't get drunk mostly," he mumbled.

"Only one," I quipped. "It's me I can't trust. But what's the occasion?"

Sadness darkened his expression. "I'm getting soft, Patrick. Liddy's to blame, but I don't fault her. Maybe I'm getting too old to be a pirate. But it's too late, Patrick. I can't get soft now. If I let my guard down for a minute, one of those wretches will cut my throat just to say he bested Sinell. That's how I'll die, you know, cut down and covered with my own blood, like all the poor bastards I've murdered. But you'll be there won't you, Patrick? You'll pray over me and take care of my woman, Liddy?"

I glanced worriedly up and down the coast. Three men on one of the ships at dock were watching curiously, but few others took note of us. "Let's get you inside, Sinell. You're more drunk than you know."

I laughed loudly as though Sinell had related some humorous tale, then with the help of Ninus, walked Sinell to his hut. Brother Ninus watched me curiously, but played along, laughing at nothing, or perhaps at me.

"What was all that about?" Brother Ninus asked after we had fed Sinell some bread and cheese and put him to bed.

"Sinell's right about those cut-throats. It won't do him any good, or Liddy either for that matter, should the pirates on this coast spot a weakness."

We stepped outside in response to the sound of Sechnall's alert. Conleng, Liddy, and Liddy's body guard stepped off the chariot.

"Where were you? Why wasn't someone here?" I demanded.

"We didn't know you were coming, Father Patrick," Liddy said perplexed, "or I would have..."

"Never mind that," I interrupted. "How long has Sinell been melancholy?"

"He's been drinking again?" Liddy asked worriedly.

"I can't say that I blame him," I said sighing, "but it's dangerous for him to be noticeably drunk on the beach two hours before noonday."

Liddy's face drained of color. "Oh, Patrick! Did anyone take notice?"

"There were three curious fellows, but I think we covered him well enough."

"I'll see that never happens again!" she declared as she hurried inside. Feeling the burden of Sinell's vulnerability shift from my shoulders to Liddy's, I turned more congenially to her companions.

"Conleng," I greeted, taking his hand, "Congratulations on that brilliant bit of horsemanship at the Beltane races. Had I the means I would have bet on you."

"Liddy tells me *you've* won a few races, yourself," Conleng responded, shaking my hand. "Brother Ninus," Conleng acknowledged, extending his hand to Ninus. By the time we had greeted her silent bodyguard, introduced Sechnall, and helped Conleng tend horses and chariots, Liddy had set out our food and drink.

We ate pleasantly until Liddy, taking advantage of our familiarity began to upbraid me. "Father Patrick, I can't understand what the problem is between you and Scothie. If ever two people were made for each other it was you two. I thought so when you almost devoured her in that slave hut thirty years ago, and she didn't mind a bit. And I was sure of it when you were still misty eyed over her six years later, and all of us had thought you were long dead. Now after more miracles than I can count here you are with no woman at all, and her a widow, still young enough to need the pleasure of a man's body..."

"Who is Scothie?" Brother Ninus interrupted as I abruptly left the table.

"He didn't tell you? Lady Gowan and her mother were servants in his father's house, before Sinell drug them all to Ireland. I can't believe, after all you've been through, Patrick, that you would hold her former station against her," she continued.

"Don't be absurd!" I barked.

"Could it be those adoring young women at the church you're attracted to?" she suggested thoughtfully. "They're sweet, but none of them can hold a candle to Scothie. She has brains, beauty, and the maturity to complete you. She'd help you, not worship you."

"Liddy! That's quite enough! I don't have to explain myself to you or anybody else. But I will assure you that I have no interest in taking up with some adolescent, with barley for brains, whose concept of God is so muddled she could confuse Him with me!"

I left them chewing over the events of my life like dogs with an old bone. Maybe my plans needed revision, I thought, as I walked among the trees. Suppose I forgot about the rest of Ireland and stayed right here? I didn't have to risk my life in every kingdom in Ireland to serve God. Let some of the Irish Scots, who felt called to be priests, take on that challenge. I could marry Scothie and enjoy the full expression of human love that couples are blessed to experience. I might even be a better priest. Most of those I counseled were troubled in their relationships.

That night as I slept near the fire outside Liddy's hut, I had a dream. I was a bishop. Before me stood hundreds of radiant people all of whom I baptized and sealed with the oil of anointing. I shared with them the mystery of Holy Communion and blessed them all, exuberant with love and joy, and confident that my Lord was pleased. --- Then I was once more a simple priest. I stood near the spring, our little Garden of Eden. I could hear it bubbling and trickling over rocks and pebbles. Graceful as a willow Scothie moved among the fern, her long auburn hair her only covering. She drew me into a bed of thick, cool clover, her crystal blue eyes sparkling with love and delight. So vivid was my dream that my body actually responded, as though I had embraced her living flesh, not just the illusion of a fantasy. I was embarrassed when I awoke. As pleasurable as the dream had been, an incomprehensible grief weighed on me. What, if anything, did it mean? I quickly rose, cleaned myself up, and plunged into my prayers.

Sinell awoke suffering a terrible headache and cursed and swore with almost every breath, his ruthlessness replacing his melancholy. So angered was he at my apparently unwelcome presence, that the only thing that kept him from driving his knife through my irritating heart, was the oath we had sworn together, or so he railed. Brother Ninus and I quietly removed ourselves and waited on the wharf for the boat from Britannia, while Sechnall readied the chariots and horses.

Brother Ninus was the first to spot the ship long before it reached its berth. The wait seemed interminable. As soon as the ship had docked and was secured to its moorings, Father Malach appeared, then an older man, followed by Father Auxilius. As they made their way toward us, my enthusiasm slowly faded. "God bless you, Father Malach, Father Auxilius," I said with genuine affection, embracing each one. As Brother Ninus did likewise, I looked with curious apprehension at their strange companion. Father Malach turned to address the older man.

"Bishop Palladius, these are our brothers, Father Patrick and Brother Iserninus," he announced. "Brothers, Bishop Palladius has been sent from Rome in response to our petition." Every organ within me seemed to shrivel, as I stared in disbelief.

Brother Ninus glanced warily at me, then greeted Palladius, "Welcome, Bishop Palladius. A chariot is waiting to carry us to Twin Hills."

The constriction in my throat made speech impossible. With only a nod to the illustrious bishop, I left them on the wharf and plodded down the beach to the rocky reef. I would never be Bishop of Ireland! Even harder to bear was the lack of freedom I now envisaged. Amicus had kept me on a leash, but without his physical oversight, I had been free to broadly interpret the phrase, "that which benefits the Christian Community," including taking risks such as those encountered at King Diarmuid's Rath. I rebelled against an overseer. One by one I hurled rocks into the sea.

"Patrick," spoke a voice beside me. I spun around. Sinell continued, "Liddy explained what you and Ninus did for me yesterday. I won't apologize for this morning..."

"Oh, go to Hell," I snapped, "but whip out that long knife and end my misery first."

"Look here, what's wrong with you?" he asked worriedly, almost like a father.

"What do you care?" I turned my back to him and hurled another rock. Sinell waited.

"In spite of all the horror and hell I've been through here, I honestly love these wretched people, even you, bastard that you are," I spewed. "I had hoped to be head of the church of Ireland. But the church has decided that I'm not the man for the job. That man over there is to be head of the church, and from now on, I'm to take orders from him."

"Do you want me to kill him for you?" he calmly inquired.

"NO!, no, Sinell," I gasped, spinning to face him, horrified that my immature outburst had generated a serious threat to Palladius. "That may be how pirate captains and kings are made, but not bishops. Swear you will do nothing to harm him. Swear it, Sinell."

"Then he's not your enemy?"

"No, Sinell, he's my brother, by blood, just like you are. Forgive me for snapping at you. And don't go to Hell." I smiled wryly "I wouldn't wish that on anyone."

"Didn't you know?" he said, laughing cynically, "I'm the devil himself. It's me that makes hell for everyone else." As he left the reef, I stared worriedly after him, then joined Bishop Palladius and my brothers who were waiting impatiently for me at the chariots. Unable to trust myself to speak civilly, I again nodded respectfully to Bishop Palladius, stepped into the chariot beside Brother Ninus, and urged my horses to a trot.

Seven children poured out of their play places and ran to greet Brother Ninus and me when we arrived at Twin Hills, hanging on our legs and arms, hugging us like we'd been gone months rather than days. "Will you tell us a story tonight, Father?" they implored.

"It's nearly bed time now. Can you be ready by the time our horses are stabled?" I challenged.

"Yes!" they all squealed, and ran, stumbling over one another to the wash pan, all but Rioc and Benignus, two little boys ages six and eight.

"Will it be a scary story, Father?" Benignus asked hopefully.

Brother Ninus frowned. "Rioc, didn't you get frightened at those monster tales the last time?" he asked.

"I'm never scared, as long as Father Patrick's there," Rioc whispered conspiratorially. "I just pretend."

"All right, after the wee ones have gone to sleep, I'll scare you good," I promised. They ran off to wash.

"Are these your children?" Palladius asked.

"Yes, aren't they marvelous?"

Bishop Palladius frowned doubtfully, then followed Father Malach to our quarters. By the time I had finished playing the filid, everyone but Brother Ninus had gone to bed. We sat watching the embers of the fire in silence.

"The bishop says he'll need separate quarters," Brother Ninus related. I chose to remain silent rather than risk a snide remark. "He's a good man, Patrick. I know it's not what you wanted, but you've said before, 'We have to accept what we can't change.'"

"I'll accept it, Ninus. It'll just take some time."

Brother Ninus patted me on the leg and stood to go. "Ninus, did they say what happened? How did we get a bishop from Rome?"

"Father Auxilius left the petition with Bishop Eusibus' secretary. It was sent to Rome, possibly by accident, with several other communications. Palladius was sent because his arguments against the Pelagian heresy have been so profound. Rome wanted to ensure that such heresy didn't take root in Ireland."

"Heresy?" I began laughing at the absurdity. "It's the sword I've been striving to preserve our heads from, not sophisticated questions of doctrine. What of Bishop Amicus? Did Father Malach say how he received my letter?"

"You'd better ask him yourself in the morning."

Bishop Palladius slept in the following morning. I could imagine the trip had been rough, the food unusual, his reception less than satisfactory. It was a relief not to have to face him.

"Father Malach," I said as we breakfasted on fish, "What was Bishop Amicus's reaction to the letter?"

"Incomprehensible. 'Is this true?' Bishop Amicus asked us irritably, 'Christians added to the church every day, nobles, Druid priests, et cetera, et cetera,' as though he was sure you had made it all up," Father Malach answered.

"I told him, 'Maybe not *every* day, but most days,'" Father Auxilius chimed in.

"Then he said, 'So he's ready to be made bishop and campaign all over Ireland. I'll see that he is. Then I'll be free of him. Let the Irish bring about justice.' An odd comment we thought," Father Malach concluded.

"He only meant that justice will follow, once I am free to spread the gospel to all Ireland," I interpreted. "So, his intention was to promote my candidacy for bishop? I just wish he'd had the opportunity."

None of the brothers commented, so I began to outline the day's tasks. "Father Malach, recruit some men to help you build a separate hut for the bishop. The best spot would be near that ash tree beyond the stream."

"Father Patrick, we have a bishop," Father Malach interrupted. "You are no longer in charge. Bishop Palladius has already requested that his hut be built near the spring, and, as I told him you were the most skilled builder among us, he wants you to build it."

I sat silently absorbing the shock. Having nothing Christian to say, I left their company, and embarked on my monthly visit to King Diarmuid's Rath. King Diarmuid was especially hospitable and I gladly succumbed to his invitation to remain another day.

CHAPTER TWENTY
Day of Disaster

It was late when I returned to Twin Hills, the eve of Bishop Palladius's first Sunday among us. His hut had been built, desecrating our little Garden of Eden. The atmosphere was charged with tension as invariably happens when power changes hands. I hadn't thought of myself as a man of power, only a zealous servant of God. Now that I had lost it, I saw how easily power takes hold and corrupts. A man not corrupted by power, I realized, is a man who can easily lay it down.

Bishop Palladius selected the scriptures and determined to provide the homily for the Sunday services. Father Malach interpreted, and Brother Ninus, Father Auxilius, and I sat in the front beside the altar ready to assist, should Bishop Palladius request it. Bishop Palladius donned what seemed elaborate robes for our primitive congregation. The people pointed and whispered, and listened expectantly as he opened his mouth to speak. Their irritation at hearing scriptures read in Latin, and the homily given through an interpreter, himself less than fluent in Gaelic, was obvious, but they were much more patient and well behaved than I feared they might be. When the service ended, however, their discontent became vocal, each one yelling, so that none could be understood. Bishop Palladius stared open-mouthed at the vociferous crowd before him. Father Malach attempted to restore order, to no avail. I was unsure exactly what I should do, what the bishop would allow, but anything was better than chaos.

I stood. The congregation immediately became silent. A dear old woman, who had attended faithfully since our first service at Twin Hills, spoke up. "We won't leave until you have told us what the scriptures mean, Father Patrick. Have you no story for us to chew on this week?"

"Bishop Palladius spoke of Heaven and Hell," I began. "Hell you know by another name. You have been taught that the abode of the dead is a place of unending hunting, warring, and feasting. Every day the wild boar are savagely hunted and slaughtered. Warriors wage war with one another until most are dead or dismembered. Those who survive feast on the champion's portion, drink until they are merry, and enjoy their women in the dimness of their feast hall. The next day they all come alive to do it once again.

"This Other World may be a place of felicity for men who love war and hate their brothers. But for men and women who joy in a beautiful sunrise, in the laughter of children, in the flight of a poor bird whose injured wing has been mended, for people of peace, it is a place of torment, a dismal Hell.

"Jesus said, 'I go to prepare a place for you.' That place is a kingdom of love, a city outside your Otherworld where only those men and women who love may enter, brilliantly lit by the glory of God. In the great hall God's saints share a love feast with our Lord. Whoever would gain the champion's portion at that feast, is he, or she, who loves most and serves best. This city we call Heaven. If you were to pass from this life today, which kingdom would you chose?" Shouts of "Heaven" and enthusiastic applause brought my tale to an end. Bishop Palladius pronounced the benediction again, and the people were dismissed.

"I want a word with you before the next service," Bishop Palladius insisted.

"Yes, Bishop Palladius," I acknowledged.

As Father Malach was helping the bishop remove his vestments, Attrachta, a young woman, who had always appeared less interested in the Lord than she was in his priests, stepped to the front and placed a gift of fine jewelry on the altar. I grabbed her arm as she turned to go.

"Your good will is appreciated, Attrachta, but if you wish to bless God, give your wealth to a widow, or an orphan, or a hungry slave." I placed the jewelry in back her hand. She pushed it away.

"It is you I wish to bless, Father Patrick," she crooned, smiling sweetly but with exaggerated innocence.

"To bless God *is* to bless me," I retorted, and frowning sternly, I forced her fingers closed around the jewelry. She tossed her head in a pout and stormed out of the church.

Father Malach railed, preening before the bishop, "The jewelry and gold you've returned to the Irish ladies could have bought two dozen cows or more. If they want to give, why refuse them? Our funds are not inexhaustab..."

"If King Diarmuid thinks we use our influence to take advantage of his people," I angrily interrupted, "tolerance will turn to bloody persecution. We Take Nothing! We can make do."

"Father Patrick, Lady Gowan is..." Ninus stopped speaking as Scothie's voice, cold and authoritative, could be heard from the doorway.

"Father Auxilius, is Father Patrick at his prayers again," she asked sarcastically, "or do you think this time he might see me?" She stepped into the church.

"If you'll excuse me Bishop Palladius," Brother Ninus said as he retreated toward the doorway. "Lady Gowan," he saluted before stepping outside.

"Lady Gowan," Father Malach gushed, "May I introduce you to our new bishop, Bishop Palladius. Bishop, this lady is our benefactress."

"Leave us," Scothie ordered turning her eyes on mine.

"But..."

"Leave us! Both of you!" she interrupted leaving no quarter for compromise.

Father Malach obediently led the perplexed bishop out. I sat down and quietly watched a beetle crawl up to and over my shoe.

"Patrick," she began, the sharpness gone from her voice, "I know you remember me, the day we landed in Ireland?"

I nodded, my eyes smiling at the memory. "A frightened, beautiful girl," I whispered. I stood and stepped toward the doorway.

Her voice arrested my steps. "Don't you want to know why I've come?"

"No," I answered simply, attempting to step outside.

Scothie grabbed my arm roughly and swung around in front of me. "I am NOW an Irish noblewoman, and you WILL hear me! No more prayers, no more excuses!" she demanded furiously. "You are invited to my home this evening. My driver will see to it that you get there!" She stormed out of the church just as Bishop Palladius reentered.

"You have a volatile effect on the women of our congregation," he said humorously. "I suppose a handsome priest always has his own special cross to bear." I said nothing. "When your bishop addresses you," he insisted, " you are expected to answer."

"Yes, sir," I barely managed to utter.

"Will you tell me what have I done to earn your contempt?" he humbly asked.

"Nothing, Bishop Palladius," I said in defeat, ashamed that this poor man had to bear with such a difficult subordinate, and in so foreign a ministry. It was, after all, our request that he had come in answer to.

"Then it's professional jealousy? Father Malach tells me you had hoped to be bishop."

My eyes met his. "Bishop Palladius, I have such vision for what should be done here, but my hands are tied."

"Share your vision with me, Patrick. Perhaps I can untie those hands." His encouragement filled me with exuberant hope. As people began filing in for the second service he insisted with a chuckle, "You take this service, Father Patrick. I want to see what they're used to. I made a disaster of the first one."

By the end of the day I felt I had climbed a huge mountain only to slip at the summit and tumble painfully back to the bottom. Preparing for my forced rendezvous with Lady Gowan, I scrubbed my face and chest with such violent frustration, that I fully expected to peel the skin off. Brother Ninus, waiting patiently for his turn at the basin, said nothing. I dried off and slammed the towel down on the table.

"Your meeting with the bishop?" he gingerly ventured. I spun around. Ninus threw up his hands in mock surrender and backed away. I sighed heavily and tossed on my shirt. Ninus began washing.

"I hoped, expected..." I kicked the rocks at my feet, then sat and began relacing my trousers. "He wouldn't believe there were Christians among the Picts, so my trip north is canceled. Missions to Connachta, Meath, anywhere are not permitted. And the children? Ninus, I'm forbidden to take them in. Am I to let their fathers kill them? Maciul, Lallocc, and the sisters who help them have never complained." I stared for a time in frustration at the children across the way, who played merrily in a mud hole. "God help me, Ninus. I feel like a horse in harness being whipped to go forward and reined back in at the same time."

Ninus sat beside me, silently for a time, then spoke with clear and simple deliberation. "When Sinell, or Totmael, or that mad prince beat you as a lad, did you beg for your life? or beg your bread when they refused you food?"

"No," I contemplated.

"Yet now you beg your life and bread from the church," he suggested. "You still see yourself a slave, Patrick. But who is your master?"

Lady Gowan's home was a neatly attended, several-room house in the center of a small rath, surrounded on three sides by quarters for slaves and servants, and a flower and vegetable garden in front. A creek gurgled nearby, lightly concealed by a few trees on either bank. The stables and chariot house, corral and stock pens were outside the enclosure.

Her driver deposited us within the rath. Slaves and servants were working excitedly around a large fire pit a short distance from the main house, as though a festival were about to be enjoyed. We approached the house and were greeted at the door by a short, round woman exuding an air of efficiency.

"A hundred thousand welcomes," Scothie sang, as she brushed by her servant and ushered us into her home. The woman began to take her leave. "Hattie," Scothie called, "take Brother Ninus to the gathering, I'm sure they would be thrilled to hear his stories. You don't mind do you, Brother Ninus?"

"Lady Gowan," I insisted, "I would prefer that he witness our discussion."

"No doubt! But I prefer otherwise!" she challenged unyieldingly. "I don't recall my invitation including Brother Ninus."

Addressing Brother Ninus she continued graciously, "There will be more than enough to eat and drink, Brother Ninus. And your stories would so add to the festival. Will you remain, or shall I arrange for you to be returned to Twin Hills?" she continued.

I glanced nervously at Brother Ninus. The arch of his eyebrow told me that Ninus had no solution to my dilemma. I reluctantly nodded.

"I'll be delighted to tell a few stories," Brother Ninus chirped.

"Wonderful!" Scothie exclaimed with considerable charm. "Have your fill and enjoy the evening. Hattie, see that he gets the best of everything." They left us.

"The matter you wish to discuss?" I began.

"Will you not sit, drink, share a few stories before business is conducted? Have you no manners at all?" Scothie chided.

"Another of my many shortcomings, Lady Gowan," I confessed. She smiled beautifully. "Yes, yes it is. But it was not your shortcomings that engendered your invitation this evening." The tenor of her voice sent a ripple from head to toe. "Please sit," she continued. "If we must begin with business, at least we can enjoy a drink while we talk." I sat across from her. She lifted her glass, and we drank.

"The business I have with you is this. I am a widow of property, title, and wealth. It is my right as an Irish noblewoman to choose a husband. I choose you." She took another drink, while I stared, speechless.

"You --- honor me, dear lady," I finally managed to breathe, "but I can't marry you."

Scothie smiled nervously then walked around the table. She slipped her arms around my neck and whispered, "I can make you a noble. Give my wealth to help in your work."

"I'm not for sale," I quietly responded.

"No?" Scothie seethed, turning to face me. She stood, rigid as an oak. "You forget who and where you are. With a snap of my fingers you *will* be for sale, or worse!" A cold chill swept over me. "There's not a man in all Leinster who wouldn't gladly trade places with you! How dare you..." She broke off, struggling determinedly to contain her angry tears.

It was a miserable recompense for the tremendous compliment she had paid me. I stood and pulled her into my arms. Her eyes flashed, as she tossed her head to repel me. Forcing her head against my chest, I held her tightly, like I would a little child in the throws of a tantrum. But she wasn't a child. She was the only woman I had ever loved, the only woman I felt incomplete without. I was grieved at the pain I had caused her, but embarrassed, that the desire I felt holding her body next to mine, was so much greater than that grief. Scothie relaxed in my arms, sobbing softly. I stroked her hair and kissed the top of her head.

"I wasn't trying to buy you," Scothie wept into my shoulder.

"I know, Scothie. That was a stupid remark."

"Can't you see that I love you?" she said, her tear filled eyes searching mine. "I can make you a good wife, Patrick. Don't you want me?"

Not want her? As if I could drink in the whole of her through one sweet exchange, I caressed her lips with mine; a deep, slow, passionate kiss. My heart pounded wildly as all my resolve began to crumble.

"Scothie," I whispered desperately, "I have always loved you, will always love you. My body aches for you. But I can't be what you need me to be. Please, if I don't go now, I..."

Her fingers stopped my lips. She whispered breathlessly, "Tomorrow."

Bishop Augustine had said, "It is one thing to fall and rise quickly, and quite another to never fall at all." I not only fell, I determined to stay fallen till the light of day illuminated my sin. That night I closed my mind to anything but Scothie and the consummate satisfaction of our love.

Like the pain of too much drink, grief gnawed at the pit of my stomach and pounded in my head the following morning. I prayed, but I knew better than to expect any comfort. Since the day Bishop Palladius had arrived, I had piled one sin upon another, until my soul needed surgery, not a just a bandage.

Scothie lay sleeping. Beautiful, her face, her form. I laced my trousers, then gently stroked her cheek and brushed the hair from her forehead. Her eyes opened. She stretched and smiled contentedly.

"We need to talk," I told her. "I'll wait outside." I tossed on my shirt and left her to dress.

Leaning against a tree near the creek and absently rolling a twig between my fingers, I considered one last time if it might be possible to change my course. I knew better. The voices that had called me to Ireland resounded almost audibly in my mind. "God, forgive me," I prayed, "for putting my hand to the plow and looking back. How crooked the furrow I have carved."

Scothie strolled happily over and leaned against the tree beside me. I turned my head to meet her eyes.

"I made a vow to God, that I would never marry," I confessed.

"What?" she gasped, ashamed and amazed. "Why? Why you, Patrick? Other priests marry. Your grandfather..." I pushed away from the tree, snapped the twig in my hand, and tossed it in the creek.

"The story I came to tell, it's for all Ireland, not just Leinster. I almost met my death in King Diarmuid's court." I said, turning to face her. "Do you imagine it will be any different in every other kingdom in Ireland? Scothie, I have no life to give you. And I couldn't bear to see you share mine."

Scothie took my hand in hers and stared into the rippling water. "You couldn't just stay here with me?"

A heavy sigh escaped my lips. I took her in my arms and lay my cheek against her hair. "Beautiful Lady, you are the most difficult temptation I have ever had to deal with. You're like a lovely dream. Any man, any man, would *love* you, even worship you. But Scothie, who else will carry this story to the Irish?" I searched her eyes for understanding. "Who else will *love* these people the way I do?"

"Take me with you," she begged as tears filled her eyes. "You don't have to stay here, or even marry me, Patrick. I'd rather be your whore than have no part of you at all."

"Oh, Scothie," I breathed. "Can you really love me so much? You deserve far better. --- A man, who would continue to dishonor you, and selfishly put your life at risk, would be lying if he said he loved you. What you suggest can never be." Sunlight sparkled like rubies from her auburn tresses. A few wisps floating on the breeze swept onto her tear soaked cheeks. She wiped them away. How desperately I loved her. How jealously I would guard every memory. One other consideration had to be made. "If a child should come from this night's passion..."

She shook her head swiftly. "The night was well planned." I felt the corners of my mouth curl with embarrassment. How easily had this game been snared. "I promise," she added with sweet sadness, "I will not plan another." There beside the creek, in the shadows of ash and oak, we consummately embraced each other one last time.

When we approached the house, Brother Ninus was waiting at the door. Scothie immediately removed her arm from around my waist and stepped away.

"Was that for my honor or yours?" I asked.

"Why, yours, Patrick," she answered, surprised.

Taking her precious face between the palms of my hands I confessed, "I was wrong, Scothie, to take the liberties of a husband, without making you my wife. For *that* I am ashamed." She started to protest, but I stopped her lips with my fingers. "But I will never be ashamed of, or deny, my love for you." I wiped a tear from her cheek and kissed her forehead. "Farewell, beautiful lady," I whispered hoarsely and turned quickly away. She hurried past Brother Ninus and into the house.

"Patrick?" Brother Ninus's voice rang behind me as he approached. I felt his hand on my shoulder, and quickly dried my face. "I heard her terrible threats last night. I was worried she'd made you a slave again."

"She very nearly has."

CHAPTER TWENTY-ONE
Last Journey Home

Bishop Palladius, Father Auxilius, and Father Malach greeted us the moment we arrived at Twin Hills. "Brother Ninus, Father Patrick, you met with Lady Gowan?" Bishop Palladius inquired. "Yes, sir," I answered.

"What did she want, Brother Ninus?"

"I can't say. I was telling stories and explaining our faith to the slaves and servants all evening. It was Father Patrick she wanted to see," Brother Ninus responded.

"Father Patrick, I should have been consulted before you met privately with this woman."

"A private meeting was not intended, Bishop Palladius."

"Was her business of such a personal nature that you couldn't share it with Brother Ninus when you retired?"

"I ...didn't retire," I hesitantly began to confess.

"Alone with that lovely vision all night long? What could you have been discussing?" Father Auxilius teased suggestively.

"I can well imagine!" Father Malach snapped self-righteously.

Instantly irritated, I called up all the charm, energy, and skill of a master storyteller, heavily seasoned with sarcasm.

"Ah! There was magic in the air! She asked me to be her husband. We made passionate love all night long. In the morning we mounted her two finest horses and rode across the whole land of Ireland and out into the Western Sea, to the land of Tir Na Nog, where no one ever grows old or ugly. And we lived happily ever after!"

Father Auxilius stared open-mouthed. Father Malach fumed.

"I should think, brothers, that you would have enough of your own sins to account for without troubling yourself with mine!" I concluded.

A gesture from the bishop sent Father Malach and Father Auxilius back to the common house.

"Have you used *your* influence, Father Patrick, to take advantage of this noblewoman?" Bishop Palladius inquired.

Brother Ninus caught my eye and shook his head cautiously. Could I add deceit to my long list of sins? My face betrayed me at any rate. Bishop Palladius patiently waited for me to answer.

"I have... *loved* her," I managed to painfully confess.

"With the intention of marriage?"

"No."

Bishop Palladius frowned in contemplation. "Father Patrick, I'm very sorry, but we cannot work together," he solemnly announced. "You are rude, ignorant, ambitious, and immoral. See that you are on the first ship back to Britannia." He turned to go.

"If you wish to destroy my life, do it honestly," I snapped in anger. "Allow me to go among the Picts. You claim there are no Christians I can corrupt, and the Picts may even oblige you by taking my head!"

"I want you out of Ireland," he calmly retorted, a master of self control, "and I'll see to it that the church never sends you back."

"Who made you God?" I exploded.

"How dare you challenge my authority!" he seethed. "Pack your things and get out ---NOW!"

I packed my things, but I didn't get out, not out of Ireland anyway. I was lost. My life was over. Everything I had lived for, worked for, prayed for, this ministry, the only thing that made any real sense or purpose out of those harrowing years in slavery. What was I to do? Where was I to go? My Lord had felt the need to fast and pray for forty days and forty nights. I determined I needed at least that much.

Brother Ninus, refusing to let me go alone, accompanied me to the foot of a great mountain, too rocky and remote to attract shepherds or herdsmen. I insisted upon climbing to the summit alone, and there I prayed and wept and struggled with my passions. Week after week the chill wind and icy rain tore through my garments, biting to the bone. Hunger gnawed at the pit of my stomach until I cramped with a pain that stretched from my throat to the calves of my legs. My skin stank and crawled for want of a bath. But my body only mirrored the torment of my soul. How corrupt I felt. How unredeemable.

"Lord God, by my gross error, I have lost the cause you called me to," I prayed. "But you knew before I started this journey, what a weak and miserable soul I am. Why did you make me dare to believe that I could be the father of these people? I rejected Scothie, because you are my first love, and *you* have made Ireland my mistress, my purpose, my passion. I can't bear to have lost her, too. What is left? What am I fit for? Please, Father, deliver me from this life which I have so miserably failed."

The cold rock beneath me seemed to drain what little warmth was left in my bones. I shivered uncontrollably. Ironically a raven fluttered to rest beside me. Our Lord had a sense of humor. To the Irish the raven is one of three manifestations of the goddess Mauve, and signified certain death. "So be it, Father." I closed my eyes and waited for sleep to come.

The fluttering of wings and the brush of feathers across my nose drew my attention outside myself. My opened eyes were greeted by, not one, but fifteen ravens perched all around me, and dozens more circling overhead. Suddenly the air, though chilling, weighed oppressively with the same indescribable aura of evil that had surrounded Lochru in his moments of madness. I thought for a moment I was hallucinating from hunger or thirst. Then one of the ravens, without provocation flew at my head, claws extended, and tore at my hair. Instantly the entire flock descended on me, screeching and clawing and tearing with their beaks.

"No!" I shouted in outrage as I leapt to my feet. Within my tired, sick body, power surged. It was to God I had surrendered. I would not surrender one drop of my blood to the demons of Hell! I slammed three or more ravens to the ground with my cape, pelted those overhead with rocks, and broke the necks of those whose claws had become tangled in my hair. Before the frantic nightmare was over thirteen broken ravens and a carpet of black feathers littered the ground around me.

I sat down, weary, but feeling remarkably elated and victorious. As the wind stirred the feathers at my feet another slowly and gently floated down to rest, a white one. Overhead a dove cooed softly before lighting on a rock nearby, illuminating God's message. I fell on my face and wept. The battle over Ireland was still mine. It was *my* challenge, weak though I was, to scatter his enemies and make way for the dove, the Spirit of the living God. Full of faith and hope, I was bathed in love once again by the God of a shepherd boy, the glorious God of the Trinity.

It had taken the full forty days to sort myself out and to finally realize, my ultimate approval, my ultimate authority, came not from men, even Godly, well meaning men, but from the voice that called me. As I made my way tiredly down the mountain, physically drained, but zealous with purpose, I puzzled at what I saw below. At the foot of the mountain there were fires burning, and shelters erected. Ninus had made his way up the mountain every Sunday to worship with me, so he said. To check on me was more accurate. Yet he had never mentioned the village that grew. When I was near the end of my descent, the people began gathering, excitedly calling my name. I felt like Moses on Mount Sinai, only embarrassed that the man they awaited was not nearly so holy. And how terrible I must have looked, smelled

"Why have you come?" I asked the people.

"We heard that you were leaving us," Sechnall explained.

"I am."

"Why?" Maciul protested painfully, his voice echoed by those of others. "Why did you bring us this new faith, only to abandon us to our old ways?"

"No, Maciul, please, don't disappoint me by falling away. I don't abandon you. Christ will never leave you nor forsake you."

"You are his priest. Yet you forsake us!" an angry brother grumbled.

"How could I forsake Ireland, her precious people? Be faithful brothers and sisters. God will bring me back. Imagine my grief if when I return all we have accomplished in the last four years has been lost."

"What would it please you for us to do, Father Patrick?" a devout old woman queried. What indeed? I prayerfully answered, "Be faithful to God, and love Bishop Palladius. He is a good man and he has given up all he ever had to care for you. Receive your baptism. Be filled with the Spirit of God. And have great tales to tell when I return."

The aged saint patted me on one cheek and kissed the other, then gathered her things and left. One by one each of my sheep similarly bid me farewell. Within a few days Brother Ninus and I departed. We were amazed to find Bishop Palladius and Father Malach waiting for us when we reached the coast.

"Father Patrick, I expected you to be off this island more than seven weeks ago," Bishop Palladius began. "Your continued presence has been extremely disruptive to the unity of this church. However, I do appreciate the Christian counsel you gave your devotees. Sechnall related the entire business to us."

"These people are dear to me, Bishop Palladius. I can't let them lose their faith in God, simply because you have lost your faith in me."

"I do pray that God will find a suitable place for you in Britannia. You have powerful gifts as a priest. But do not delude yourself. You will have no place of ministry here as long as I am Bishop of Ireland.

"Brother Ninus," Bishop Palladius said turning away from me, "after Father Patrick departs, we need to explore..."

"Forgive me, Bishop Palladius," Ninus interrupted. "I have the greatest respect for you, sir. However, I am not one of your priests, but a monk. My community sent me, not to serve the Irish church, but to serve Father Patrick. Where he goes, I will go."

"I'm sorry to lose you," Bishop Palladius sincerely responded.

"I fear you will be sorry to have lost us both. God be with you."

We boarded the ship and set sail for home. Sinell had offered to transport us, but memories of our previous voyages had made me reluctant to trust him. So long as I remained in Ireland his oath was binding, but who could say if he still felt an obligation beyond these shores? On the other hand, if his conviction remained, what might become of Bishop Palladius? I had fervently insisted that *God* was directing me out of Ireland, not Bishop Palladius. I could only pray that Liddy might discourage our bloody champion from becoming Palladius' nemeses.

We arrived at Bannaventa Berniae unannounced and quietly made our way to my father's house. Victoricus opened the door to us, not smartly dressed or efficiently prompt as I had expected, but with the casual air of a landowner at his leisure.

"Upon my word, Master Sucat... Father Patrick, this is so unexpected. Your father is in the sitting room."

"Thank you, Victoricus," I acknowledged, puzzled that he had not troubled to announce us. Brother Ninus and I went immediately to the sitting room. The gentleman reclining on the couch was a stranger to me, gaunt and pale, his bony fingers rigidly clutching a well worn blanket. Tears sprang immediately to my eyes.

"Sucat?" he questioned weakly.

"Yes, Father." I pulled a chair next to the couch and sat before him.

"The only thing I ever prayed for, and here you are!" he sighed smiling. "You're looking good, Sucat. Ireland agrees with you."

"I'm so glad to be home," I encouraged.

"Are you?" he responded skeptically. "You always thought yourself so clever. But you never learned to lie convincingly."

"I am glad to see you," I corrected myself.

"Yes, yes, but you don't see me. You see an apparition. Something vile within eats away bit by bit, day after day, until now I scarcely have strength even to speak. Is that Ninus with you?" he asked as he wearily closed his eyes.

"Yes, Lord Calpornius," Brother Ninus confirmed, taking Father's hand.

"Welcome, brother, to my pitiful palace. Forgive my lack of hospitality, but sleep commands my obedient compliance." Father drifted off. I went immediately to Father's study. The disorder was so uncharacteristic of Father, that I stared in amazement as one might at the carnage of war.

"Victoricus!" I bellowed. "Where are Father's ledgers?"

For the remainder of the year Brother Ninus and I worked night and day pulling the estates back to their productive best. Everything needed repair. Slaves who had toiled enthusiastically in the past hoping to earn their freedom had become discouraged with the lack of profits generated after Father had taken ill. Their lackluster efforts were counter to productivity, but I knew them to be good men.

"Every slave willing to work as hard as I do will have his freedom before the end of the year, and every freeman will have his section of land," I pledged.

The enthusiasm was contagious. Both estates suddenly swarmed with zealous laborers like worker ants before a rain. The results were almost miraculous. Father was so pleased. He never regained his strength sufficiently to inspect our progress, but what he did see and his review of the ledgers gave him peace of mind. He knew there would be an inheritance for his children. He could die a success.

"Sucat," he had barely managed to utter one afternoon, as I told him of my troubles in Ireland, "I made you believe you were a disappointment to me. That's not true. There's a greatness in you, Sucat, that I can't understand." Instantly the burden of my father's displeasure, which I had borne so long unaware, lifted from me like the shedding of a heavy cloak. "Whatever your obstacles," Father advised, "*you do what you have to do, and that will be right.*" I slowly nodded, recognizing the voice of the Spirit in the counsel he gave. His face suddenly twisted with pain. "Will you hear my confession now, Father Patrick?" he gasped.

"Of course," I answered with difficulty.

Before the dawn broke he was gone.

Once all our possessions and estates had been sold I presented Lupait with her share of the proceeds. Having married into a family of considerable means, she generously refused all but a token of the sum. "Without Rome, every church must provide somehow for its own protection from foreign raids and native criminals," Lupait explained. "I'm sure, no matter how great your success, the British churches will no longer be able to support you. Take my share as an offering to your ministry, Sucat. And keep me informed. Your letters touch me deeply." I gratefully accepted her gift without admitting to her that I returned to Ireland without either the church's support or blessing.

Having sold everything else, I at last sold my title, my rank as a noble, to a promising young man. I then loaded all my coins in battered old bags, strapped them to the backs of two donkeys, and boarded the boat with Brother Ninus for our return to Ireland. This time I would go north as far as Dalaridia or possibly just to Meath.

Coroticus, who had paid only the briefest of visits while Father was ill, and Ami, whom I had avoided during most of my stay rather than explain my break with Palladius, now appeared unexpectedly on the dock.

"I used to envy you, Sucat," Coroticus gloated uneasily. "You had everything I wanted, even Audrey. Now look at you. You've sold your fortune and your nobility to waste on Irish peasants. Should a man of such talents come to so ignoble an end? Forget serving those Irish savages and stay here to serve your king."

"It is my King who commands me to serve the Irish," I responded carefully, "but I appreciate your offer, old friend, and your concern."

"*I* am your King!" Coroticus exclaimed, his face flushed with anger.

"Why didn't you inform me of your plans to leave?" Bishop Amicus irritably intervened. "I expected a full report before you returned to Ireland."

"Now that Ireland has a bishop I assume all reports will be made by him," I suggested. "Farewell, Ami."

"You sound as if..." Ami began, but shouts from a ship pulling into port captured our attention.

"Bishop Amicus! Father Patrick! Wait!" screeched the anxious voice of Father Malach. He leapt onto the dock and hurried toward us, with Father Auxilius at his heels. "Bishop Palladius..." Father Malach breathed excitedly when he stood before us, "he's dead! Martyred!"

"What!? How could that happen?" I asked, horrified that perhaps Sinell...

"Things were going so well," Father Malach explained. "Then Bishop Palladius became concerned about the Christians you had spoken of in Dalaridia."

"Dalaridia? *You let him go among the Picts?*" I gasped in disbelief.

"You were planning to go! How could we know what might happen?"

"Oh, God! Oh ignorant brothers, what have you done? Have you forgotten so soon King Diarmuid's court? How very nearly we lost our heads? What better could be expected from the Picts?"

Father Malach and Father Auxilius lowered their wounded eyes. My outburst had been insensitive and uncalled for. "Forgive me, Brothers. Were you informed as to how he died?" I gently inquired.

"Some Pictish ritual we were told," Father Auxilius answered. I shuddered and turned away from them. "You were at odds with Bishop Palladius. Why are you so distressed?"

"Whatever he thought of me," I whispered hoarsely, "he was a good man, and he paid with his life for that goodness."

"I'll call a council of bishops to determine what's to be done," Ami stated soberly. "Meet me after the noon hour in two days time at Bishop Eusibus' church."

Two hours after noon Ami stepped through the chapel doors and into the large sanctuary where we waited. "Father Patrick, the bishops would like to examine you." I followed him into the office beside the chapel. Bishop Eusibus and two other bishops sat behind a desk looking over several pieces of correspondence. As their eyes lighted on my unusual apparel the contempt on their faces was painfully evident. Never intending to return, I had sold all my Roman garments.

"Bishop Amicus, how can you promote this ---savage?" Bishop Victor exclaimed.

"We have to be very careful here, Bishop Amicus," Eusibus quietly posed. "One day this man may stand in our place. Will the British church accept such a man as bishop? And this correspondence, here are glowing reports and scathing criticisms, almost as though two very different people were being evaluated. I just don't see..."

I shook my head and turned to go. "Speak to them, Patrick," Ami begged. It was unforgivably disrespectful to walk out on a council of bishops. An address of some kind was in order.

"Fathers," I began reluctantly, "The people of Ireland are hungry for this gospel. They are sheep desperate for a shepherd, and I have been called to feed and lead them. A vine is known by its fruit. Judge me by three hundred Irish souls reborn in the waters of baptism, not by my Irish trousers or my ignorance of Cicero. And while you wrestle with prayer and fasting to determine how God's will can be so in opposition to your prejudice, do not expect me to wait. I have wasted too much time already. I have one Master. I follow Him, *with or without* your blessing. Today I leave for Ireland, and I will never return. God's blessings on each of you." I left them gaping and speechless.

"What happened?" Brother Ninus inquired as we walked through the sanctuary to the street. "I'm either a heretic or apostate, but definitely not bishop," I answered dismally. "Let's be off."

As we made our way to the hostel the voices of Father Malach and Father Auxilius resounded behind us, "Father Patrick, may we come with you?" I cast a puzzled eye toward Brother Ninus.

"Brothers," I responded as they met us, "I thought you'd be delighted to be free of me."

"I thought so too," Father Malach began, "but..."

Our laughter covered his words. "How can we deny such an honest man? But are you sure, brothers?" I more soberly challenged, "We go to the very heart of Ireland, without..."

"Patrick! Wait!" Ami shouted, running toward us. "They've agreed, Patrick!" he panted. "You are to be Bishop of Ireland!"

The service of ordination was brief. The three bishops anointed me with oil, placed their hands on my head, and prayed, each in turn, for wisdom and constancy in my faith and receptive hearts in those I would shepherd. I was at peace at last. The voice of my vision and the voice of the church finally spoke as one. All Ireland was open to me, and as her bishop I could evangelize, baptize, ordain priests and deacons, and administer the sacraments. How long I had waited for this liberty to be the happy slave of my God.

It was Ami's persuasive arguments that had won the council's grudging acquiescence. "Who else wants to be Bishop of Ireland?" he had challenged. "Can we just abandon the Irish church when this man feels so strongly called to go to her aid? What possible relevance is his appearance or education, since he never expects to return? As for his reputation, I can personally assure you that this man has *never* done anything compromising, immoral, or illegal, a man of highest principle and devotion." So Ami related as we feasted together after the service. His casual attitude toward this less than accurate depiction concerned me.

"To distort the truth is to compromise your integrity, Ami. I would not have...

"There's been no harm done," he snipped in irritation. "We both got what we wanted, and Ireland got you. Now you're free to follow Palladius. Run off and play the martyr. I wish you God speed." Ami abruptly rose and left the hall.

"Ami, wait!" I called as I hurried after him, "Please, forgive me. I wasn't judging you. I just feel guilty that your kindness to me should have cost you so much. Stay and celebrate with me ...one last time."

Ami's usually stoic face was a study in conflicting emotions. He embraced me briefly. In the end he only whispered, "Farewell, Sucat," then walked quickly away. I never saw him again. We sailed for Ireland the following morning.

BOOK THREE

BISHOPS, BUTCHERS, AND BETRAYALS

"I, Patrick, a Sinner..."

CHAPTER TWENTY-TWO
The Paschal Flame

The weight of their burdens caused our donkeys no small difficulty as we crossed the sandy beach to Sinell's hut.

"Father Patrick!" Liddy exclaimed.

"Bishop Patrick," Brother Ninus gently corrected.

"Bishop? The Lord be praised! You men come on in and make yourselves at home." We placed the bags of Roman coins onto the floor of the hut, and sat down to rest. "It was terrible what happened to Bishop Palladius," Liddy said as she filled our mugs. "Sinell offered to go with him, but Palladius said it would compromise his witness to be seen with a man with such a violent reputation. He said it kindly, of course." Liddy served Father Malach and Father Auxilius.

"I'm encouraged that Sinell would offer. He's a better man than I had judged," I confessed.

"Who drinks my ale and troubles my woman!!" Sinell roared as he entered the hut. But for the twinkle in his eye and the almost imperceptible curl of his lips at the corners, I might have been as terrified as Father Auxilius. I laughed and stood to greet him. Swallowing me in his powerful arms, Sinell hugged me like a long awaited son returned home.

"What's this?" Sinell inquired stooping to examine the bag at his feet. After contemplating the contents of both, Sinell looked at me in amazement. "All this is yours?"

"Ours now. Will you be our banker, Sinell?"

"I should have held you for ransom," he said with chilling ruthlessness, "instead of selling you as a slave." The hair on the back of my neck tingled. "Sorry, Patrick," he grimaced. "For a moment I forgot we were brothers."

"I'd appreciate it if these little slips of memory didn't happen too often," I only half teased.

"You would trust all this to me?"

"Sinell, with your reputation that gold could stay on your doorstep and no one would dare touch it."

Sinell laughed loudly, then eyed the bags with wary and calculated interest.

"I know you're an old pirate. If the accounts run short from time to time, I won't fault you," I suggested. "But this is all I have. It will have to last me the rest of my life."

Sinell stood to his feet and absently rubbed the back of his neck as a worried frown creased his brow. "If you were anybody else, I'd say, 'yes,' and steal the lot of it two minutes after you'd gone." He scowled silently for several moments then extended his left hand. "But I can't steal from you, Patrick." As our scared palms met he declared, "You've got a banker."

We enjoyed Sinell's hospitality for the remainder of the day. I was encouraged by Liddy's revelations. The church had grown. Three hundred catechumens had been baptized and as many awaited baptism, six men had been ordained as priests, and, with the necessary consent of King Diarmuid, two new churches had been built. Bishop Palladius had left an admirable legacy. A fitting memorial and mass would be my first order of business.

The following morning we left for Twin Hills. The rhythmic creaking of the ox cart and the warmth of the morning sun lulled my companions and me into quiet contemplations. Ireland was mine to win, I thought, her people my children and I their father. But how to proceed with the winning? There was no formal overall structure to the government of Ireland. Each kingdom was totally independent of the others unless specific agreements were made between the individual kings. Fear of the Druids and respect for the brehons provided a kind of universal standard of justice. Fear also of the bard, who could establish a man's reputation with his songs and stories of heroism (or cowardice), motivated men to noble deeds. This was the extent of their unity. But even in this unstructured society, men of distinction, simply by virtue of the greatness of their character, commanded, without force, the allegiance of those wise enough to perceive their greatness. Such a man was Loguaire, or so the stories said, poetically entitled "High King of Ireland." If we were to succeed in Ireland Loguaire's favor would have to be secured. Our sojourn at Twin Hills would be a short one.

The journey took longer by cart than when we traveled by chariot. Already anxious to be "home," I could hardly contain my zeal when Twin Hills came in sight. To my profound amazement, standing ready to receive us was a multitude of Christian brothers and sisters, a host of dignitaries, and King Diarmuid at their head.

"A Hundred Thousand Welcomes, Patrick!" King Diarmuid said in greeting, as I knelt before him.

"Thank you, King Diarmuid. Your presence honors me above my merit."

"So it does," King Diarmuid concurred, "but since your influence has been felt the length and breadth of Leinster, I'm forced to make this gesture."

"Then you still judge the influence to be positive?" I asked, standing to face him.

King Diarmuid shrugged, "The services you Christians provide the sick and the poor keep the rest of my subjects content."

"I'm glad you approve." We walked together through the retinue of well-wishers.

"I also appreciate that you and your people stay out of my affairs and don't expect to be royally entertained, unlike the Druids," he continued. "I only question your teaching them letters. How can I know the affect that will have? But until I see good reason, I won't interfere."

"King Diarmuid, I hope I find the rest of the kings of Ireland to be as wise and clever as you have shown yourself to be."

"The rest of Ireland? ---The rest of Ireland? Mark my words, Patrick. Were it not for that clever vixen, Lord Gowan's widow, I'd have had your head, and you know it. The rest of Ireland doesn't want another holy man. She'll chew you up and spit you out like vomit."

"Ireland may not want me, King Diarmuid, but my God wants her. Brother Ninus and I leave well before Beltane."

"I advise you to stay in Leinster. Besides I've missed your monthly visits to my rath. My court enjoys your tales. Stay and tend your church," he insisted.

"The church has fared quite well without me," I said, gesturing to all the people. "The Irish priests are competent to tend this mission. But, God willing, we shall return from time to time to oversee her progress and encourage her faith."

"Humpf! If not Leinster, where will you make your home?".

"Home? I doubt any one place will claim me for long. A place on a river, or rivers, near the heart of Ireland might facilitate travel."

"So you will confront King Loguaire and the kings of the north? A bold if foolhardy scheme," he scolded. "Before you lose your head in some other feast hall, come and dine with me. When you've told all my favorite stories and a new one or two besides, if I haven't talked you out of it, I'll give you leave to go. I'll expect you the evening of the new moon."

"It will be my pleasure, as always, King Diarmuid."

After he departed, Brother Ninus, Father Malach, Father Auxilius, and I were overrun with other zealous well wishers. A feast was announced, fires lit, and fish and fowl set to roast above them. Mead, ale, and wine were gathered in abundance. Pipes and cymbals, bodhrans and bones played merrily. A more Irish welcome I could not have wished for. Sechnall, now Father Sechnall, Brother Maciul, Sister Lallocc, the little orphan boys, Rioc and Benignus, two newly ordained Irish priests, Father Mactaleus and Father Justanus, and so many more friendly, familiar faces greeted us with hugs and kisses and amazing tales.

I managed, finally, to slip unnoticed into the little church for a few moments of quiet reminiscing and thanksgiving. When I stood to leave another figure kneeling in prayer was just visible in the candlelight. The figure rose as I approached.

"Beautiful, beautiful Lady," I breathed as the candlelight fell across Scothie's face.

Her crystal blue eyes captivated mine. "Can you spare a moment, Bishop Patrick?" I nodded. "When you went away, I did a lot of thinking about my life," she volunteered, "a lot of praying. After making my confession..."

"Your confession?"

"Hear me out, Patrick. After hearing my confession, Bishop Palladius helped me to understand your position, even confessed that he had misjudged you. When he inquired after you, Bishop Amicus related that your father was extremely ill, and you had taken over managing the estate."

"I wonder why Ami never mentioned it?"

"It's just as well. You needed to be with your father, and I needed to be away from you. You set a fire in my heart Patrick. Love, for God, for you. I wanted to serve you both. I just didn't know how."

"Oh, Scothie, I..."

"Listen! I want you to understand." She smiled radiantly. "I've chosen, I've been called, to be a bride of Christ, one of the sisters here."

A bride of Christ? My joy at her words, was it a reverent joy, because she had chosen the best of all possible roads? Or a selfish, perverse joy, because no other man would take my place in her affections? Was this really right for Scothie?

"I have to applaud your choice but can you be sure?" I counseled. "Those vows. You're a woman of such marvelous passion, Scothie, surely a husband..."

"That's quite a compliment coming from a man of yours," she purred teasingly. I felt my cheeks flush with humiliation. How could I presume to counsel her? "Oh, I'm sorry, Patrick." It was her turn to blush. "Forgive me. Of course I understand your concern. But don't underestimate my determination to direct all that I am to the service and love of God, including my passion; including my love for you."

My heart felt as if it divided and beat against itself. "I spoke from my own weakness, Scothie. I don't doubt that, with God's grace, you can accomplish whatever you put your mind to."

"Well don't vainly imagine that I'm just chasing after you. My call to this life is every bit as valid and genuine as yours. Bishop Palladius wouldn't permit..."

"I believe you," I chuckled, and taking that remarkable, confident face between the palms of my hands I gently kissed her forehead. "A bride of Christ! You couldn't have done better, Scothie."

"I'm obviously not as holy as you now imagine." She sighed nervously and moved away from me. "If we are to work together, fond embraces and holy kisses will have to be abandoned. I'm not willing or able to wrestle with the temptations they will arouse... And neither should you be."

"Work together?" I asked in amazement.

"Yes, Bishop, you will need women in your company if you plan, as I know you do, to traipse all over Ireland. Who will mend your clothes and sew new garments, make the altar cloths and vestments, gather medicinal herbs and nurse the sick, prepare the meals and wash the clothes, and minister to women converts?"

"Well, I don't know, but God will provide."

Scothie approached the altar table, made reverence, and ran her fingers along the beautifully embroidered trim on the altar cloth. "Has it never occurred to you that *I* have overseen those chores since the day this church was founded? Even before I believed in God, I believed in you."

All those anonymous gifts; years of love, labor, and artistry, even when she avoided me and I ran scared of her. How could I have known? I joined her at the altar.

"Several of the sisters have been preparing for this mission, believing your promise to return," she continued. "They are young, full of energy and zeal, but lacking in mature wisdom. For this reason Bishop Palladius put them under my authority. I have been their mother for almost a year now. I believe God wants me to continue to guide them on this journey."

Who better for God to choose? There was no more remarkable woman in all of Leinster. I could feel in my soul that she was right, but in my body I could feel other things, too. Was God amused? Was he worried that I was under challenged? Or maybe two people, so perfectly suited for such a mission, would by their very natures be attracted to each other.

"You could be a valuable asset to this mission," I admitted. "But to me personally?" I stroked her cheek with my fingers and tucked a wisp of auburn tresses under her veil. "I can't begin to imagine the nightmare, Scothie. Seeing you every morning, every evening. Smelling your hair, hearing your voice, knowing you were sleeping near by, yet not able to touch you. Worrying about your safety every time we met a challenge." I turned painfully away.

"We each have our cross to bear, mine no lighter than yours," Scothie sighed sympathetically. "I am sorry. I know what I've done to you, but this interview was necessary. You'll be amazed at the brevity of our discourses in the future. Pray about it, Patrick. I have.

"The feast is certain to be ready," she suggested as she walked to the door, "Will you come soon?" I nodded. "One other thing. It will help if you call me 'Mother Scothie'. And I will call you Bishop." Scothie disappeared, and I went in search of a cold bath and a long conversation with God.

Six months later, having comforted and encouraged the churches in Leinster, and having enjoyed the most cordial relations with King Diarmuid, I made plans to visit King Loguaire at Tara. Our company on this journey consisted of Father Malach, Father Auxilius, Brother Ninus, Father Sechnall, Benignus, Rioc, Mother Scothie, and three other sisters, Cadhla, Cas, and Boin. The two little boys, now ten and eight, had been running wild, since the orphan home at Twin Hills had been closed by Palladius. Now, though the home had been reopened, they felt they were too old to be looked after, so I invited them to travel with us.

We determined to travel north by sea. Before we cast off, Sinell (reluctantly remaining behind to insure our resources) had given me a superfluity of advice and cautions, along with a fine collection of tribute, which he hoped would endear us to Loguaire.

Sailing north along the coast, we made good time until we reached a harbor in Meath. Unfortunately, rumors about our party had preceded us, and the natives of that settlement were so hostile for fear of the Druids, that Father Sechnall, Brother Ninus, and I were driven from the beach, pelted by sticks and stones.

We continued north, hugging the coastline, until a shallow, uninhabited inlet presented itself. We disembarked, paid the ship's captain a generous fee, and began traveling overland toward Tara.

As the days passed I grew more and more impressed with the women who worked so silently among us. They kept completely to themselves, and never said a word except in prayer, or occasionally to one another. Any compliment we paid them was answered with a modest nod of the head. Their piety inspired greater devotion in all of us.

As for being tormented by Scothie's presence, I never saw her. The younger women performed the services we required, cooking, mending, etc. while Mother Scothie devoted her time to prayer and the guidance they required, and so remained apart and unseen, her face hidden behind her cowl. But hadn't she been a master at hiding herself since childhood?

We were six weeks into spring. It was almost Easter by the Celtic church calendar, though the Romans had already celebrated their Easter more than a week ago. This difference caused Brother Ninus some consternation as he had lived so long at Lerins where the Roman calendar was used. But it was the Celtic church that had sent me to Ireland, and I chose to align our celebration with theirs. This year the Celtic Easter coincided with Beltane, signifying to me that the glory of the risen Christ would overcome the fires of Beltane this year and for all time.

By the end of Holy Week Tara was in sight. Even from a distance, it was an impressive structure by Irish standards, encompassing the entire upper surface of the broadest and tallest hill for miles in every direction. We made camp early in the day in order to prepare for the most beautiful and moving celebration of the Christian year. It was Holy Saturday the evening of our all night Easter vigil and the festival of lights.

We began to ascend the lower slope of a sizeable rise almost entirely covered with multitudes of rocks and stones that shifted precariously with every step, and plummeted to the valley like an avalanche of snow. Forced to stop, we waited while Father Sechnall surveyed the circumference. He soon found a small avenue to the summit that was slightly less treacherous, which we scaled. From the height all Ireland seemed to stretch out before us, our view only impeded by the mound of Tara. Oh, glorious Ireland! At once I was filled with praise for the God who had created such a masterpiece. Here we would worship, our cathedral, the vault of the heavens, our altar the stones. I began to arrange candles and a fire pit for the service.

"Shouldn't we forego the festival of lights, Patrick?" Brother Ninus challenged. "It's Beltane. Dare we risk offending King Loguaire?"

"Dare we risk offending God?" I asked incredulously. "Where is my faith, Ninus, if, like a coward, I bow to the Beltane gods, failing to worship the risen Christ with all the glory and festival this night requires?" Brother Ninus reluctantly nodded his head, but the worry behind his eyes betrayed his doubts. "I only speak for myself, Ninus," I added. "If you and the others would rather worship privately at the foot of the mountain, I can respect that. For me, I cannot do otherwise."

Brother Ninus smiled causing the freckles to dance on his cheeks. "Is it your *faith in God* or your *fear of God* that makes you so reckless, Patrick?

"Neither faith nor fear," I answered, "just love."

All the doubt left his eyes. "No man lights a candle and puts it under a bushel. Beltane or not, my light will be shining alongside yours." Given the same option, each of the others deliberately determined to participate in our celebration on the mount.

To represent the darkness of the tomb and the absence of light in a world without Christ, we began our worship in the dark. There was an unusual eerie blackness that night. The moon did not give her light, and clouds shrouded the twinkling stars from view. Not a fire burned or candle flickered from the Rath of Tara or any settlement within our broad view. The silence of night birds and insects added a dismal feeling of isolation. Each of us held an unlit candle awaiting the moment when grief would turn to joy, death into resurrection, despair into hope, darkness into light. With strong conviction we chanted the Psalms of penitence and mourning, and recited the scriptures recording Christ's passion. The awful reality, terror, of Christ's death, cut off from God and man, utterly alone, weighed heavily on us all in the blackness.

At last the moment of light had come, the record of Christ's resurrection recited. God and man had been reconciled, driving out the darkness in men's hearts, and wiping away the tears from every eye. The fire was kindled, and the Paschal candle lit. When each of us had lit his candle from the Paschal flame, and those candles and torches on and near the altar were set ablaze, the moon and stars, too, suddenly stripped of their clouds, shone brilliantly, as if in reflection of the light below. Inexpressible joy ignited our hearts. We held our lights aloft and sang with magnificent enthusiasm a hymn of the resurrection, sounding and resounding from every hill like the strains of a great choir.

In the silence of prayer that followed, we became aware of a low rumble which grew steadily in volume, until finally it assumed the unmistakable thunder of chariots. We continued our worship, raising our voices over the din until the thunder ceased.

"What godless traitor breaks the darkness before King Loguaire has lit the fires of Beltane?" the well-trained voice of a herald boomed up from below. The distracting noise of rocks grating and sliding beneath the feet of many ascending warriors filled our ears. We concluded our worship in full voice. Then, holding the Paschal candle high, I took a position visible to those below.

"Put out that fire! Who are you, who would dare to offend our gods?" the herald inquired.

"I am Patrick, who dares not offend the one true God," I answered. "He wishes to make himself known to you, and to all the bold men of Ireland. For this reason I have come."

"Heresy!" yelled an ancient Druid priest, noticeable by his white beard and robes. "Sons of Ireland, drag him down!!"

Three of the warriors had managed to attain the summit and lunged for me. Beneath their feet the shifting rocks gave way, preventing their success, and causing, in spite of their great efforts, their gradual descent. The entire mountain seemed to tremble. Suddenly, tumbling one onto another, a cascade of rocks, stones, and boulders in ever increasing volume and velocity bounded punishingly toward the valley below, dragging the warriors in their wake. Screams of men and horses unable to escape the avalanche were barely heard above the rumbling chaos. The terrible echoes resounded from hilltop to hilltop for what seemed a long time.

As the dust finally settled, another voice called out, "I am King Loguaire. Your coming was expected, *Christian* Patrick. Come down! Make yourself known."

I carefully worked my way down the shifting mountainside by Father Sechnall's safer route with Ninus following. The others of our party remained safely out of sight. At the foot of the mountain we stepped over and around broken boulders, bodies, and chariots. As we approached King Loguaire, his warriors deliberately dropped their heads, a sign of respect. Loguaire made a guttural grunt of disapproval and the warriors nervously resumed their alert posture.

Standing in his exquisitely ornamented chariot, Loguaire looked every bit a king. He was tall, almost a head taller than most men, and his posture exuded the confidence that always emanates from a powerful physique carefully dominated by an even more powerful will. I sensed also in him a sensitivity that guaranteed not sentimentality, but an exceptionally acute intuition. As I carefully committed these observations to memory, King Loguaire was taking mental note of me as well. I wondered what he read.

Beside Loguaire stood a lady who could only have been his queen, confident, elegantly dressed, and beautiful, but possibly as shrewd as Loguaire himself.

"My Lord King," I saluted as I went down respectfully on one knee. Ninus followed suit.

"Do you honor the king now with your words? Your actions have greatly offended me!" King Loguaire seethed, attempting to suppress his fury. "You enter my kingdom uninvited and openly defy the king's commands. I should repay your arrogance by severing your heads in the most painful way imaginable."

"My lord," the queen interrupted, taking his arm, "remember the prophecy." King Loguaire's arm rippled like the flesh of a horse attempting to discourage an irritating fly.

"Prophecy?" I queried.

"That this light of yours will consume all Ireland!" King Loguaire snapped. "Preposterous!"

So Ono MacOengusa's words were heard as far north as Tara. What else might they have heard?

"It was not our intention to offend you, King Loguaire, but to honor the one true God," I submitted. "Was I wrong to believe it was the Druids' convention, and not King Loguaire's command, that no fires be lit until the sacrifice was kindled?"

After several moments of careful scrutiny a sly smile curled the corners of Loguaire's mouth. "Why, it was the Druids, certainly," he responded. "You think yourself a shrewd man, Christian Patrick. But you may discover it more expedient to offend the king than to challenge the Druids. Come. Ride with me to Tara. The hour is late, and Beltane waits to be initiated."

"Thank you, but no, King Loguaire. This is also a Holy Day for us." King Loguaire glared irritably. "It was an invitation and not a command, I trust?"

His scowl faded into a grimace, "An invitation, surely."

"My companions and I travel to Tara within the week. At that time we will gratefully embrace whatever hospitality you are pleased to extend." I handed his driver a small satchel containing expensive ornaments. "Please accept this token of the tribute we bring."

"So be it," Loguaire pronounced crossly. "But if I don't see you before the dust has settled from the last of the Beltane races, you will not find me so agreeable at our next meeting."

We exchanged wary nods. King Loguaire and his company thundered away, leaving behind only those who were attending to the injured and the dead. The rest of our company joined us and we assisted in freeing the injured from their rocky prisons. The sisters ministered to their wounds and we helped them into the chariots that would return them to Tara. Then we prayed for their souls, and all ascended the hill to continue our worship. What a poignant Easter celebration that was!

"I, Patrick, a Sinner..."

CHAPTER TWENTY-THREE
Dichru's Barn

Two days later as we made our way to Tara a young man, riding with the grace and style of a born horseman, approached rapidly. His mount was magnificent. She swiftly traversed the countryside, neither driven nor restrained by her rider, with such ease that lather had yet to appear on her neck or hindquarters.

"Who is the holy prophet called Patrick?" the rider queried as he trotted into our midst.

"I am called Patrick," I said as I stroked the mare's nose. "And who is the lad who so skillfully commands this exquisite horse?"

The young man smiled broadly. "I am Mor, with a message for Patrick. But, sir," he frowned quizzically, "you do not look like a prophet or a holy man."

All my brothers broke into laughter.

"I am neither of those. I am a Christian priest..." I began to explain.

"A Christian *bishop*!" Father Malach interrupted.

"What is the message?" I asked ignoring Malach's attempt at making a tedious point once more about my office and my attire.

"Lochru, Chief Druid from Milchu's Rath, visits King Loguaire. He demands you come before him and demonstrate the power of your god by making it snow this fine spring day."

"Lochru!?"

How successfully I had suppressed his memory. Lochru! Now that his name rang in my ears, I realized my appalling desire that he be the one man who would never hear of God's mercy, the one man I wanted doomed to Hell for all eternity. Mor handed me a piece of fine colored cloth with King Loguaire's crest embroidered on it, ending my disturbing bout of self-examination.

"This is an official challenge, then. When?" I forced myself to ask.

"Now, on the king's high hill," Mor responded.

"What will you do, Patrick?" Brother Ninus asked guardedly.

"He'll pray and God will send the snow," Little Rioc stated loudly with innocent confidence. Benignus jabbed him with his elbow.

"Can I ask God to jump through hoops just to amuse Lochru?" I asked tousling Rioc's hair.

"Why not?" interjected Father Auxilius, "Look at Moses and the Red Sea."

"Do you see a *Moses* here?" I snapped, immediately regretting my short temper. "Tell the king I come." I placed in Mor's hand the king's crest. Mor looked at once surprised and delighted, as he urged his pony into a spirited gallop. "Ninus, it's the Prince of Darkness himself I'll be facing. You're to stay here. All of you."

"Lochru?" Brother Ninus puzzled. "The same man you were enslaved to?"

"Still am by Irish law," I concurred.

"No, Bishop," Brother Ninus retorted with authority. "If we don't share the battle, we'll have no part in the victory. We all go!"

"And for this battle you will look like a bishop and not a peasant!" Father Malach insisted.

The uncompromising looks in all their eyes convinced me I must yield or face a mutiny. Father Auxilius unrolled a measure of white spring wool that had been beautifully woven into a robe and matching cloak and cowl. On the front and back of both cloak and robe were crosses embroidered in gold and scarlet thread.

"It's beautiful! Such artistry. Where did this come from?" I puzzled aloud. Father Sechnall and Father Malach glanced quickly at Mother Scothie.

"Scothie? Your fingers crafted this garment?"

"You won't impress King Loguaire and his Druids in your peasant's garb, Bishop," Mother Scothie quietly but determinedly insisted. "Wear what you like when you travel or visit among the people. But at the king's court dress in a manner befitting the head of Christ's church."

"This is much too..."

"Please, Patrick, I understand these nobles," she interrupted, unable to completely mask her anxiety. "If you value your head..."

"Brother Ninus, help me to put it on."

"After years of trying to get through to you," Father Malach touted, "it takes one word from Lady...Mother Scothie and you..."

"Gloating is prideful, Father Malach," I barked, generating chuckles from my fine companions.

I felt as awkward as David must have felt when he tried to don Saul's armor. Mother Scothie nodded approvingly, once more masterfully serene, then disappeared among her sisters. Father Malach, Father Auxilius, and Brother Ninus slapped me on the back and marveled profusely at the transformation. Was it such a dreadful a visage I had presented before? As we resumed walking, Father Sechnall removed the tired old walking stick from my hand and replaced it with a beautifully carved and polished crook. Thus the caterpillar, dressed up like a butterfly, led his little party uncertainly to face the nearest thing I knew to the devil himself.

Finding the king's high hill presented no difficulty, as the entire population of Tara seemed to have turned out for the spectacle. The way was lined with curious eyes who stared with fear and contempt at the unwelcome strangers in their midst. "He's the one," an old woman croaked to her companions, as I passed. "Sure, he cursed old Lucetmael. Flung him up unto the air and smashed his head against the rocks without lifting a finger, so they tell me."

Lucetmael? In my mind's eye I could plainly see on the hem of his skirt, snakes intertwined and unending in perfect symmetry, as his feet circled my little altar so very long ago. Could he have still been alive after so many years?

Upon gaining the summit all the Christians followed me in approaching Loguaire and kneeling in respect. I am forced to admit that he was noticeably impressed with my appearance. He said nothing at all, but gestured toward a company of Druids who stood to the right of his throne and were huddled together in intense debate.

"Brother Ninus, stand our company to the left of the throne, and let me confront him alone. But don't forget to pray." Brother Ninus nodded and did as I asked.

"Chief Druid Lochru!" I addressed. "You have wasted my time and yours, for the Great and Mighty God of heaven and earth has no obligation to perform for you or anybody else."

From the midst of the Druids stepped forth Lochru. His thinning hair was streaked with black and grey as was his scraggled beard. Multitudes of wrinkles creased his face. He might have been unrecognizable but for those mad eyes the color of cold daggers, which had only become more intense with age. I was inclined to shiver but calmly prayed for peace instead.

Lochru squinted as his eyes searched mine. I had been a young man in slave's garments, with a full head of hair and a bushy beard when last I saw Lochru. Now middle aged, clean shaven, balding, and dressed like a powerful holy man he would never know me, unless my eyes gave me away.

Thankfully there was no indication of recognition. I turned my appeal to King Loguaire. "Great and wise Loguaire, High King of all Ireland, I appeal to your wisdom. Shall I ask God, who caused these trees to bud and these flowers to bloom, to destroy all this new life by sending snow out of season, just to placate Lochru?"

King Loguaire's eyes twinkled merrily as he shrugged his shoulders and quipped, "Why not?"

"And if I refuse to present God with this absurd request? If it doesn't snow?"

"Then you will be exposed as a lying fraud, a false prophet who only pretends to have power," Lochru charged.

"I have no power. That I readily admit. But my God has all power in heaven and earth. Power for good, not evil. To bring the death of winter to the new life of spring, can that be good?"

"Pray that it is, Christian," Lochru pronounced chillingly. "For if you fail, you and your followers will beg for more than snow to quench the fires I have prepared to receive you."

As I glanced toward Brother Ninus and the others, my eyes were captivated by Rioc's confident, expectant expression, his lips moving in prayer. If only I had the faith of that child, I mused. I bowed my head praying silently that God's will be done, whether it be to send the snow, or.... A cool gentle breeze kissed my cheek. I glanced quickly at Rioc's beaming face, then upward

"Your powers are too weak!" Lochru shouted almost hysterically. Like manna from heaven, large feathery snowflakes greeted my upraised eyes. I smiled within myself at the goodness of God. "See, I have brought the snow! You could not, but I have brought the snow! Seize the imposter!" Lochru screeched.

Fury exploded within me. What deplorable prevarication! That worm would claim for himself a miracle of God? My arms were immediately pinned behind me and I was forced to my knees by a stout and powerfully muscular warrior, the point of his blade nearly penetrating the flesh of my neck.

"Any power, your conceit imagines to be yours, can only be for evil, you blasphemous peacock!" I roared so furiously that the warrior's blade inadvertently sliced my neck. "Glorious and jealous Father in heaven," I prayed in full voice, "You who will not exchange your glory for the proud and vain boasts of this serpent, Lochru, remove the snow before one blossom withers or one bud freezes on the trees."

As suddenly as it started, the snow stopped. The sun bore down with such intensity that the white carpet at our feet disappeared almost instantly. The warrior restraining me released his hold and backed away.

"Thanks be to God," I humbly acknowledged, then rose and turned to King Loguaire. "My Lord?"

The King smiled impishly then glanced at Lochru, his Druids, and the company of Christians. He shrugged and motioned our dismissal without a word. Brother Ninus and the others surrounded me with triumphant smiles, hugs, and pats on the back.

"I knew if you asked him, God would send the snow," Rioc stated with almost arrogant confidence. I smiled and lay my finger against his nose.

"It was your prayer God answered!"

"Really?" he asked amazed.

"Without a doubt."

Mother Scothie passed me a cloth to stop the bleeding of my neck wound, and dressed it more satisfactorily when we arrived at the quarters King Loguaire had provided in Tara.

"I promise to avoid staining these fine garments with my rusty old blood whenever possible," I teased. Mother Scothie's kind grimace told me she didn't put much store in my promise. "You're quite a healer," I added.

"Any Irish noble woman worthy of the title could do as well," she responded as she returned the medicinal herbs to her pouch.

"Scothie, I was wrong. I thought your presence would weaken me. It hasn't. You only make me stronger."

"We all strengthen each other," she said smiling, then closed her bag and returned to the women's hut.

Food and refreshment were delivered early in the day, "a gift from King Loguaire," the servant related, so we all enjoyed the rich fare then rested until evening. As Loguaire's invited guests to Tara, an invitation to the feast that evening was assured by custom. To keep a sharp wit for the evening's feast, we set aside the wine for a less critical occasion.

King Loguaire's hall was larger than any I had seen. More than a thousand people could easily be seated at any one time, with wide aisles remaining for servers, musicians, jugglers, filids, and a friendly dog or two. Most of the guests were already seated by the time we entered. We stood, quietly awaiting direction. A servant appraised King Loguaire of our presence, and he rose slowly to his feet.

"Patrick, what a surprise! I was told not to expect you this evening," King Loguaire announced loudly from the end of the hall.

"Not expect us, my lord?" I asked bewildered.

"You don't appear at all indisposed," he continued. "Evidently a slight misunderstanding on Chief Druid Lochru's part. Servers, set another table here beside me. Come forward Patrick, you and your companions."

As we crossed the long hall hushed whispers could be heard all around. Mother Scothie, like the noble lady she was, dressed simply, but elegantly, as did the sisters under her care. I wore the bishop's robe she had made. Father Malach and Father Auxilius wore their finest Roman robes. Brother Ninus still wore his monk's garb, and the little boys dressed like most any Irish lad might. We were a mixed bag, but not a shabby one, as Father Malach had judged before we entered.

As we approached the throne, Father Malach and Father Auxilius placed the additional bags of tribute before King Loguaire, then we took our seats. King Loguaire was noticeably impressed by the valuables, which Sinell had so wisely purchased for tribute. Fine silk in various colors, golden torques and jeweled armbands, rare spices and fine wine inspired gasps of awe from those nobles near enough to view them.

"Patrick, you've come to share more than tribute. Entertain my nobles with your claims. Afterwards we will consider what you desire in return for these gifts." And so, encouraged to present for the nobles' consideration the principles of the Christian faith, this filid priest set before them those stories of error and death, redemption and resurrection that so often ignite men's hearts with the love of God. Several immediately perceived the truth and embraced the faith that evening. By Brother Ninus' calculations, fully a third of those within the sound of my voice desired to know more about our God. Even those who were not convicted must have felt they had been admirably entertained as they called for more stories. King Loguaire was not one of them. However, he was kindly disposed to tolerate the new religion.

One of King Loguaire's nobles, a man named Dichru who actually lived in the realm of a lesser king a good distance to the north, offered the land we needed to establish a church and community. King Loguaire and the other nobles consented, and the covenant was sealed.

The Druids and their honored guest, Lochru, came late to the feast and missed the gospel story. Our presence both alarmed and infuriated them, especially Chief Druid Lochru. "The wine you were sent was not to your liking?" Lochru asked with a sneer. "How dare a foreign wizard, so rudely refuse the king's gift!"

"The wine was very much appreciated, Chief Druid Lochru, but how would you know if we drank it or not?" I challenged.

Ignoring my challenge, he addressed the entire assembly, "If you allow this gross deceiver to plant his root in Meath, know that the Druids will not permit his vine to take over their fields. We will cut it down, burn it out, and cast the ashes to the wind." A burst of flame leapt from his hand onto the table before me. There were gasps throughout the hall. I had previously seen such tricks of magic, and calmly watched it die away. "A curse on these charlatans, these parasites, and all who are in league with them to deceive the people of Ireland!" Lochru roared. With pompous indignation he tossed his cloak about him. In a puff of dust he disappeared through a secret door hidden in the side of the hall. It was a more impressive performance than my storytelling had been. Had I not depended on God to move men's hearts rather than skillful performances, I might have been discouraged. I rose to my feet.

"You have heard the Druids' position. Will you still honor our covenant?" I asked.

The nobles looked from one to the other all around the hall. King Loguaire stood. "I rule by law. The covenant we have made stands. If the Druid's have been unable to discredit you publicly or to dispose of you privately, both which they swore they would do, then let the contest continue until we know better what course we should follow."

By God's grace Lochru left for King Milchu's Rath the following morning, while our company left for Lord Dichru's barn, our new home. Towards the end of the first week we were nearly through reworking the barn to serve as our new church and had begun constructing our dwellings. While Father Malach, Father Sechnall, and I broke ground, Brother Ninus and Father Auxilius hauled rock and laid foundations. Mother Scothie and Sister Cadhla prepared the wattle. Sister Cas, Sister Boin, and Benignus cut and hauled turf. And Rioc ran amongst us as our water boy. How swiftly and smoothly the building was assembled. And how merry our company, forced to sweat, strain, laugh, and sometimes, unfortunately, swear together.

Like true Irish women, the sisters worked at least as hard as the men and probably harder. Drenched with perspiration and smelling as ripe as any of us, they inspired admiration, not lust. Like true brothers and sisters, we were able to laugh, tease, and converse without that distracting demon, and I found in their companionship a depth of friendship unhindered by expectations, that I had only thought possible between men.

Our community finally consisted of two common houses one for the fathers and brothers and one for the sisters; two separate apartments, one for Mother Scothie and one for me, (a luxury I could have done without, but which the others insisted I needed); a house for the children 'rescued from the fairies'; a storage house for grain and other supplies; and the sanctuary.

King Loguaire, his nobles, and the Druids received an invitation to the first service held in our new church. Most attended out of curiosity as much as etiquette. The ritual appeared to impress them, the storytelling to delight them, but it was the reading that captured King Loguaire's interest.

"The words, do you hear them from the paper?" he asked following the service.

"No, there is no magic here. Each symbol represents a sound, which put together make words. I can teach you, your sons, to read, and to write your own words as well," I responded.

"So the laws you read, the Ten Commandments of your faith, they will be the same each time you read them?" he asked.

"Yes."

"I wish to make a record of law for Ireland. You will see that my sons learn to interpret these symbols," he commanded.

"As you wish, King Loguaire. Will you at some time consider embracing my faith, and not just my letters?" I carefully inquired.

King Loguaire laughed, "You presume too much, Christian. 'Adze head will come, a cowl upon his shoulders, a crook within his hand, shouting blasphemies against the gods of Ireland from his table.' So the prophecy comes to pass. Should I stand like a sheet in the wind hoping to resist the gale? No. But neither will I abandon the religion whose priests have long prophesied your coming. Let your fire consume all Ireland, as it surely will, but leave me to the gods of my fathers."

King Loguaire was never converted, though his daughter-in-law, I discovered, was a Christian captive from Britannia who had already raised her sons to know Christ, and would lead her husband to the faith as well. In response to King Loguaire's request a school was constructed in our compound, and in every compound we built from that day forward.

Overall the success we enjoyed in Meath was no less than in Leinster, but the trials slightly greater. Brother Ninus sent word to the brothers in Lerins informing them of my ordination as bishop and the growth of the Irish church. I sent word to Bishop Amicus, rejoicing in everything that God had done.

Within the year eighty catechumens had passed through the waters of baptism, three men felt possibly called to become priests, and eight women and thirteen men wished to follow the examples of Mother Scothie and Brother Ninus in lives set apart to pray and serve.

This in spite of the fact that the homes of these people often suffered vandalism or conflagration. Their families frequently rejected them. And they were occasionally waylaid, robbed, and assaulted on their way to and from the church.

These assaults and any personal illnesses or other misfortunes were touted to be curses laid on us by the jealous gods of Ireland. It was the ill will of the Druids that generated such persecution and superstition. No wise sage like Ono MacOengusa was to be found here. Lochru may have long since returned to the forests of Voclut, and Lucetmael to the Otherworld, but their animosity lingered.

The answer to prayer came one Sunday morning when several knights of King Loguaire's court and King Loguaire's two oldest sons came forward en mass to profess their allegiance to the new god. With knights accompanying Christian travelers, acts of piracy all but stopped, and acts of vandalism began to decline.

By the end of the second year our congregation had grown so that it could scarcely be served by our modest facilities. One of the Christian clansmen expelled the Druids from a sacred oak grove on his lands and donated that place for another church. It was much nearer Tara. We immediately took possession, consecrated the grounds for God's purpose, and built a second house for worship. In the minds of the common folk, this constituted a greater miracle than causing snow to fall, or overcoming Lochru's attempt to poison me, or transforming myself and those with me into deer to hide from King Loguaire's assassins (a fantastic story for which I can't account, but the people almost swear by). No, in their minds, to triumph over the sacred oaks was to assure the supremacy of my God. The church was securely established. It was almost time to move on.

"I, Patrick, a Sinner..."

CHAPTER TWENTY-FOUR
Every Tale Worth Telling

"Patrick! Come and see!" Brother Ninus shouted excitedly, drawing all of us from our early morning tasks. Down the path came a number of men in monks' habits escorted by the knights of King Loguaire.

"Our brothers from Lerins!?! Sisters, can you prepare a feast? Sechnall, we'll need some game. Malach, have the boys gather peat and wood for a long, long fire. Where are the instruments, Ninus? Some of our new brothers play a mean pipe. Auxilius, we'll need plenty to drink. A gifted bard or two would sure be welcome," I rattled in my enthusiasm.

"Peace, Bishop Patrick, they're monks, not Irish dignitaries," Brother Ninus chortled officiously.

"And all the more precious to me," I retorted. "Brother Bernicius! Brother Aurelius! A hundred thousand welcomes!" I exclaimed as the brothers came near. Brother Ninus and I greeted every one with embraces and a kiss on each cheek, then introduced them to the rest of our company. "Where is Brother Mathias?" I asked, suddenly sobered by his absence.

"He went to be with the Lord two weeks before we sailed," Brother Bernicius volunteered.

"I would so like to have seen him again," I said regretfully, "but I suppose he is seeing us all. I'll remember him tomorrow morning at the table of our Lord."

"We'll remember him together," Brother Ninus confirmed. "Come, brothers, enjoy the hospitality of our little community and a rest from your travels." Brother Ninus led the others to our sleeping quarters, all of them chattering uncharacteristically for monks.

"Accept our profound thanks for bringing our brothers safely from Tara," I said to the knights. "Will you stay and feast with us?"

"No, thank you, Bishop Patrick, the king requires our attendance," an officer related.

"So be it," I allowed. "God go with you, and give our fond regards to King Loguaire." The officer and his men nodded respectfully and departed.

A delightfully pleasant evening unfolded, the feast only excelled by the fellowship.

The brothers brought news of Gaul. The Vandals had moved south to Ibernia, only to be replaced by Visigoth raids plaguing Gaul. Roman forces were continually struggling to maintain Roman order. Equally unsettling was news that heretical factions fractured the church not only in Gaul, but throughout the empire. Yet Roman civilization and catholic Christianity continued to survive. The news of Britannia was less certain, but could not have greatly changed since I left three years ago. It all seemed worlds away from me now.

As the darkness deepened, several brothers treated our guests to the rhythmic delight of Irish music. I prepared to tell a tale or two. Brother Ninus strongly suggested that, as a Bishop, I should be much more circumspect with regard to the tales I related, so, in answer to my prayers, a filid just happened down the road and was attracted by our fire. A hearty meal, a strong drink, and a trinket or two loosens any filid's tongue and this filid's went to wagging for most of the night. What a marvelous teller he was. Tales I had heard time and time again he delivered with such skill and imagination that I might have heard them for the first time, so delightful was the hearing. Father Malach, Father Auxilius, and Brother Ninus translated for the brothers who had probably not laughed as much in all their years at Lerins.

One by one the revelers surrendered to their exhaustion, all but the filid. Alone together, I shared the story of God in Christ with the filid. Behind the gifted performer, I discovered a sad and empty man who enthusiastically desired to embrace the selfless love of Christ. Having wept and prayed, he fell peacefully asleep, leaving me to enjoy the sparkling coals of the dwindling fire in solitude. The first warm rays of the morning sun stirred Ninus, Malach, and Bernicius awake.

"They were great stories, all of them," I suggested.

"Amazing stories," Brother Bernicius added laughing.

"I want them written down. Every one. Every word."

"What? Patrick, surely not pagan stories?" Brother Ninus exclaimed.

"They're *stories*, Ninus." I responded. "The heart of these people beats through the stories they tell. You're an Irishman. Can't you feel it?"

"But in Gaul the bishops forbid recording..."

"Where is the harm? Do you imagine that God is threatened by these tales?" I interrupted.

"Such liberty was also forbidden in Britannia, as you well know," Father Malach chided with irritating self-righteousness. "More learned men than you have condemned perpetuating these myths and legends, many of them far more innocent than those told here last night. You can't just presume to..."

"Am I the *BISHOP OF IRELAND*?!" I exploded, rising to my feet. "Am I? I say write them down, *every Tale Worth Telling*! Would we lose the treasures of Ireland by the prejudice of simple-minded piety? Not while I am her father... her bishop! Rather, these jewels should be preserved by her saints! I'd record them myself if I had the skill. Give this filid whatever accommodations he requires, and set a scribe to the task every waking hour! If that offends your piety I'll find someone else who will!"

"Perhaps my piety needs offending," Father Malach humbly replied. "I'll put a scribe to the task as soon as our guest awakens."

"It's good that God gave Ireland a man of vision rather than a man of letters," Brother Ninus allowed as he stood to face me. "I, too, will add as many tales as I can to that record."

"Letters!? Bishop Patrick," Brother Bernicius announced with some embarrassment, "there was a letter for you on the ship. Forgive me for not remembering until now."

"You're forgiven, just give me the letter. 'Anno Domini 432,'" I read good-humoredly. "A year old! I doubt one day's delay made a great deal of difference." I wandered a few feet from the fire circle and silently read on.

Anno Domini 432

"To Bishop Patrick of Ireland, from Bishop Amicus of Britannia, greetings.

"It was kind of you to keep me informed. Your letter was quite illuminating. I trust mine will be as well. Unlike the church in Ireland (as you describe it), the churches in Britannia are static, her people confused by the disturbing changes and uncertainties of these times. I would, of course, prefer the fervor, the excitement, of building new frontier churches to watching old ones deteriorate without enough money or manpower to prevent or erase the ravages of time. However, this seems to be where the Lord would have me continue to serve, and I endeavor to be content.

"The tenor of your news concerned me greatly. I wish I could rejoice without reservation at all the impossible victories for the faith you claim to have amassed. Have you truly won single-handedly another Irish kingdom for Christ and his church? I fear the storyteller must be given to exaggeration. You surely could not have forgotten the terrible price you paid for such arrogance and self love in the past. Repent of your pride and temper your letters in the future with more honest humility. Yes, and out of love for me have Brother Iserninus or Father Malach rewrite them. I wade through mounds of correspondence daily. To have to suffer through your vulgar Latin is such an irritant that I must force myself to the task.

"If you are still at Tara when this letter finds you then I am disappointed. Have you become lazy? Are you so content with the good will you receive at Loguaire's court that you have become disloyal to the mission to convert all Ireland? And why have you begun in Meath, obviously a lesser, more comfortable, challenge than Palladius' mission to the Picts? Where is your courage? Your faith?

"Send me no letters about comfortable churches and great kings' favors. Tell me the savages are tamed, the Druids discredited, the blood of martyrs purifies the land!

"I hope, my dear friend, that you are capable of receiving this correspondence with enough humility to realize I only speak uncomfortably to preserve your soul. I pray God's richest blessings on your bold and courageous efforts to take up the cross of Christ and give your all for Him. I remain you dearest friend.

"Bishop Amicus"

I stared with unfocused eyes. Had my letter been so offensive? The sight of Ami's name had so delighted me. Now...

"What is it, Patrick? You're pale as bleached wool," Brother Ninus asked.

I could only shake my head. Ami had meant well, I'm sure of it. I owed more to him than to any other man alive. However painful, there had to be truth in what he said.

"Truth?" Mother Scothie mused, as I confided in her that evening. "Oh, for the love of God! Bishop Patrick, if you must remember your old friend with such blind devotion, imagine he suffered from gout or indigestion when he wrote that refuse." She smiled a crooked smile, kissed me gently on the forehead, then gracefully slipped away. The damage from Ami's words was instantly healed.

It wasn't long before I was, once more, ready to embrace the challenge that Ami's letter had posed. With the assistance of the brothers from Gaul and the oversight of Father Auxilius, the newly ordained priests began to effectively direct all the ministries we had established in Meath. Care of the sick, of the orphans, of the students of Latin, of the catechumens was well directed. The fields were producing sufficiently to feed our community and the cattle were breeding alarmingly well.

"Brother Ninus, we leave before the week is out."

"Our destination?"

"Milchu's Rath. There's a debt I have to pay."

"What if Lochru is still there?"

"What if he is?"

Brother Ninus raised an eyebrow and frowned, but said nothing.

Three days later our party gathered for the journey to the western sea. Ninus and I rode one chariot. Father Sechnall took the reins of another, and Sister Cas and Sister Boin took their seats on the well loaded ox cart behind Father Malach. Rioc and Benignus herded the cattle, needed as currency, onto the road behind the ox cart and our caravan began. Since the new sisters in Meath still required guidance, Mother Scothie remained behind along with Sister Cadhla and Father Auxilius.

Our guide, Prince Caerwin, King Loguaire's seventeen-year-old son, arrived on a magnificent mount. Prince Caerwin proved to be an excellent guide but an unbearable companion. He despised everyone in our company and brazenly said so. I patiently tolerated his mockery and crude humor. After all I had been a rich, arrogant, young fool once myself. However, Rioc and Benignus, now eleven and thirteen, and strongly opinionated, endured without much charity his belittling remarks and unwarranted criticisms.

Unlike the boys, Sisters Cas and Boin endured in silence his degrading insults, which he had been very careful to make outside my hearing. Like a watchful father, I had wondered with relief at his seeming disinterest in the sisters. How nearly disastrous for Cas that assumption had been. But that is her story to tell. I will say that I had sufficient provocation to preach with unbridled ferocity the fire of Hell to that young man.

The smell of the sea can be perceived miles away by those who love her. We were nearly two weeks into our journey when that faint saltiness tickled my nostrils, signaling the last leg of our trip. The focus of my prayers now turned from Prince Caerwin to my meeting with King Milchu, and possibly Chief Druid Lochru.

About mid morning the fifteenth day, young Prince Caerwin exuded a dangerously arrogant but uneasy confidence as he led our caravan into a shallow and narrow ravine. The moment Rioc and Benignus had driven the last cow into the ravine, warriors descended the slopes, arrested our chariots, and forced us to the ground, all but Prince Caerwin. What wicked treachery. Prince Caerwin's purse stood to gain substantially.

"You planned this well, Prince Caerwin," I quietly accused. Caerwin looked away. At least he wasn't gloating.

At the top of the rise, sitting tall upon a beautiful mount, was a young man wearing the seven colors of the king's family. It was not Lochru, but as Chief Druid he could never be king. Could King Milchu have died and another king been chosen?

"What king rides so magnificent a horse?" I shouted, lifting my head from the dirt. The knobby toes of a warrior slammed into my jaw. I spit the blood from my mouth.

"Who is the stranger who dares to speak?" the king called back.

I slowly rose, watchful of the warriors. "No stranger," I shouted. "Former slave of King Milchu, come to repay the freedom I stole."

The king prodded his horse and soon towered above me in the ravine. "What is your name, slave?"

"I am no longer a slave."

"We'll soon see! What were you called when you were a slave?"

"A number of *colorful* things."

"No doubt," he quipped with a smile. He gracefully swung down from his mount and stood before me. "What did they call you *most* of the time?"

"Sucat, sometimes Holy Boy," I replied, instantly sobered by painful memories. My response must have sobered the king as well. He studied me for several moments, then reached for the leather cord on my neck. The worn and weathered book of verses appeared from within my shirt.

"A story, Sucat. Tell me a story," he almost whispered.

"Prince Gosacht? Can this tall bearded man be little Prince Gosacht?"

"He can if this old, bald, chariot driver is Sucat."

We broke into laughter and embraced. All my brothers and sisters were allowed to rise. They surrounded us staring curiously.

"Prince Caerwin, son of Loguaire," Prince Gosacht called, "Who did you think you brought to us?"

"A Christian prophet named Patrick," he answered meekly.

"A Christian prophet? Yes, of course. With such power he commands the lightning and the snow! He speaks and the mountains fall on his enemies! His stories make all who hear them Christian! The Druids tell of such a prophet. And *You* are that man!"

"No, Prince Gosacht. Those are a filid's fables or else they speak of another. Does King Milchu still live?"

"Yes, he's well beyond sixty, but still rules with power and cunning."

"I must settle my account with King Milchu," I insisted, "but afterwards might we swap a tale or two?"

"Agreed! I'll ride ahead to begin preparations for a feast. My warriors will lead you to the settlement. A hundred thousand welcomes, Sucat." Gosacht leapt upon his mount and rode swiftly away.

Much relieved our party resumed their travel appointments and followed the warriors out of the valley and over several foothills. Prince Caerwin seemed to be strangely sobered, whether from the loss to his pocket, or the guilt of his treachery, I couldn't discern. As we crested the last mountain, Prince Gosacht and another rider began ascending.

I felt a sudden heaviness. The settlement below was almost unchanged after nearly thirty years. The chariot house and stables at the southern end of the valley hosted one additional corral. There were two sheepfolds now. The old hollow tree half way down the mountain must have finally rotted away. But the punishment pole still grimly stood near the green, and the large rock, the filid's perch remained on the opposite end of the field. The slave huts and fire circles were unchanged. I hated being there. The sooner this account was settled the better.

King Milchu's larger dwelling and feast hall still stood with the other nobles' dwellings across the green from the slaves' quarters. King Milchu, it must have been, stood in the doorway of his looking up the mountain toward us. Then, as if he were at once in a great hurry, he began fetching things into the house. Back and forth he went, like a worker ant before the rain.

"Holy Boy!" a gruff voice shouted, drawing my attention from King Milchu's strange behavior. Leading his horse toward me was Lord Totmael. He had seemed so much older when I was a slave, now he was about fifty-eight. The little more than ten years difference in ages seemed almost negligible.

"You still wear that talisman, Holy Boy?" he asked, pointing to the book hanging from my neck.

"Thanks to you, old friend," I responded. Lord Totmael gripped my hand and nodded, the most emotion I was likely to see from him, if memory served.

"Why do you return?" he asked worriedly.

"He came to pay Milchu for the slave he stole," Prince Gosacht chimed in laughing.

"Enough good humor at my expense, Prince Gosacht. Shall I now introduce you both to my poor companions, nearly expired from curiosity, or shall we continue to the valley?" Glancing below as I gestured, I saw King Milchu, curiously dressed in ceremonial armor, setting a torch ablaze. "Something's wrong," I breathed to no one and whipped my horse to run.

The chariot rocked dangerously as we raced to the valley floor, the hoofbeats of Lord Totmael and Prince Gosacht thundering behind us. I reined the horses to a trot, passed the reins to Brother Ninus, and leapt from the chariot, Lord Totmael and Prince Gosacht at my heels.

King Milchu stood in his doorway, a helmet on his head, and leather girdle about his waist, a sword raised in one hand and the torch in the other.

"King Milchu, hear me, please," I begged, carefully walking toward him.

"Am I to be humiliated?" King Milchu's voice boomed defiantly. "Milchu a Christian? A former slave my master? I will not abandon the old ways!" He tossed the torch within. I began running, Gosacht and Totmael at my heels. "My ears will never again hear your stories!" he declared, then disappeared inside.

"NO!" Prince Gosacht screamed.

"LORDS OF THE OTHER WORLD, WELCOME ME!" carried from within the house on the swirling ashes, as smoke gave way to fire. Like that flash of fire in Lochru's hand at Tara, the entire dwelling burst instantly into flame. So intense was the blaze that, though we tried, none could enter. Every man, woman and child joined in as we frantically hauled water to throw on the fire or beat the flames with blankets and cloaks. The long tremulous groans of pain, that a man, too brave to cry out, could not contain, rose eerily as though the fire itself had a voice, until the chilling silence within finally signaled the uselessness of our efforts. Another victim of a fire my presence had kindled, I miserably thought. I fell to my knees and wept. Brother Ninus, Prince Caerwin, and the boys collapsed beside me.

"Why, Patrick?" Brother Ninus asked.

"Fear?" I suggested brokenly. "Superstitious people are easily frightened."

"King Milchu was afraid of nothing!" Prince Gosacht spewed venomously as he turned on me. "You bewitched him. You made King Milchu die. We were warned of your sorcery. How glad I was to see you. Foolish childhood dreams! Now the king is dead and you will pay."

CHAPTER TWENTY-FIVE
Trial by Fire

"Chief Druid Lochru will determine the trial!" Prince Gosacht proclaimed and drew his sword. All the other warriors did likewise. I stood and turned my appeal to Lord Totmael, but he shook his head.

"Why else would you return, if not to wield power over those who once had power over you?" he proposed. At once I felt convicted.

"May God forgive me, if there is any truth in what you say."

Prince Gosacht signaled the warriors and my hands were bound in front, along with those of all my companions, all but Prince Caerwin. As Prince Gosacht rode near I asked, "If I'm the one to be tried, can't we leave these others to..." I was silenced with the back of his hand. Rioc and Benignus swiftly positioned themselves protectively next to me, my bold young sons in the faith.

The warriors herded us toward the long road to King Milchu's Rath, another day's journey on. It was then that I noticed Prince Caerwin, still in our company.

"You have no part in this, Caerwin. Go home to your father."

"That man, King Milchu, burning alive, just like you told me about Hell. You did that?" he asked pitifully.

"Even if I had the power, which I don't, I didn't wish his death, Caerwin. Nor do I wish yours." He wasn't convinced. "Listen, lad, the curse of Hell is on all men who hate love and love evil. You want to be free? Just love God, son. Then you'll be free of the fear of Hell. Just love God. Now go, and God go with you." Prince Caerwin nodded slowly and returned to his mount. A glance over my shoulder saw him cresting the mountain long before we were out of the valley.

"I wish I could have sent you boys along with him," I told Rioc and Benignus.

"We wouldn't have gone," Benignus retorted defiantly. My hard working, obedient lads? Their defiant attitudes left me speechless.

The brilliance of the full moon gave sufficient light to travel well after sunset. Prince Gosacht led us to the great gnarled oak that stood as sentinel to the Druid's sacred grove. In spite of the dim light the hideous figures carved in its trunk were terrifyingly visible, or perhaps because of it. The warriors refused to enter the grove, but prodded us at spear point to do so. The putrescent smell of flesh and blood, both fresh and rotting, singed hair, and soot assaulted our nostrils as we stepped into the heavy darkness of the grove. The spongy ground beneath our felt abnormally damp and cold.

"Is it wrong for me to be so frightened?" Benignus asked anxiously.

"Right or wrong, it's a fact. Don't deny it, nor condemn yourself for it," I responded.

"But how do I overcome it?"

"When I am terrified, I..."

"But you're not afraid of anything, Father," Rioc insisted irritably.

"No? My spirit has absolute confidence in God. But a man is both spirit and flesh. As long as I am in this body, Rioc, I share the same fear that you feel, and always will."

"No you don't! You don't even look frightened!"

"Well, I pray, Rioc!" I retorted.

Eerie groans emanated from deeper within the grove. I could feel the shudders of both boys, and the pressure of bodies all around me as our party huddled together.

"What do you pray, Father Patrick? Maybe that prayer can help me, too," Benignus begged.

"Let's go no further. Sit down, brothers and sisters." We did. "Pray with me, Benignus, 'Christ be with me, Christ within me, Christ behind me, Christ before me, Christ beside me, Christ to win me, Christ to comfort and restore me."

"That was beautiful, Bishop Patrick," Sister Boin breathed tremulously. The sisters were always so remarkably self possessed, that I had failed to consider how anxious they had to be in our dismal surroundings. Two more low groans from the center of the grove sent another shudder throughout our party.

"Perhaps, Brother Ninus, you have another?" I asked. "We have a good while before the Druids come for us, and I doubt that any of us will sleep in this evil place."

"I bind unto myself today the strong name of the Trinity," Brother Ninus recited, defiant of the evil that threatened, "by invocation of the same, the Three in One and One in Three."

"That's a powerful prayer, Ninus," Father Sechnall remarked. "I would bind also my salvation, the Word of God..."

"Yes, and the prayers and faith of all the saints," Father Malach added thoughtfully.

"The Druids sing their ritual incantations, frightening everyone with their magic and curses. Could we put together our own chant, a prayer? Like Brother Ninus said, an invocation instead of an evil spell?" Sister Cas brilliantly posed.

"We could include all of the Bishop's prayer and work in these others," Sister Boin offered.

What more creative and edifying use could such a night serve? We set at once to the task. Everyone made contributions and Brother Ninus set them all together in a poetic prayer.

"I bind unto myself today the strong Name of the Trinity, by invocation of the same, the Three in One and One in Three.

"I bind this day to me forever, by power of faith, Christ's incarnation; his baptism in the Jordan river; his death on the cross for my salvation; his bursting from the spiced tomb; his riding up the heavenly way; his coming at the day of doom: I bind unto myself today.

"I bind unto myself the power of the great love of the Cherubim; the sweet "Well Done" in judgment hour; the service of the Seraphim; confessors' faith, apostles' word, the patriarchs' prayers, the prophets' scrolls; all good deeds done unto to the Lord, and purity of virgin souls.

"I bind unto myself today the virtues of the starlit heaven, the glorious sun's life giving ray, the whiteness of the moon at even, the flashing of the lightning free, the whirling wind's tempestuous shocks, the stable earth, the deep salt sea, around the old eternal rocks.

"I bind unto myself today the power of God to hold and lead, his eye to watch, his might to stay, his ear to hearken to my need; the wisdom of my God to teach, his hand to guide, his shield to ward; the word of God to give me speech, his heavenly host to be my guard.

"Christ be with me, Christ within me, Christ behind me, Christ before me, Christ beside me, Christ to win me, Christ to comfort and restore me.

"Christ beneath me, Christ above me, Christ in quiet, Christ in danger, Christ in hearts of all that love me, Christ in mouth of friend and stranger.

"I bind unto myself the Name, the strong Name of the Trinity, by invocation of the same, the Three in One and One in Three. Of Whom all nature hath creation, eternal Father, Spirit, Word: praise to the Lord of my salvation, salvation is of Christ the Lord."

By morning we had memorized every line. Each recitation sent surging throughout our little band a strong sense of faith and victory. Only God could have wrought such a miracle from a night that promised only terror. As light filtered through the trees we were able to see beyond our noses and into the center of the grove. Our imaginations had provided ample material to try the faint-hearted, now our eyes only reinforced those images. Every tree bore it's own masterful, but sickening figure, faces of men and beasts contorted with hate or terror, along with other symbols of earth and sky. In the open space at the heart of the grove the ground crawled with rats climbing over and around a mound of fleshy limbs, the discarded portions of ritual sacrifices. As our little band approached, the rats scurried in every direction, illuminating the femininity of our stalwart sisters, who gasped and climbed into the arms of Brother Ninus and Father Sechnall.

The entire company jolted as one the next moment, for a loud and piteous groan fell on our ears. Instinctively we turned our eyes upward, to the source of the outcry. Several bodies had been ritually stabbed and hung in the branches, one apparently lifeless, another near death, and a third still doomed to several days' agony before death would claim him.

"Such obscene barbarism!" Father Malach judged contemptuously.

"Is it, Father Malach? Or possibly the Irish answer to Roman crucifixion," I responded. As I glanced from one horror stricken face to the other, I began to pray, "I bind unto myself today the strong Name of the Trinity..." The others immediately took up the prayer.

Lifting a hard stone from the ground, I approached an oak bearing the circle of the sun. With tremendous difficulty and much perspiration, I endeavored to carve over that pagan idol the cross of Christ. "What are you doing, Father?" Benignus asked when the chant had reached its end. "What kind of cross is that?"

"The Son of God is greater than the sun they worship, and his cross will prevail over all these images of darkness, now and forever," I answered, wiping the perspiration from my forehead.

From the shadows of the grove whined an unpleasantly familiar voice, "My worthless, insolent, slave has returned." Chief Druid Lochru stepped forward with a delegation of Druids, followed by Prince Gosacht and Lord Totmael. "Had I recognized you in Tara I would have had your head!"

"You have no power over me, Lochru, unless God wills it," I said, looking into the blackness of his soul through the cold windows of his steel-gray eyes.

Lochru's hands gripped both his arms, as though suddenly chilled by the coldness of his own heart. His eyes began to twitch, and he cast them nervously from face to face. Lochru walked deliberately beneath the dangling feet of the groaning victim, then fixed his scheming gaze on the two boys. Benignus glared defiantly back at him, but Rioc fearfully stepped behind me.

"See what power I do have," Lochru declared. He nodded to the other Druids. Immediately they jerked Rioc from our circle and stood him in front of Chief Druid Lochru.

"You wouldn't want anything to happen to this child, would you, Sucat?" Lochru sneered. "No, I didn't think so. Well hear this, if your magic saves this lad, that will prove you had the power to *make my father die*. Then you will suffer the fate of these other murderers..." With brutal viciousness he twisted the dangling leg, causing the grove to echo with dying man's screams. "...a slow and miserable death. --- On the other hand, if you cannot save him, if the lad is consumed in the flames, it will prove that you have NO power, your religion's a farce, corrupting the true faith of Ireland. Then you and all your deluded followers will die for your heresy!"

"How convenient for you, Lochru. Either way, I die," I retorted, honestly impressed by the sophisticated brilliance his wickedness had acquired. "But, do you imagine the priests of all true religions have power to save a man from the fire?"

"The Druids do. If the others can't, then they are false," he declared.

"Then demonstrate that power. Convince my poor followers that they are fools following a fool. I challenge YOU, Chief Druid Lochru, just you and me - in the fire. Leave the lad out of it."

Lochru froze. My determined eyes held him for a moment. Then fiendish laughter spewed from his mouth, while his eyes, totally absent of humor, stared vacantly like the eyes of the dead. "You've always had a soft heart for children, Sucat. Don't you remember, Gosacht?" he called over his shoulder. "No, the lad will make a much more... compelling victim."

My eyes briefly caught a flicker of doubt behind Gosacht's eyes, but he said nothing.

Lochru set his face to leave. I quickly blocked his path. "Is this fair?" I challenged. "Which of *your* disciples would stand alongside mine? Or do *you* not have the power to save him?"

The Druids began mumbling one to another. Lochru glanced nervously at his doubting followers. "Caplait!" he announced. The other Druids seized one of their young novices, a boy of about eleven.

"No, Lochru! Are you such a coward that you make boys endure what you will not?" Lochru continued unmoved into the clearing. We could only follow, every breath a prayer. In the clearing was a wicker frame, the rectangular base of an incomplete much larger sculpture obviously being prepared for the coming festivals. Rioc and Caplait were locked within the wicker. The Druids' slaves piled high the straw around its base. I quickly studied the movement of the clouds, then broke free and ran to Rioc.

"Hold on to this, Rioc," I ordered, lacing his fingers around the wicker on the west side of the structure. "And keep your eyes on that big rock at the top of the mountain. Don't look at anything else, no matter what you hear, smell... or feel. Can you do that?"

He nodded. "Will you be praying, Father?" he asked fearfully.

"With everything that's in me," I answered with some difficulty. "But remember the snow, Rioc? You look at that mountain and pray. 'I bind unto myself today...'" Rioc took up the prayer.

"ENOUGH!" Lochru shouted in annoyance. "Light the fire!"

A warrior and two Druids forced me away as the straw was set ablaze. The thick smoke and unpleasant smell that rose from beneath Caplait exposed their deception in wetting down the straw. The west side, where Rioc stood, immediately ignited. I glanced at my fellows who had been surrounded by warriors and held, as I was, at knife point. The intensity of their prayers could almost be felt.

Suddenly a strong wind blew from the west. Rioc obediently stared at the mountain, reciting our prayer, while the blazing fire swept away from him, its heat overcoming the wetness of the remaining straw. A cry of fear could be heard through the Caplait's coughing.

"Save him, Lochru!" I challenged. "Save him by your great power!"

Lochru began dancing with lifted arms and chanting unintelligible syllables. A burst of flame shot forth as the newly dried straw ignited. Caplait screamed, this time from pain.

"LOCHRU!" I roared. He was lost in his mystical madness.

I violently pushed aside the two Druids and bounded toward the structure, only to be intercepted by the warrior. A sharp pain in my left side halted my steps. I smashed my tethered hands against the warrior's face, knocking him off balance, and planted my right knee in his groin. When I reached the blazing structure, Father Sechnall, who had also overpowered his guard, met me. He painfully wrenched the knife from my side, then cut our hands free. Our beating against the weakened structure with stout branches, sent Caplait and a shower of blazing wicker crashing down upon us. I threw myself on the lad, smothering the flames on his hair and clothing. His continual screams tore at the inside of me, as surely as that warrior's knife had torn my flesh. A soft, steady rain began to fall.

"Patrick, see to Rioc," Brother Ninus said calmly, as his hands took my shoulders. I left the lad, still screaming, in the care of Brother Ninus and approached the west side of the structure. It stood in spite of being weakened by the blaze. Father Sechnall stared bewilderedly at Rioc, who remained vacantly lost in his prayers as the rain washed his face.

"It's over, Rioc. You can let go now," I said quietly. Rioc seemed not to hear. He continued mumbling the words of the prayer and staring at the mountain. I covered his hands with my own. A slight jerk was his only response. "Rioc," I called again to deaf ears. Injured, bleeding, and rain soaked, waves of chills and exhaustion surged through me. I turned helplessly to Father Sechnall. He began prying Rioc's fingers from the wicker.

Several Druids were helping Brother Ninus and the sisters treat young Caplait's burns, I noticed, casting my eyes around the green. Caplait's clothes had been removed and, with the help of the waning rain, the fragments carefully worked out of his wounds. Some kind of dressing had been swabbed over most of his burns and bandages were being applied. Standing aloof near the entrance to the grove was Chief Druid Lochru, Prince Gosacht, and several warriors. Fury gave me the strength to address him.

"LOCHRU!" I shouted. "Not *your* power! Not *my* power spared these lads. God's mercy worked in the hearts of these men. Do you still challenge me? Speak Lochru! What other contest do you demand?" The only sounds to be heard were the low murmur of Rioc's continuing prayers, the groans from poor Caplait, and the soft dripping of the rain. Prince Gosacht turned away and disappeared into the grove.

A strong arm suddenly arrested my fall as I slumped weakly against the wicker. "Steady, Holy Boy," the commanding voice of Lord Totmael insisted. I had wondered where he disappeared to. Leaning heavily against him, I forced myself to shout above the increasing rain.

"Since you no longer challenge me, Lochru, I demand, in the name of God, an end to these deplorable rituals and the freedom to teach this new faith."

Lochru turned away, and, followed by his warriors, he disappeared among the oaks.

CHAPTER TWENTY-SIX
No Greater Love

I awoke in a foggy cold sweat. The smell of musty earth and firepits, the pattern of thatching in the roof above my head, the pain in my body, convinced me I was sixteen and a slave of Lochru once more. My heart pounded furiously.

"Bishop Patrick?" the soothing voice of Sister Boin sang.

I sighed and wiped my face with the palm of my sweaty hand. "Yes, Sister Boin," I answered more weakly than I expected.

"You looked as though you were a million miles away."

She and Sister Cas removed the bandage from my side. I suddenly realized that I was exposed far more than was comfortable in the presence of these two ladies. Sister Cas began laughing.

"The blushing bishop," she teased. "We'll work as quickly as we can, but you know Mother Scothie would be furious if we didn't care for you as certainly as she would." I silently accepted the humiliation of their ministrations. Sister Cas began smearing ointment on my wound, while Sister Boin washed the sweat from my back.

"How many days have I been sleeping?"

"Two days. You'll want to know that Caplait, the Druid boy, is still with us and getting better. That burly man, Lord Totmael, brought us back to King Milchu's settlement, but that king or noble never returned. We haven't heard a thing from Chief Druid Lochru either. Two other Druids come by now and again to check on Caplait. Lord Totmael won't let them take him. And Rioc... well Rioc is no better," Sister Cas candidly admitted.

"Thank you, Sister."

"Bishop Patrick, forgive me if it's none of my business, but I'll just keep wondering. These scars on your back, you really were a slave and that evil man was your master?" I nodded. "How do you keep from hating him?"

I didn't answer. Sister Boin blushed, obviously embarrassed at being so forward. They completed their nursing in silence.

As they collected their things I responded soberly, "I have no other option, Sister Boin. If I don't forgive Lochru, then God can't forgive me. How do I not hate him? God, help me. That is something, dear sisters, to add to your prayers. I'm not certain that I don't."

"Well, how can our Lord ask such a hard thing of you?" Sister Boin protested.

"Perhaps because others who have had cause to hate me, forgave me instead. Certainly because Christ suffered a hard thing for me," I explained.

"That monster, I hate him for what he did to Rioc and Caplait," Sister Boin confessed. "And now that I see what he did to you..."

"Sweet sister, don't let that tender heart grow weeds of bitterness," I interrupted. "God will change Lochru or deal with him more terribly than we might wish for any man, monster or not. And now that you angels have done your work so well, I think I shall look in on those boys."

The sisters modestly kissed my cheeks (a familiarity I never encouraged, but which under the circumstances was a comfort) and left with their bags. I stood unsteadily, quickly gained my balance, and ventured to locate the boys' hut.

Caplait stirred fitfully in his sleep. His bed was closest to the doorway. Between his and Rioc's bed, Father Malach sat watch. Rioc lay, wide-eyed but staring at nothing, gripping the blanket as forcefully as he had the wicker, his lips moving without sound. Brother Ninus sat on the other side of his bed, and Benignus lay weeping in the bed beyond. The air felt oppressively heavy but cold as the grave. No one spoke as I crossed the room to Benignus and gently stroked his back.

"It isn't fair!" Benignus blurted out between his sobs. "Why didn't God save him? Why did *you* let it happen? What kind of love drives a little boy to madness? He was my brother, my friend!"

I had no answers for him. Those were questions my own heart was screaming to the Father in Heaven. I thought my life was the greatest sacrifice I would ever be expected to make. But to lose a son! To lose a son! I gasped. Hadn't our Heavenly Father given his? Still, could God require this sacrifice? His love for Rioc was so much greater than mine. Or might this be the poisoned fruit of my unconquered hate for Lochru? I sat heavily on Rioc's bed and took his rigid little hands in mine.

"You know, Lord God, if the power were mine, I would heal this lad," I prayed, tears silently wetting my cheeks. "Won't you heal him, Father? Or can I give my life in trade for his? He's such a fine, fine boy. I know 'my ways are not your ways; my thoughts are not your thoughts.' If his madness must remain, God, help me to bear it. Help me to accept, without resentment and without continual grief, this bitter... bitter cup." I felt Rioc's hands go limp. God in his mercy had taken him on.

"Is it... all over?" a raspy voice asked. I glanced anxiously at Rioc, his eyes as big as kneecaps. "Is it, Father Patrick?" Rioc asked again.

I pulled him into my arms and sent up a thousand silent prayers of thanks to God, while making an impressive effort to stop those irritating tears.

"Yes, it's all over, Rioc. At least for today."

After praying over the sleeping Caplait, I left Benignus to answer all Rioc's questions and Father Malach and Brother Ninus to see to his feeding. Still feeling weak, but too full of gratitude and joy to rest, I wandered along the stream in the twilight. A few stones remained one on top of the other, where my first altar had stood thirty-five years ago, and I thought to kneel for a moment.

"Sucat!" an angry voice challenged from behind. I turned to see Prince Gosacht, his eyes filled with confused fury and sorrow, and in his hand an unsheathed knife.

"God spared my little son tonight, Gosacht," I confided. "If I am to lose my life in return, so be it."

Prince Gosacht breathed heavily for several moments. "I'm glad the boy is well," he said softly. "Why should he lose a father, too?" He slowly sheathed his knife, and dropped his head. "I don't know what to think anymore, what I should feel or do."

"Can I tell you a story, Gosacht?" I asked, "the one Old Milchu was afraid to hear?"

Concerned that King Milchu's settlement by right belonged to Chief Druid Lochru, Lord Totmael moved us to an abandoned settlement on his family's section of land the following week. There were three huts in desperate need of repair, half a corral, and an over grown fire pit. We set to work immediately. By Sunday all the repairs had been made, and we were relatively comfortable. Until a new king was selected, we could do nothing but wait. The time proved good for healing.

Lord Totmael, Prince Gosacht, and I spent a few evenings sharing all that had happened in the intervening years, the races won, wars fought, lasses wooed. Often they reflected back on our years together. Those times had been pleasant for them, especially for Prince Gosacht, but I seldom shared their joy in those remembrances.

"Lord Totmael, how is it that King Milchu didn't pursue me the morning I left?" I finally asked.

"He didn't know you had gone."

"You knew."

"No," he said evasively. "I knew I didn't see you. There was a boy who needed to learn how to shepherd, so I gave him your job. Why, I didn't miss you till the following day when Prince Lochru asked where you were. It must have been all that drinking from the night before."

"King Milchu believed that story?" I asked with a chuckle.

"Not completely, but he didn't want to see you burn any more than I did. Chief Druid Lucetmael divined that you had vanished into the Other World to be reunited to your father. Milchu chose to believe that. He was a good man, Milchu, a good friend, and a good king."

"He was a great king, just, wise, and careful not to abuse his power. And he loved me, and you, too, Sucat," Prince Gosacht insisted.

"You were a little boy, Gosacht. How little you knew," I replied.

"Maybe more than you think," Lord Totmael interjected. "King Milchu couldn't face failure as a father, so he looked the other way when Lochru behaved ignobly. But do you imagine he didn't know that I slipped you food, that I lashed you as lightly as could be done and still fool Prince Lochru. Why do you think I insisted on beating you myself? Still it was a cruel thing we did. King Milchu was wrong to indulge Lochru. He suffered for it. A good man can't see injustice and not suffer for allowing it. You may not be able to appreciate that."

"No, I can't generate much sympathy for him, Totmael. The only thing I can appreciate is that slavery might have been as unbearable every year as it was those first two." I took a deep breath and fought the pain of those memories. "I don't think it's helpful to review that nightmare." I stood to go.

"Hear me a bit longer," Lord Totmael forcefully encouraged. I reluctantly sat down. "After watching you endure Prince Lochru's outrageous pranks with such courage and nobility, King Milchu determined to adopt you as his foster son. You were a British prince, after all. I knew it was a disastrous idea, but he refused to hear me. The night you won the Beltane races, he told Lochru his intentions. He was too drunk, too happy, and too blind to realize what that decision would cost you. Even I was alarmed at Prince Lochru's depravities.When King Milchu finally learned the whole ugly truth, how much you had suffered, it nearly killed him. He grieved as though he had lost two sons. Once Prince Lochru had recovered from his madness, do you remember that?" I nodded. "King Milchu told him if he ever repeated his sordid and brutal behavior, if he even came close to killing you again, he would be turned out of the kingdom with nothing but the clothes he wore.

"Prince Lochru knew it wasn't an empty threat. That, but mostly his fear of the curse you put on him, insured you a slightly improved life, though not a comfortable one. Even so, a slave might suffer from any number of *accidents*. So, rather than further antagonize Prince Lochru, King Milchu hardened his heart and left you to suffer in slavery, denying himself the son he wanted out of loyalty to blood."

"I never knew any of this," Prince Gosacht remarked soberly.

"It's hardly a story worth repeating," I responded. "Still I am glad you shared it with me. Understanding makes forgiving easier. God help me to understand Lochru."

"There's little I could tell you," Lord Totmael replied. "His mother died giving him birth. King Milchu blamed Lochru for her death, probably until the day he died. The hateful old crone who raised Lochru put nothing but poison in his head. When Prince Lochru was five King Milchu finally sent her away, but by then the die was cast."

"That does help, if only a little. But Totmael, all those years ago, I put no curse on Prince Lochru. Nor did I cast a spell to send King Milchu to his death. Don't perpetuate such villainous lies. They only frighten away those I hope to draw near."

"I can understand that guilt and fear drove King Milchu to do what he did," Lord Totmael allowed. "But there *was* a curse on Prince Lochru, until the day you walked off. Maybe you don't know what power you generate."

"I yield myself only to God and his power. He's much too jealous to give it to unscrupulous rascals, who would go about carelessly pronouncing curses and casting spells."

"So you say. But I've never known *you* to be an unscrupulous rascal," Lord Totmael suggested warily.

"If you men are to be Christians," I sighed, "there's much of the Druid religion you need to let loose of. But we'll speak of that another day."

The following week a messenger rode into our settlement with an invitation from the council of nobles to the election of the new king. It was an unexpected honor. Sisters Cas and Boin immediately set to work examining my courtly bishop's robes for dirt, flaws, or wrinkles, and tending Brother Ninus' better monastic garment as well. I busied myself inspecting the items we had brought for tribute. Father Sechnall and Father Malach cleaned and polished the chariot, and Lord Totmael and Brother Ninus dressed the horses.

Two days later, scrubbed and dressed, I loaded a bag of tribute onto the chariot and was startled by Prince Gosacht's appearance in the distance. Dressed like a king he rode between two warriors, his horse burdened with the necessary supplies for a long trip.

"A hundred thousand welcomes, Prince Gosacht!" I called up to him as he reined in his mount.

"A good day to you, Sucat!" As we shook hands, my whole community turned out to welcome Prince Gosacht and his companions.

"Won't you come down, stay awhile?" Father Sechnall suggested.

"No, I'm going home, north to Ailech, to the rath of my father, King Madden. With King Milchu dead there's no place for me here. The ride is long and I'm anxious to be off. But I had to warn you, Sucat. Avoid the ceremony today. Lochru has somehow arranged your death."

"Thank you, Gosacht," I responded thoughtfully.

Lord Totmael gave Prince Gosacht and his companions a drink, and Rioc and Benignus watered their horses.

"You'll receive a royal welcome when you come to Ailech," Prince Gosacht proclaimed. "My word upon it. Don't tarry too long here."

"As soon as God allows, we'll take you up on that promise," I said smiling, then shook his hand once more and watched him ride away.

As I resumed loading the chariot, Lord Totmael demanded with some concern, "You can't still be planning to go?"

"If I stop living for fear of dying, Lord Totmael, I am dead already," I answered. I placed the beautiful shepherd's crook into it's holder. Glancing past Lord Totmael, the faces of Father Sechnall, Brother Ninus, and Father Malach looked gravely into mine.

"Lochru is too great a coward to confront me again. He will more likely strike at the lads while I'm away, especially as we now have Caplait with us. Father Sechnall, I want you and Father Malach to remain here with Lord Totmael and watch over these lads while we're gone. Keep the sisters in sight as well. Make it a pleasant evening. Benignus needs to practice his storytelling, and Sister Cas plays a fine flute."

"You and Brother Ninus will break your necks trying to drive an Irish chariot in those fancy robes." Father Sechnall challenged. "Who is to drive you?"

"My neck's not so easily broken," I retorted.

"I'm not so old I can't drive a chariot," Lord Totmael insisted. "That would suit me better than being shut in with rowdy boys."

The issue settled, Brother Ninus and I took our seats behind Lord Totmael in the chariot and began the long ride to King Milchu's rath, a name that was soon to change.

It was well after noon when we came near the Valley of the Laughing Springs, a narrow ravine, heavily wooded on either side. Paralleling the river the entire length of the ravine was the rough road. At one end, the river was fed by the pristine water from a prolific spring, which gurgled over and cascaded down a large rock wall, sounding magically like the voices of laughter in a great feast hall. Every traveler not foreign to the area looked forward to being refreshed at this spring.

Without warning Lord Totmael reined in the horses and sat heavily in the bed of the chariot.

"I was wrong," he sighed, "I am too old. I can't go on. Take me back at least as far as Milchu's settlement," he commanded.

"We're more than half-way there, Lord Totmael," I discounted. "Once we're in the valley and cool ourselves at the spring, you'll feel better." I stood to take the reins.

"No! No, take me back. My bones ache in every joint, and I'm so cold, chilled to the bone. Please, it's a sickness," Lord Totmael begged.

I did begin to worry. "You will fare better in the hands of a skilled herbalist. One can be found at the rath."

"Then cover me with your cloak," Totmael insisted irritably, still barking orders like a man in charge. If his body were as strong as his will he would never be sick I mused. I removed my cloak and robe.

"These will keep off the chill until we get to the rath. I can drive better without them anyway. Ninus, alert me if he gets worse."

Brother Ninus nodded. I tied my long shirt at the waist to free my knees from its folds, and took up the reins.

Within minutes we were clipping along the valley floor, the sparkling river running alongside. A glance at Lord Totmael assured me he was fine. His characteristic scowl once more defined his face, and he had dressed himself in my clothes, providing him much more warmth than blankets. I turned my attention back to the road and the measured slow trotting of the horses.

A sharp, resonant crack split the air as the chariot tipped up on one wheel, then crashed back down again. I hadn't seen any obstacles...

"Patrick, get us out of here!" Brother Ninus shouted with authority, as he moved urgently behind me.

I cracked the whip and raced the horses the entire length of the valley and out onto the plain before reining them down to a trot. Finally free to glance back at Ninus, I saw Totmael, the huge shaft of a spear piercing through his heart and into the side of the chariot behind him. I was almost numb. As soon as the horses could be safely brought to a halt, I leapt from the chariot, and wandered aimlessly through the heather. Too many tragedies in too few days had left me depleted. I wanted to cry, to yell, to rage, but I could do none of those things. I couldn't even pray. I simply fell to my knees and stared, as Rioc had, with vacant eyes. Brother Ninus joined me after a time, and we sat together in silence. Finally he spoke.

"Patrick, Lord Totmael purposely put himself in your place. Don't sit here like you're the one who's dead and waste his sacrifice."

His challenge brought life back into me with all its sorrow, fury, and passion. I knew instantly what I had to do.

CHAPTER TWENTY-SEVEN
You and Every Other Snake

The feast hall buzzed with excitement. Outside the common folk listened near the doors and windows, anxious to know which warrior the nobles would select. Some were placing bets on the outcome. Slaves and servants bustled in and out with platters and mugs. Dogs ran under and between the legs of men and children to get whatever scraps fell. As we approached, we were cautiously scrutinized by these onlookers. We were late. The guests had already been seated. The doorkeeper frowned as I presented the required token, then let us pass into the hall. Brother Ninus entered first, carrying the bag of tribute. I slipped in behind him.

A noble, my age or older, stood to his feet and addressed the guests. "It has been decided! Honor Amalgaid, our new king!"

The entire company rose, lifted their glasses, and repeated the charge, "Honor Amalgaid! Long life and Prosperity to our New King!" A few men with anxious expressions hurried from the hall. Apparently they had supported another candidate.

A young man of about thirty stood to his feet. He was tall, handsome, and powerfully built. His eyes revealed above average intelligence, as did his manner. He nodded respectfully to the company of nobles and made his way to the throne, where a multicolored cloak was draped about his shoulders, and a band of gold was placed upon his brow.

The nobles took their seats and one by one began presenting him with gifts. Brother Ninus and I took our place at the end of the line of tribute bearers. Music and feasting began. The line moved slowly. We received some peculiar stares from those who were close enough to see my untidy robes. As we neared the head of the table, Chief Druid Lochru could be heard boasting proudly to all those within the sound of his voice.

"This Patrick, is no prophet, but a slave! He has no power! He stood like a fool in the pouring rain shouting orders."

"What did you do?" an eager listener inquired.

"Nothing at all. I enjoyed the ridiculous spectacle," Lochru laughed. "But he will not challenge me for long. After today the deceiver's power will be broken."

Standing behind him I whispered, "You speak the truth, Chief Druid Lochru." I dropped the book of verses into his plate. He greedily snatched the book, leapt to his feet, and turned with triumphant enthusiasm, his wide-eyed grin replaced by the pale face of horror as his eyes met mine. The entire hall gradually fell silent.

"Sucat!" he uttered soundlessly. He looked from my eyes to the rend over my heart. With trembling fingers he felt the wetness of the fresh blood. "You should be d...." The book of verses fell to the floor. I grabbed him by the collar of his garment, artistically decorated with a symmetrical, winding snake in unending knot work.

"I thought there were no snakes in Ireland, but look here is one," I falsely marveled, straining to control my fury. "Have you ever seen a snake, Lochru? They can be beautiful, shiny, colorful." I gritted my teeth. "But they can't stand like a man. Ever crawl on your belly, Lochru? That's what a snake does, hides in the bush and STRIKES! when you least expect it, with fangs sharper than any needle." I pressed two fingers, like fangs, into his neck. "Through those fangs he fills a man with poison." Lochru bolted toward the door. I seized him by the shoulders and slammed his back against the wall.

"It's right that you wear snakes!" my voice suddenly boomed. "Be warned! Unless you change your heart... by the grace of God, I'll drive *YOU* and *EVERY OTHER SNAKE* out of Ireland!" I propelled him violently toward the door. Lochru stumbled several times, then ran out into the night. The nobles all stared in stunned amazement. I respectfully addressed the hall.

"I mean no dishonor to the rest of King Milchu's clan. My quarrel is with Chief Druid Lochru, whose assassin's spear pierced the heart of my friend tonight, and whose lies poison us all. King Amalgaid," I added as I dropped to one knee, "forgive me for casting so solemn a shadow on this festive occasion."

King Amalgaid stood. "You are the Christian Prophet whose coming was foretold!" he declared.

I took a deep breath and stood to my feet. "I am Patrick, shepherd of God's people in Ireland." King Amalgaid motioned me to the Chief Druid's seat, and the feasting resumed.

We left the celebration hours later, exhausted, but content with the progress we had made. The Druids, disillusioned by Lochru's cowardly performance at the trial, expressed great interest in our faith. King Amalgaid was curious, not hostile. Thus, after sharing a tale or two, we had won a promise of tolerance, property, and protection by law for our community, as long as we could afford King Amalgaid's generosity. The price of these privileges varied from kingdom to kingdom. King Amalgaid proved reasonable in his expectations. But this night of victory, how unpleasant it was, seasoned by the blood of Totmael.

A number of people crowded around us as we left the hall. They were shouting excitedly, and pointing to the top of a rise that sheltered this rath from the strong breezes of the Western Sea. "Chief Druid Lochru, he calls for you," they were saying. Under the bright light of the moon, the outlines of a few people could be seen at the summit. By the time we had reached the height and reined in our horses, the crowd had grown quite sizable. Lochru, his hair disheveled, clothes tattered, danced like a wild man, running and leaping precariously close to the edge of the cliff. I tried, without success, to feel some pity for him. The closest thing I could manage was a cautious reserve. I could will to love, even act in love, but God would have to work a miracle if I were to feel any love for that wicked wizard.

I carefully approached him. He spun around and sprang like a predatory animal, nails bared, eyes flashing. Catching his wrists, I barely avoided his claws rending my face, but his teeth sunk painfully into the side of my hand. I slammed him to the ground. He laughed madly, then amazingly transformed. There was nothing mad or demented about the man who rose up before me, his eyes calm, his voice quiet, steady, and accusing. "You stole my father's affections. Outshined every thing I attempted. Even the wenches I bedded would have preferred to lie with you. Then came the curse. Milchu wouldn't let me kill you to break it, so I needed power. As a Druid I had that power. You left and the curse with you. I finally became somebody, respected, even by Milchu. Chief Druid Lochru, one of the most powerful Druids in all Ireland! Now you bring death to Milchu, overpower my magic, humiliate me before my kinsmen and disciples..."

"Am I to feel guilty?" I stormed incredulously. "You ripped me from my father's arms, stripped away my nobility, starved and shamefully humiliated me, then beat me so viciously, that my only prayer was for death. And you want *me* to accept responsibility for your failures? Look to the dark forces of evil you serve for the villain here."

"We could have been brothers, Lochru, sharing your father's good will. But with every decision you chose evil over good, hate over love, jealousy over charity. Should you be amazed that the evil you prefer has come upon your own head?"

Lochru turned away. A fragment of pity stirred within me. "I admit that I destroyed you today, Lochru. But you can turn away from that dark past and begin a new life." I rested my hand on his shoulder. "We might yet be brothers."

Lochru squirmed out from under my hand and spun to face me, his eyes flashing dementedly once again. "I have a new life, you pathetic worm," he sneered, as around and around he circled, his face only inches from my own. "I'm a snake. Sssssss! Don't you remember? But I'm not alone. You won't live long enough to drive us all out of Ireland."

He leapt, knocking me to the ground and began rolling us over and over the stony ground, toward the edge of the precipice. Instinctively I grasped for anything as we tumbled over the side. My arms caught hold of a protruding rock, and my feet dug into the face of the cliff. The sudden arrest broke Lochru's grip. He grappled to hold on, clawing at my garments as he slid past me, barely grasping my ankles with his bony fingers. My arms ached and trembled under the burden of supporting Lochru, flailing below.

Ninus peered over the edge, then lay on his belly and reached for me. The distance was too great. He disappeared and others tried the same. Lochru's left hand slid an inch, then another, then slipped off all together, until he dangled perilously by one arm. The sudden shift knocked my feet from their footing. Barely able to hang on, I glanced down at the craggy rocks below. As my eyes met his, Lochru screamed defiantly, "Die, Slave! Die with your master!"

"Gladly!" I yelled back, "But YOU are not my master."

His eyes grew large, his face panic stricken. His fingers lost their strength. Chilling, piercing screams of terror echoed from every stone as he plummeted, thrashing desperately, to his death on the rocks below. A wave of dizziness passed over me. I feared I was soon to join him. My feet began to search methodically for a foothold. My sweaty arms and fingers slipped little by little. The end of a stout rope struck me as it fell over the side of the cliff. I twisted my foot securely in it's knots, grabbed it first with one hand, and then another. By the time I had been drug to secure footing, the beautiful bishop's robes, rent, blood stained, dirty and hopelessly tattered were only a sad shadow of Scothie's artistic masterpiece.

Scothie, I suddenly missed her so very much. Feeling too weak to stand I glanced at the moonlight reflected in the billowing waves of the distant sea, then rested my forehead on my knees.

"You can't save a man who won't save himself, Patrick," Brother Ninus said comfortingly, as he gathered the tinker's rope. I nodded. But my mind was not on Lochru; nor, for the moment, on Scothie. I was seeing another cliff; another pointless death on the rocky shore below.

Within three months we were well settled into our community on the land I had haggled long and hard to purchase. At its heart stood that sinister Druid grove. The healing that took place, as we cleared away the profane and claimed the grove for God, strengthened and uplifted us all. We had sent word to Meath of our success, and eagerly watched down the road the approaching company of Father Auxilius and several new priests and sisters who felt called to serve the new church in its infancy.

"Welcome! Welcome! A hundred thousand welcomes!" I shouted, as I soundly embraced each man and gently kissed the hands of each sister, all but one.

"Scothie!" I exclaimed in surprise, hugging her tightly. "How I have missed you! I'd kiss you if I thought I could stop with a kiss." She laughed, blushing as I released her. Aware of the scandalized faces of Father Malach and Father Auxilius, I addressed her with more restraint. "Pardon my enthusiasm, but I've felt so great a need of late to remind one of Ireland's daughters how very much I love her, how much strength she gives me, how greatly I value her counsel, her piety."

"Never have I received so marvelous a welcome," Mother Scothie softly responded, smiling beautifully through those pale blue eyes. "Thank you, Bishop. Now what is this I hear about you shredding, staining, and rolling that elegant robe I worked so hard to make in the dirt of Connachta?" she scolded teasingly. I opened my mouth to answer, but she cut me off. "I don't want to hear the story. Just show me the robe. That'll be hard enough to bear."

"Sister Cas," I called, "show Mother Scothie the disaster." They embraced and set off for the sisters' quarters. Father Malach and Sister Boin led the other travelers into the compound to enjoy refreshments.

Alone together, Ninus' silence spoke more loudly than any rebuke. "Ninus, my dear friend," I confided "you, are like my right arm. Your love gives me courage, confidence, power. But Scothie! Scothie's like part of my inmost being. Her very presence heals my soul, builds my faith, clears away my doubts..."

"Her presence does a great deal more than that. You always live on the edge, Patrick. Be very careful not to fall. So many fragile souls look up to you."

"I know, Ninus. I know. But I have a strong conviction that selfless love is never wrong, and too precious not to be expressed."

"Expressed? Do you imagine yourself so holy? Can you openly love the beauty of her soul without aching for the intimacy of her body? I can't. What of your vows, Patrick?"

"You, Ninus? I... I've not forgotten that Ireland's my mistress. And fornication is never a true expression of love, even if love inspires the appetite. The joining of two bodies should seal the joining of two lives. Not satisfy an itch."

"Since that is not a commitment you are free to make, Patrick..."

"...my relationship with Scothie must remain something unique." The arch of his eyebrow indicated Ninus' considerable reservations. He was right, of course. "If I have to sleep every night in a cold mountain stream, Ninus, I will not do anything to embarrass you or the church. I appreciate your counsel, beloved brother, and I covet your prayers."

The following month Captain Sinell sought us out, concerned that our resources might be dwindling (or more likely that our heads might be dangling). On the contrary our livestock had thrived well, and we had all kept our heads, even me. However, we welcomed his visit as well as the fine fabrics, jeweled goblets, and other treasures he brought to impress the next king we might encounter.

Mother Scothie had crafted two superb sets of courtly bishop's robes for me during her stay. "These won't survive unless you stop being so reckless," she teased as I walked her to Sinell's curraugh. "There's little hope of that, is there?" she sighed heavily. The sea breeze whipped a few strands of hair across her cheek. Good-byes were not necessary, for I had learned to read her eyes as surely as she read mine. "Should God will that one day you return to Leinster, Bishop Patrick, I shall have two brand new robes sewn and waiting for you."

Mother Scothie, Father Malach, and Father Auxilius returned to Leinster with Sinell in response to that church's request. I was relieved that their route by sea would not be as lengthy and hazardous as overland always proved to be. As they pulled out of the harbor, I was not alone in feeling a keen loss at Scothie's absence. Her influence had been an inspiration to the entire community. What surprised me was the melancholy effect it had on Brother Ninus.

With the guidance of the Irish priests from Meath the new church was soon strong enough to flourish without the leadership of Brother Ninus, Father Sechnall, and I. We set our course to meet Prince Gosacht and King Madden in Ailech.

"I, Patrick, a Sinner..."

CHAPTER TWENTY-EIGHT
The Noise of Battle

Prince Gosacht made good his promise of a warm welcome. Ailech was easily the most cooperative kingdom in the establishment of a Christian church. King Madden, like all the other kings of Ireland seemed stubbornly resistant to the new faith, he nevertheless recognized what Ono MacOengusa had understood, the Druid faith and every other belief was destined to fall before the Christian God. Prince Gosacht was himself called to be a priest and immediately undertook studies to that end. When the church was secure, and we moved on, Gosacht went with us.

In every kingdom we entered we faced challenges, dangers, trials, and victories. Brother Ninus, and I and those in our company were at different times imprisoned, flogged, used to bait wild boar, and laced to pillars to be drowned in the rising tide. Captain Sinell just happened along that last time. We were betrayed twice more by king's sons we had hired as guides. One arranged an ambush by a robber band, the other sold us into slavery. Surprisingly it was Prince Caerwin, Loguaire's son, who instigated our release. (Whatever positive changes God had wrought in that lad through my stumbling efforts seemed to be permanent.)

Fortunately I had learned not to venture into new territory with the boys or sisters in our company. Once good relations had been established, I would send for those who felt God was leading them. Without this anxiety I was free to be as reckless as necessary to get the job done, more reckless than necessary Brother Ninus often thought.

Dalaridia was the last pagan stronghold. Since the surrounding kingdoms had allowed the new faith, the Picts eventually capitulated, though their good will came at a much higher price. Glorious tales of the confident faith and indomitable courage of Dalaridia's secret Christian community, inspired me. Julia, I learned had been part of that community. She died in Anno Domini 432 having been run through by a warrior for relieving the pain of Palladius's tortures. There's your martyrs' blood, Amicus, I thought sadly; Totmael's in the west and Julia's in the east, and how many others unknown.

The whole church in Ireland was now relatively secure. As I remained the only man in Ireland with the authority of the church catholic to baptize converts and administer the feast of the Lord, Bishop Patrick, the evangelist, had to defer to Bishop Patrick, the baptist. The Irish priests were bold, devout, and passionate for their missions, so everywhere we went large numbers of new converts had been made and eagerly awaited our arrival. Confirmations, baptisms, ordinations, and admissions to the ascetic vocation consumed our time.

In addition, kings had to continuously be courted and judges placated. (Failing to visit the king immediately upon arrival resulted in four days imprisonment once.) We traveled constantly and worked tirelessly, and I developed a deplorable aversion to cold water. After an absence of nearly eight years, we finally returned to Leinster.

"Bishop Patrick! From what I've heard, I expected you to fly into Leinster on the backs of two fire breathing dragons, not slip in unannounced like some common herdsman," King Diarmuid exclaimed jovially on our arrival. "And what an old man you've gotten to be. Or is it that gray beard you're wearing?"

"What do think, King Diarmuid, is it an improvement over that beardless chin?" I bantered.

"The only beardless chins I like have soft round breasts below," he chuckled. "We're neither of us too old to appreciate that. Ah, but you Christians suppose a man should settle for only one pair of breasts in his life, apart from his mother's of course. Are you still fond of the same pair?"

I didn't answer. King Diarmuid laughed good-naturedly, then waited.

"If you mean, do I still love the same woman, the answer is 'yes'. But her breasts have little to do with it," I finally admitted.

"I fancied those breasts... no, you have it right. I fancied that woman once, still do. Gowan was a lucky old goat. But we both lost out. She's a feast for the gods now. Besides, she's surely skinny, old, and gray. What nonsense I talk. It must be your bad influence."

"Undoubtedly," I agreed.

We feasted with King Diarmuid for a week before he would allow our departure to Twin Hills. He had praise for much that the church had done to benefit his kingdom, and strong complaints regarding several incidents that engendered unrest. The church's giving sanctuary to an abused, runaway slave especially angered him.

"King Diarmuid, before I left Leinster I was dangerously candid with you. You know me well. Can I be expected to do other than agree with the church's position in this matter?" I asked.

"I expected you would," he shrugged. "Still I can't just have slaves running loose all over Leinster. This is my proposition. If your people will assume the responsibility of trying these matters fairly, and will recompense the masters in part for their losses, then we will see if my irritation subsides."

"A wise and creative proposal, King Diarmuid. I accept that challenge."

With most of King Diarmuid's concerns similarly addressed, we left for Twin Hills. Rioc and Benignus were eighteen and twenty now, seasoned travelers, excellent chariot drivers, and somewhat overzealous Christian witnesses, as young men are likely to be. They also had a fine command of Latin, due to Brother Ninus's scholarship and training. They brought me as much joy as any sons might.

Brother Ninus and I rode in the chariot behind Benignus. Father Gosacht rode his horse. And Father Sechnall drove the second chariot carrying Rioc, who was irritated at the arrangement. Rioc could have driven, but was more reckless than Father Sechnall would tolerate.

Word of our arrival had reached Twin Hills, and I expected a warm welcome, but the sight that met my eyes sent such a shock through me that I was physically sick. A thousand, no, much more people lined the road, cheering, waving banners, and calling my name. Lovely young women and strong handsome men reached out their hands to touch us as we passed. Children, too young even to have known me, ran alongside the chariots throwing flowers.

"Aren't you excited?" Brother Ninus asked, grinning from ear to ear. "Just look at the people."

"Excited? Frightened! I feel like a god. Drop me in front of the church Benignus," I ordered.

There was a new church where the old one had stood, much larger and beautifully decorated with brilliant and colorful designs. I stepped off the chariot and went immediately inside, leaving the others to deal with the crowds. I imagined Mother Scothie chiding, "Have you no manners at all?"

"One of my many shortcomings," I answered to no one. I sat down heavily on the bench against the wall. The good people meant well. They always meant well. But to feast at the king's table, then praise and applaud the servant who sets the meal before you, more generously than the Lord who provides the feast, is a dangerous mistake. A servant who accepted such adulation, rather than direct that praise to his master, could well expect to feel the king's displeasure, if not his wrath. And what of the king's fury toward those guests?

I stood and walked the length of the building. The artwork within rivaled the beauty of that on the exterior. The painted walls, magnificent carved altar, crucifix, and candleholders impressed me with the love these people had for the church. I was encouraged. The church was Christ's body, and this building her garment. It was right to love her. But how dearly did they love the head, Christ the Lord himself? To love the body and not the head is perverse, selfish, misdirected. Any woman could attest to that.

Standing at the altar I noticed for the first time the inscription over the doorway:

IN HONOR OF PATRICIUS MAGONUS SUCATUS
BISHOP OF IRELAND

"Bishop Patrick! There you are! I hardly recognized you with that hair all over your face. Come outside. Everyone wants to see you!" Father Malach exclaimed enthusiastically, as he burst through the doorway.

"Father Malach, I would like to see all the clergy, and the religious orders. Could you gather them?"

"Certainly, Patrick. They'd love to meet you privately before losing you to that crowd. What an excellent idea."

"And, Father Malach, could you bring me a hammer?"

Father Malach frowned but nodded and slipped out. The clergy entered one by one as they heard the summons. I personally greeted them. The atmosphere was charged but sobering. They felt it but didn't understand, not yet. Finally Malach assured me they were all present, including Brother Ninus and our company, Mother Scothie and the sisters of Leinster, Father Auxilius, Brother Maciul, Sister Lallocc, everyone.

Standing under the inscription I asked, "Brothers and sisters, whose church is this?"

"Why, this is your church, Patrick. You are the Bishop of Ireland," Father Malach insisted grandly.

My heart sank.

"Then I will tear it down!" I lifted the hammer above my head and powerfully cracked it against the wall, sending a chunk of wattle that bore part of my name flying across the sanctuary. "Every stone!" I struck the wall again. "Every splinter of wood!"

"Why?" Father Auxilius gasped. "Why, Patrick? *THIS* is what you came to Ireland to build!"

"Is it? Is it, Auxilius? Malach? Brothers and Sisters? --- I thought I came," I dropped the hammer and sighed heavily, "to build our *LORD'S* church."

"This is... our Lord's church," Father Malach replied.

"You confuse our wise, powerful, beautiful Lord with this ignorant slave?" I looked gravely from face to face. "Dear brothers and sisters, how can our people know what to believe, when you, who should know better, make of God's house a monument to a man?" There was no attempt to answer. A few feet shuffled nervously. "You will remove my name from that wall. Only God is worthy of our worship. And you will tell those good people, that I expect to hear tomorrow in this sanctuary the praises of *GOD*, sung, shouted, and prayed with no less enthusiasm than has been misdirected to this servant today. Now I wish to retire."

For a moment no one moved. "Come, Bishop," Mother Scothie volunteered quietly. She led me out the back door, away from the crowds, to a worn rock bench by the spring. I felt instantly relieved. We sat quietly, the gurgling of the spring bringing calm to my soul.

"How is it you always know what I need?" I asked after several moments. She didn't answer. "Was I too harsh with them, Scothie?"

"No, you had to be true to your convictions. That's what makes you the man you are," she answered quietly. "But you're not likely to be as popular tomorrow as you were today."

"Thanks be to God!" I breathed in relief.

Like a thousand tinkling bells, spontaneous laughter rang from her soul. It was contagious, sending merriment rolling from the heart of me as well. How wrong Diarmuid had been. Skinny, old, and gray? Not Scothie. At fifty-three she was only more beautiful with creases of wisdom softly lining her eyes and streaks of silver highlighting those wisps of auburn hair that slipped from under her veil. Or maybe it was the beauty of her soul I was seeing, especially in those crystal blue eyes. Ten years seemed like only yesterday.

Our laughter attracted Brother Ninus and several others to our company. "This is the kind of retirement I covet," Brother Ninus announced, and we roared with laughter again.

Mother Scothie and Brother Ninus wouldn't allow me to retire. Instead Mother Scothie led us quietly from fire circle to fire circle, where the people were enjoying the feasts they had prepared in honor of the occasion. She graciously introduced us to everyone, like the noble woman she was.

Before long it was easy to see why they were so overawed by our presence. Outrageously embellished tales spun by wandering bards and filids had presented me as a water-walking, fire-breathing, holy man, and these simple, superstitious people had believed every word. After listening in amazement, and enjoying a belly laugh or two, Brother Ninus good-humoredly attempted to dismantle their error in the light of truth. From his accounts I was neither water-walking, fire-breathing, nor overly holy. God, not Patrick, was the miracle worker.

As the days passed and I plunged myself into the tasks a bishop must assume, I considered what a mistake I had made in leaving the church in Leinster for so long. Such a subtle decline into near idolatry might have been prevented by more frequent visits. But like the lambs they were, the people and their priests were easily led aright to lift their eyes from the church and her ministers and glorify Christ instead.

The enormous numbers of catechumens who had amassed over the years presented a problem not so easily addressed. I set about to examine them in groups of fifty, and baptize a hundred at a time. Even so, that promised to take several months.

The pond we used for baptisms was at one end of a small valley, not more than a mile long and half a mile wide, and was fed by pure spring water. The vegetation was lush and beautiful in late spring, making an inspiring backdrop for the services. Today it was especially glorious.

Brother Ninus and I walked past all the fire circles where brothers and sisters were preparing feasts to celebrate the occasion. As we approached the little pond we saw Liddy, Mother Scothie, and several of the sisters who had prepared the white baptismal robes, standing with Sinell, Conleng, Father Mactaleus, Father Justanus, Father Gosacht, and Father Sechnall on one side of the pond. Father Malach, Father Auxilius, Brother Maciul, and Sister Lallocc stood with all the baptismal candidates on the other. I stood on the bank of the pond and addressed them.

"Today you will seal a decision you have made to lay down your lives and become part of Christ's body. Your life for His life; your blood for His blood; to forever live in Him and He in you."

Brother Ninus and I removed our boots and shirts. I prayed silently then plunged along with Brother Ninus into the nearly freezing water. At least it felt nearly freezing to me.

"Cold enough to keep you awake, old man?" Brother Ninus teased. I didn't share his good humor. With every year the cold became harder for me to bear. I motioned to the first candidate, a little girl of eight. She slipped, giggling, into the water, and I had to smile.

As I took her hands in mine I said the familiar words, "In this sacrament of baptism, you are buried with Christ, and like him, you are raised, born again to a new life." She nodded her head. Her little face beamed. Such a little girl, yet she had memorized the principles of the faith so well, and had as much understanding as many of the adults.

I dipped her head under the water. "In the name of the Father." I dipped her under again. "In the name of the Son." For the third time, "In the name of the Holy Spirit."

I passed her on to Brother Ninus, who dried her face with the towel on his shoulder and, dipping his finger into a vial of oil, made a glistening sign of the cross on her forehead. "Now walk in this new life," Ninus encouraged as he moved her toward the shore, where Liddy had a robe ready to cover her shiny wet limbs. As the child knelt before Fathers Mactaleus, Justanus, Gosacht and Sechnall to receive through their prayers the gift of the Holy Spirit's indwelling presence, I motioned to the next candidate. And just so each of them filed before us, the children, the men, then the women, one after another, until all one hundred had received the rite. After weeks of instruction and examination, I knew every one, and felt such joy at their baptisms that the pain in my feet hardly mattered. Turning to follow Ninus out of the pond, however, I found myself unable to move my legs, and fell face first into the water. Sechnall leapt in and lifted me out. I had to be carried to a fire circle, where I might dry myself off and warm my feet. From just behind my kneecap to the tips of my toes the pain was nearly incapacitating. I couldn't even stand as I administered the feast of the Lord's body and blood.

With the sacraments over, the music and feasting began. I had little appetite, but conversation with so many old friends was tremendously satisfying. Liddy was as profound as ever, Sinell remarkably insightful, and both amazingly well for their more than seventy years. After tending to other duties, Mother Scothie approached, and immediately appraised my blue feet.

"May I?" She asked, and without waiting for an answer, she lifted a foot into her lap. "This foot's like ice!" She declared in shocked amazement.

"And that's the warm one!" I laughed.

She felt the other and shook her head, "You need blood in those feet. Get up. We're going for a walk."

"But my feet hurt," I barked.

"Brother Ninus, the bishop needs to walk, I imagine you do, too," she ordered, ignoring my protest.

"Benignus," I said turning to face him, "get Father Mactaleus, Father Justanus, Father Gosacht and a few of the sisters, and carry our wee ones home. And Benignus, play the filid for them, so they won't feel they've missed the party."

"Yes, Father," he answered. He tossed back his drink, grabbed another fish from the skewer, and walked off toward Father Gosacht.

"All right, Mother Scothie," I grudgingly capitulated, as Brother Ninus and Mother Scothie helped me up, "but I'm not enjoying one minute." My feet felt like two stubs instead of feet.

"Where are you going, Patrick?" Sinell asked as he ripped another piece of meat from the spit.

"We'll go over that hill. If I have to be humiliated, it doesn't have to be in front of two hundred and fifty people."

"Come now Bishop, humility is a cross we all must bear," Mother Scothie scolded with a laugh.

"Don't wander too far. An old friend of yours I ran into by accident should be here later, sort of a surprise, he said, in honor of an old priest and a special lady you both knew," Sinell revealed.

"Who?"

"He made me swear not to tell. I'll let you know if he shows." My curiosity was enormous, but Mother Scothie and Brother Ninus were committed to this walk.

One step and I stumbled so pitifully, that only Brother Ninus' swift intervention arrested Scothie's plummet toward the ground. Fathers Sechnall, Malach, and Auxilius saw the near disaster and rushed to relieve Mother Scothie's burden. Everyone enjoyed a laugh at my expense. I didn't notice my pain decreasing, but the good humor made it easier to bear. We strolled, and hobbled, over the hill, laughing, singing, and collecting several sisters and brothers as we went. I made every effort to enjoy their merriment. But the dull pain soon gave way to a thousand slender needles sharply piercing feet and calves. I gritted my teeth, as irritating tears filled my eyes, and would have crumbled to the ground, but Mother Scothie insisted they keep me walking, only slower. My companions were no longer laughing. As Mother Scothie knelt to rub my feet and legs I suddenly felt as though I stood in the blazing heat of a fire pit.

"That's all I can bear, Scothie!" I shouted. "Let it be!"

"Hush!" Father Sechnall ordered. I turned angrily toward him. Immediately alarmed by the look on his face, I began to listen. "The noise of battle!" he exclaimed in disbelief. He began running back toward the valley.

Grateful that I could at least feel my feet under me, I ran after him with all the others in our band. At the crest of the hill Father Sechnall forced us to stop. A blood washed field stretched out before us. At the far end, surrounded by Roman British soldiers, stood Sinell, alone, sword in hand, at his feet nearly twenty dead. Bit by bit, like an object of sport, the soldiers whittled him down. Courageously he raised his sword high over his head. "I was a fool to trust a British king," his voice boomed across the valley. "May God make Hell seven times hotter before you get there." He swung at the king, too weak to make his mark. The king struck him down.

"No...!" I screamed from the depths of my being, as I raced down the hill.

The king and his soldiers made a quick retreat into the dense woods. Liddy emerged from hiding, stumbled and crawled over the dead, and reached Sinell before we did. Sinell was covered in blood; splattered over his face, running down his arms, congealing on the hilt of his sword. His legs bore so many lacerations, that his trousers lay in shreds. How he could possibly have been alive baffled us all. Liddy had Sinell's head cradled in her lap. Barely breathing, Sinell turned to spit the blood from his mouth, then looked into Liddy's face.

"I fooled you, Liddy," he said hoarsely. "You think I'm a bloody pagan. I was too proud to tell you. Ask Patrick. I'll be waiting for you, Liddy."

"See that you are," she scolded through her tears. "Don't you go running off with the first pretty face you see, you bloody..." She dissolved in tears as his body slumped in death. Mother Scothie and I knelt beside her.

Father Sechnall and Father Malach searched the field for the wounded. None were found. The butchers had been efficient.

When she could speak again, I asked, "Can you tell me what happened, Liddy?"

"We were all happy, laughing." she related. "Sinell stood up suddenly, looking pale as a lamb. 'You're free, Liddy,' he said, and handed me my token of freedom. 'Now get the lasses over the hill,' he ordered. 'Quickly!' He grabbed his sword and ran toward Conleng, and Maciul. I did as he said, but not even half got away before the soldiers fell on us." Liddy took a deep breath, fought back her tears, and staring vacantly, continued, "I hid behind a fallen log and watched as they murdered the old men and women and any who resisted at all.

"They shackled our baby Christians, still so sweet in their white robes, the crosses shining on their foreheads. As they marched them out of the valley, Rioc's strong voice could just be heard from the head of the line, 'I bind unto myself today the strong Name of the Trinity...'"

"Rioc is captive?" I asked anxiously, but Liddy was lost in her own thoughts. She continued narrating with little emotion.

"Sinell, Conleng, and Maciul fought like champions. Every soldier they struck down gave another Irishman a sword, until eight were fighting back to back, circled by nearly twenty of the enemy. They knew they were dead men, but they were buying time for those who might escape. One by one they fell. Finally Maciul and Conleng were run through, and Sinell alone was left. Can you imagine, seventy-one years old and still such a warrior."

Her grief overwhelmed her. Filled with such anxiety, it was hard to be patient, but the villains had to wait for the tide to make their escape. I could give Liddy another moment. I needed one myself.

"Who was it, Liddy? Do you know?" I finally asked.

"Your *friend*, Coroticus!" she sneered.

"Coroticus!?" I gasped in fury. "He'll answer to me for this!" Liddy's firm grasp held me, as I attempted to stand.

"No! That's just what he'd like!" she protested "Look around you. This raid wasn't for profit, Patrick. He came for you."

I slowly stood and surveyed the carnage. Liddy's observations were astute. This was not business but mindless slaughter. Why? Revenge? What had I done to cost these dear lambs their lives and the others their liberty? How heavily the burden of grief and uncertain guilt weighed upon me.

"The dead at least... rest in the bosom of our Lord," I confessed brokenly, as much to console myself as the others. "It is the captives who face hell. Surely, I can persuade Coroticus to release them. I have to reason with him, Liddy."

"Are butchers *reasonable* men?" Ninus snapped defiantly.

"You expect me to do nothing?!" I exploded. "Forty saints lie slaughtered. Rioc, my own dear son in the faith, and how many others face slavery. And all because a British king wants revenge, for God knows what. I *will* challenge this man!"

"The Irish church doesn't need another martyr, Patrick," Scothie declared uncompromisingly, as she stood to her feet. "She needs her bishop, especially now."

"And what of those who are enslaved? Do they need their bishop any less?"

"If you give this bloody bastard everything he came for, what can we hope to bargain with? You're not going!" Father Sechnall commanded like an old warrior. "Even if Father Gosacht and I have to tie you up until they sail out of here!"

"Malach and I will go to Coroticus," Father Auxilius volunteered. "He won't bargain with an Irishman, I'm sure of it. Just tell us what to say."

Given no other option, I agreed. We returned to Twin Hills to collect a bag of tribute. Against my better judgement, I allowed Benignus to accompany Father Malach and Father Auxilius. I understood the cry in his heart to see Rioc, and I knew he would have gone even without my permission.

"If Coroticus won't yield," I told him, "though he *must* see reason, he is a Christian king. Still, if Rioc doesn't return with you, tell him I am praying day and night, and give him this." I removed the little book of verses from my neck and gave it to Benignus. "Be very careful," I added. "I don't think I could bear to lose two sons in one day." Benignus nodded gravely, and we embraced.

They returned the next morning without Rioc, and without my grandfather's book.

"I, Patrick, a Sinner..."

CHAPTER TWENTY-NINE
King's Bishop or King's Pawn?

"Tell me everything," I directed Father Malach and Father Auxilius as we met in the privacy of my quarters. My room was little more than twice the size of a monk's cell. Furnished with a bed, a desk, a rack of scrolls, a closet, and two chairs, one for the occasional visitor.

"We implored King Coroticus, for the love of God, to release his brothers and sisters in the faith," Father Auxilius began, slumping onto the bed. "'Brothers and sisters? Hah!' he shouted back at me. 'They're Irish! I could just as easily sell my dogs.'"

"What of the money?" I queried.

"Coroticus said it wasn't your money he was after," Father Malach reported. "So I said, 'If your appetite will be satisfied in no other way, we are prepared to offer you the Bishop of Ireland in exchange for these twenty-two captives."

"And?"

"He laughed at us. 'Patrick's idea, do doubt,' he said. 'What would I do with Patrick? Run him through and end his misery? No, you can't buy me gentlemen, I have what I want.'"

"But what is it he wants? What does he have?" I asked bewildered.

"He said to tell you," Father Auxilius seethed, "that after his soldiers had ravaged the 'little Irish tarts,' he planned to sell them to the *Picts*. 'I thought I knew you, Coroticus,' I shouted at him. 'It's Sucat you don't know,' he sneered, then sent us away."

"The Picts!" I sunk down into my chair. "Oh, God, Oh God!"

"The soldiers allowed us a few minutes to pray with our brothers. Some were even ashamed at what they'd done, unlike their despicable king!"

"Benignus had several moments with Rioc," Father Malach reported. "You would have been so blessed to see the change that came over him when Rioc hung that book of verses from his neck. 'Somehow all things work together for good,' he confidently told Benignus. 'I have to believe that, and so do you, brother.'"

"What good?" I muttered.

For days I struggled with my grief, unable to see anything clearly, unable to function, unable to hate God for what had happened, or even Coroticus. Like all those ravens on the mountain years ago, terrible accusations flew in my face and tore at my heart. Was it my fault? Had I, perhaps, loved Rioc more than God? Was my love for Scothie not as innocent as I pretended? Did I secretly enjoy and covet all the cheers and adulation of the crowds? Were my prayers only a pretense at holiness? What proud arrogance, that I had ever imagined this sinful, ignorant slave could represent the perfect beauty and holiness that is God. Still, if it was for my sins, why were others made to suffer? I had forgotten Aesop's moral, "any excuse will serve a tyrant." Evil requires no reason. On my knees, feeling too wretched to pray, I wept and wept. Nothing I could ever do would reverse the disaster. The faces of the dead and captive promised to haunt me with undefined guilt the rest of my life.

"We've all suffered a great tragedy," Mother Scothie's strong, commanding voice rang outside my window, "but there's work to be done here! I don't want to see another tear fall unless you work while you weep... and that includes your bishop!"

The next moment she was standing inside my room frowning crossly, with a full platter and a mug of ale. Her frown dissolved as my swollen eyes met hers. "Bishop Patrick, won't you eat something?" she asked kindly, her voice like velvet to my ears.

I stood and walked toward the window. "My stomach stays in knots," I confessed. "I can't sleep or eat. What is it I have done Scothie? What would cause a man, who was my friend, to..."

"You are not responsible for the evil in that man," she declared, cutting me off.

"I *FEEL* responsible," I yelled back at her. "*Dear God*, I *feel* responsible. Every time I look into their faces, a dagger seems to rip my heart. I can't live with this grief, this anguish. Scothie, I'm leaving Ireland... for the monastery in Lerins." I turned away. Scothie stepped toward me, and laying her palms against my cheeks, she gently forced me to look into those crystal eyes. I wilted, knowing how skillfully she was reading every dark doubt.

"Oh, Patrick," she said sadly, "Because a wolf devours the lambs, you would leave the whole flock without a shepherd?"

"A fine shepherd I am," I said despairingly.

"But the only one we have. Fight those demons, Patrick. You're still God's man in Ireland."

Scothie smiled irresistibly and dried my wet cheeks with her thumbs. How selfishly I wanted to take her in my arms and dull my pain with the pleasure of her body, to know after all these years that she would still have me. I took her hands in mine.

"Beautiful, Beautiful Lady," I asked apprehensively, "do you still love me? The way you once did?"

The sudden flush of her cheeks and the rapid rise and fall of her breasts anticipated her response. "You blind, old man," she chided breathlessly, "I love you so much more." Those crystal blue pools, which she so frequently turned away, were now wide open to me. I plunged in, reading as surely the fabric of her heart as she was reading mine, feeling the love surge in waves between us. The balm of healing swept over me. I kissed her fingertips, still pressed between my palms.

"Thank you, Scothie. How desperately I needed to know that. How desperately I need you. Now I suppose you've let my dinner get cold," I teased to break the tension.

"Cold or not," she whispered, "you'd better eat every bite." From scalp to toenail my entire body tingled as her warm lips unexpectedly caressed mine. "Take care when you're on the edge, Patrick," she advised slowly, still flushed. "Some of us slip more easily than you do." She handed me the plate, and, once again the master of control, she smiled briefly and left.

Immediately following the raid it was Mother Scothie, Liddy and a number of other stouthearted sisters who had prepared all the dead for burial. Fathers Sechnall, Gosacht, Mactaleus, and Justanus had directed the services for the dead. I had been too overwrought by grief to attend to this necessary ministry. A fine shepherd I was, indeed. But my self-pity and condemnation were behind me. Those demons had been slaughtered as surely as the ravens. It was time to move ahead.

Resuming my duties, I wrote several letters to King Coroticus, begging that he release the captives, pleading for him to see his error and, for the sake of his own soul, to repent. He never responded. Even the letters I sent to Bishops Amicus, Eusibus, and Victor brought only a brief dismissal.

"Anno Domini 444

"To Patrick, Bishop of Ireland, from Bishop Amicus, greetings.
" I sympathize with your sorrow. However, as long as Irish kings raid the coasts of Britannia, how can we censure British kings who raid the Irish?

"I did speak to Coroticus. I told him he had gone too far; that his rash response was terrible, inequitable, brutal; that I would have no part in it. I never imagined that innocent people would suffer; that after all these years the man would feel so passionate. He refused to change his position, or even to tell me where he had sold your people, so that I might redeem them with the money you sent.

"As to your realization that this raid was personally directed at you, we all reap what we sow, Patrick, Christian or not. It is unavoidable. Sometimes innocent people do suffer for our mistakes, a frequent occurrence in your case, I believe. Isn't the boy, Rioc, the same lad who almost gave in to madness on the occasion of another error? That account, by the way, and your references to Pictish horrors and martyrs' blood was excessively melodramatic. I am amazed that Brother Ninus and Father Malach would agree to record such appalling rubbish. You may derive from this the reason I failed to respond.

"But to the issue at hand, be very careful you don't overstep your authority. Coroticus is not answerable for his faith to any bishop of Ireland. Nor am I answerable for Coroticus' foul deeds.

"Personally, my words can't adequately express my grief at this tragedy. May God have mercy on us all.

"Amicus"

"Coroticus' response to what? You'd think he might tell me. Amicus may not be answerable for his deeds, but what about his soul? And how can he compare the raids of *pagan* Irish kings to a Catholic King's slaughter of innocent Christians during the celebration of baptism? Has he lost all perception of the mystical body of Christ? He's a bishop after all!" I railed furiously.

"Patrick, if that's their position, what can we do?" Brother Ninus asked.

"We can sail to Britannia ourselves and remind them that we have *one* Father, and that he will judge them for everything they have done to even the least of our brothers," Benignus asserted.

"That might not be a wise..." Father Malach began.

"Benignus is right," I interrupted. "We'll try one more time. The people can't be as blind as their bishops."

I sat down and, with the help of Brother Ninus and Father Auxilius, composed the following letter:

"Anno Domini 444

"I, Patrick, a poorly educated sinner, promoted by God's grace to Bishop of Ireland, and compelled by zeal for God and his people in Ireland, whom I have given up home and kindred to win for Christ, write to the citizens of King Coroticus, regarding a grave matter. King Coroticus cannot be deemed a Christian Roman. What brother of Christ would put to slaughter and sell into brothels fellow brothers and sisters, babes in Christ, still wearing the holy robes of baptism, anointing oil glistening upon their brows? Not brothers but greedy wolves, devouring the people of the Lord, and refusing even to allow us to purchase their freedom.

"You who are holy and humble in heart, consider this. Haven't we the same Father? Are we less than brothers because we are Irish? Did not Christ die also for us?

"It is written, 'He who hates his brother is a murderer, and He who does not love his brother remains in death.' How much more guilty is he who has defiled his hands with the blood of God's children, recently gathered unto Him from the very ends of the earth.

"Know that Coroticus is estranged from me and from Christ my God on whose behalf I have led these precious children into our Christian faith. 'Not only those who do evil, but those who consent to evil are damned.' Whoever, therefore, feasts or fellowships with Coroticus, or dances attendance upon him, consents to his evil and shares his damnation. What Christian would not shrink from making merry with a man of this sort, whose house is filled with the spoil of dead Christians?

"Unlike the Roman Gauls who send suitable Christian men with so many thousand solidi to ransom baptized people from the Franks, your King Coroticus murders them and sells the freeborn captives to barbaric races with no knowledge of God, where sin prevails openly, terribly, shamelessly, especially among the lowest, vilest outlaws, the Picts. Can a man escape judgement who distributes baptized Christian women as prizes to such outlandish peoples for personal profit? Could not the women at least have been redeemed that they might live to God and be made whole?

"I earnestly request that this letter be read in the presence of all the tribes and when Coroticus and his gang of criminals, rebels against Christ, are also present. Perhaps, by God's grace, they will repent, free those saints, who have not yet been put to the slaughter, and save their own souls from the fires of Hell. The peace of God, Father, Son, and Holy Spirit be on all who hear and comply.

"Patrick"

"Father Malach, Father Auxilius, you will sail on the next ship to Britannia," I instructed. "In every tavern, school, church, meeting house, you will post this letter and read it aloud. You are to leave it on gates and doorposts, barracks and wharves. We will see how loudly God speaks to the hearts of the common man."

We worked tirelessly, day and night, making all the copies we could before the next boat sailed. Father Malach and Father Auxilius left, burdened by almost more than they could carry, but full of eager expectations.

Benignus joined me at breakfast the next morning, obviously troubled, but then who wasn't still suffering? "Father Patrick," Benignus began, "the book of verses that Rioc wears, you were planning for him to take your place one day, weren't you?"

What was the question behind the question, I wondered, as I attempted to respond to his simple inquiry and disturbed countenance. "Rioc is a man of faith, Benignus, unswerving, dynamic faith. He is courageous, loyal, a strong right arm, a dependable follower. But he is not a leader. I pray that he will be led to a man of God who needs a strong right arm, and the two of them, like Brother Ninus and I, will see God accomplish great things. No, I hesitate to place so great a burden on your young shoulders, but as you have asked, it was always you, Benignus, you who would assume the mantle I wear. You have doubts, but you face them and work them out. You are prudent, but you don't lack the courage to be reckless should the need arise. You rebel and defy authority you don't understand, until the understanding comes. I don't say this is good, I only see that a man who is to lead others must struggle to see clearly, not blindly, all that he can. And more importantly, when understanding does come, you humbly accept your responsibility and your correction. One day, Benignus, the shillelagh I pass to you will be my bishop's crook."

"For so many years I've wanted nothing else," Benignus confessed, "but I thought I'd missed God, and harbored some mysterious and selfish motive. I imagined you preferred Rioc. Since the day he was taken, I've felt such terrible guilt. Perhaps, I'd secretly wanted him removed."

"So you've had your demons to fight, as well. If he looks hard enough, Benignus, every man can find an evil or selfish motive for any good thing he ever did or ever hopes to do. Should we stop doing good? No, we should remember that only God initiates good thoughts, good deeds, and good desires, and thank him that he trusts those things to we poor men of mixed motives and confused virtue. God doesn't condemn us. Should we condemn ourselves? Kick that demon in the teeth, Benignus. You are called because God has called you, and that is good enough."

From that day forward with Benignus at my side, I resumed instructing the catechumens, directing worship, celebrating the feast of the Lord, training the clergy, and counseling with the bereaved. In all the activity, I failed to notice how wan Liddy had become.

Mother Scothie called me to Liddy's bedside only three weeks after the massacre. She was dying. Her heart and her strength were broken. I pulled up a chair next to Scothie's, and we recalled with Liddy every time over the years that our paths and hers had crossed from the very first day we had landed in Ireland. We remembered how her practical and solid faith in God had given us hope, her courage had inspired us, and her unimaginable love for Sinell had baffled us completely. She laughed. And she laughed at all the messes we had gotten ourselves into over the years, only to be rescued by that old pirate, or else delivered by the miraculous hand of God. What a marvelous afternoon we spent. Liddy died with a smile on her face, and the peace of victory in her heart.

A few days later we gathered to put her remains to rest. As we turned the last shovelful of earth, the dust of seven horsemen rose on the hill a mile to the west. We watched in silence as King Diarmuid and his six best knights rode into the midst of us. Two of the warriors leapt from their mounts and forced me to my knees, to the alarm of the other Christians present. It was no surprise to me. I had ignored three times the King's summons.

King Diarmuid planted his feet before me. "Three times I inquire, three times the same unsatisfactory answer, three times you refuse to come," he ranted furiously. "Look at me when I address you!" He struck my face soundly with the back of his hand. My eyes reluctantly met his. "Oh, stand up man!" he ordered agitatedly. The warriors released me, and I stood to face him. "Do you think me a fool? Am I to believe that YOU are responsible for this raid? YOU? Why would you insult me with so ludicrous an answer?"

"These people follow me, King Diarmuid. I am responsible for everything that happens to them," I answered.

"I AM THEIR KING! Do you imagine that I am less responsible?" he shouted. "In our long years of association, Patrick, I have never known you to practice deceit. Who is it you presume to protect?"

I didn't answer immediately, but King Diarmuid was a master at patience. "If I give you a name, King Diarmuid, hundreds more may die in your vengeance."

King Diarmuid sighed heavily, "Yes, Patrick, hundreds more may die. But this is a matter for kings, not holy men. Have you forgotten my son, Maciul, was among those slaughtered, his wife taken captive?"

"Father Patrick!" Benignus called breathlessly, running toward us, "a letter comes from Father Malach." Upon seeing King Diarmuid and his knights, Benignus dropped down on one knee.

Diarmuid motioned him to rise and continue, then inquired, "Who do you bury now?"

"Sinell's good woman, Liddy," Brother Ninus answered. King Diarmuid nodded soberly.

Benignus handed me the letter. I ripped it open, overjoyed at the message within. "'The good people here are outraged,'" I read with unbridled enthusiasm. "'Even the barmaids avoid Coroticus. Soldiers have left his service. Priests call their people to pray for his soul, and for the lives of our brothers and sisters as well.' The bishops will have to support us now!" I charged.

"*King* Coroticus?" Diarmuid asked. My stomach turned. "Just what do you hope to accomplish?"

"That Coroticus might repent of his evil before God and men, and return our people to us."

"No king would so humiliate himself."

"A Christian king would."

"Then I doubt whether any king would be Christian!" King Diarmuid mounted his horse and his warriors followed suit. "Your gesture was noble, Patrick. But, in the future, stay out of the business of kings, and I will stay out of the business of holy men." He shook my hand firmly and rode away from Twin Hills, leaving my heart filled with foreboding for the people of Britannia.

By the end of the following week Father Malach and Father Auxilius were due to return. The seafaring men along the coast who would have cut Sinell's throat to steal his gold or win a reputation, now, because Sinell had died a hero's death, honored the man who had shared his blood oath. I was welcome in any hut along the beach and had nothing to fear from them but a plethora of crude and vulgar humor. Brother Ninus, Benignus, and I enjoyed a few drinks with two dockhands as we eagerly awaited Father Malach and Father Auxilius. The hands were generous with the latest news from the continent.

Valentinian III, the emperor of the Western Roman Empire was now twenty-five, but the real power lay with a General Aetius who had achieved a good measure of success restoring order in Gaul. I was encouraged for my brothers in Lerins. However, no attempt was being made to restore Roman order in Britannia. The fate of her people was left in the hands of tyrants, like Coroticus, and holy men of the measure of Eusibus, Victor, and Amicus. Other news was even less encouraging. The Vandals had conquered the North African Provinces of Rome, including the city of Carthage. It was a long way from Ireland, but Bishop Augustine, if he still lived, served in North Africa, and I felt I owed him a great debt for the books he had written. How I would like to have known him.

Brother Ninus was the first to notice the ship's mast. We hurried out of the hut and onto the dock. "Father Malach! Father Auxilius!" Benignus shouted exuberantly down to them as the ship came to rest. They turned weary eyes on us, and I instantly excused their poor manners in not waving. This voyage had obviously not agreed with either of them.

"You're letter was such an encouragement," I said, as I lifted their bags over the ship's rail and handed them to Brother Ninus.

"We could hardly sleep for imagining how the bishops responded," Brother Ninus said laughing.

"It's good to be home," Father Malach responded gravely. Father Auxilius said nothing.

What herald of victory ever bore so sober a countenance? "You must be tired," I suggested. "We'll speak of all that later."

As we drove our chariots, Brother Ninus chattered on about the good number of calves our cows had birthed, promising a comfortable winter. Finances always interested Father Malach. Benignus described the work that several exceptional artists had contributed to the interior of a little church about thirty-five miles south of Twin Hills. A fact certain to capture Father Auxilius' attention. Nothing was said of their mission.

The following morning, after morning prayers and the celebration of Holy Communion, I called Fathers Malach and Auxilius to my quarters. Father Malach sat heavily on my bed, while Father Auxilius crumbled neatly into my spare chair. I sat at the desk.

"Did our efforts at least force the bishops to meet in council?" I asked.

"Yes, a council of bishops was called, followed by an inquiry before the entire ecclesiastical assembly," Father Malach responded.

"Then why the defeated countenance, Malach, Auxilius?" I chided. "Take heart. Obviously the captives weren't returned. But you must not feel that you have failed. If the bishops met, the pressure on Coroticus to..."

"King Coroticus was not the object of the inquiry," Father Auxilius interrupted.

"I'm not sure I understand."

"Here is a transcript of the proceedings." Father Malach said as he handed me the record. "Please believe that Auxilius and I were completely unaware of the council's objective when we were interrogated."

I carefully unrolled its pages and began to read.

Anno Domini 444
Ecclesiastical Council of Bishops, Clergy, and Religious Orders - An Inquiry

BISHOP VICTOR: *"We have met to reconsider the appointment of Patricius Magonus Sucatus, currently serving Christ's church as Bishop of Ireland".*

BISHOP EUSIBUS: *"Bishop Patrick has exceeded his authority in presuming to excommunicate our good King Coroticus. We have reason to believe he misuses his office in other matters as well."*

HERALD: *"The council calls Father Malach!"*

BISHOP EUSIBUS: *"Father Malach, thank you for a wonderful time last evening. Your stories about Ireland were charming. We've asked you to help us understand Patrick's position more clearly."*

FATHER MALACH: *"Yes, sir."*

BISHOP EUSIBUS: *"Fine. Now you thought Patrick an ignoramus, demanding and careless for your welfare when first you landed in Ireland. Is that correct?"*

FATHER MALACH: *"Well, yes, at first, but he..."*

BISHOP EUSIBUS: *"He purchased gifts with church funds, Christian money, to squander on pagan Irish kings. Isn't that correct?"*

FATHER MALACH: "Well the funds weren't entirely..."

BISHOP EUSIBUS: "He showered gifts on pagans! Isn't that correct? Yes or no."

FATHER MALACH: "Yes."

BISHOP EUSIBUS: "Patrick not only gives generously to pagans, he presumes to dress like them, rather than wear the decent traditional robes of a Christian Roman. Is that correct?"

FATHER MALACH: "Why should his garments..."

BISHOP EUSIBUS: "And isn't it true that he required you and other Christians to record pagan legends and myths, when every other bishop in Christendom expressly forbids it?"

FATHER MALACH: "How can I know what EVERY other bishop requires?"

BISHOP EUSIBUS: "You don't deny it? That will be all."

HERALD: "The council calls Father Auxilius!"

BISHOP EUSIBUS: "Last night, didn't you tell me that hundreds of people line the roads, cheering and waving banners when Patrick enters a kingdom? As though he were a god?"

FATHER AUXILIUS: "Yes, it's very upsetting to..."

BISHOP EUSIBUS: "And didn't he take a hammer to the walls of a church, defacing the house of God?"

FATHER AUXILIUS: "His name was on..."

BISHOP EUSIBUS: "Just answer, yes or no."

FATHER AUXILIUS: "Yes."

BISHOP EUSIBUS: *"The Irish women find Patrick attractive, you said. Isn't it true, they lay jewelry and other valuables on the altar when Patrick preaches, this holy man in his tightly laced Irish trousers?"*

FATHER AUXILIUS: *"Yes."*

BISHOP EUSIBUS: *"He enriches himself with their favors?"*

FATHER AUXILIUS: *"No! He returns their gifts."*

BISHOP EUSIBUS: *"Privately, I'm sure. That might explain all those children the Irish church supports. He calls them HIS, does he not?"*

FATHER AUXILIUS: *"The pagans in Ireland are more honest than the lot of you. Patrick..."*

BISHOP EUSIBUS: *"No further questions."*

HERALD: *"The council calls Bishop Amicus."*

BISHOP EUSIBUS: *"Bishop Amicus, you helped Patrick become a priest and later promoted his cause to become a bishop, all the while concealing something about Patrick's character, something that would have prevented his being considered ...even for the priesthood. We all admire and respect you, Bishop Amicus, your loyalty to an old friend. But, out of loyalty to the church, I ask you to tell us now what you once concealed."*

BISHOP AMICUS: *"You've all heard the romantic ballad that King Coroticus has made so popular. My sister, Audrey, and Sucat, Bishop Patrick, were the subjects of that tragedy. When he returned from Ireland his guilt was so great that he confessed the truth..."*

I could read no further.

"Before the whole ecclesiastical assembly... he repeated my confessions before the entire assembly? Those vicious lies don't matter, but the truth... Oh, my dearest, dearest friend, why have you betrayed me?"

Father Auxilius' hand gently rested on my shoulder. "There's more, Patrick."

He handed me a scroll. It read:

𝔄 𝔓𝔲𝔟𝔩𝔦𝔠 𝔓𝔯𝔬𝔠𝔩𝔞𝔪𝔞𝔱𝔦𝔬𝔫
to be read aloud in every church
throughout Ireland and Britannia

I scarcely needed guess at the contents. "Assemble the saints," I directed.

"No, Patrick. Let them spew that poison all over Britannia. We don't need a drop of it here," Father Malach protested.

"The spray will carry across the water, Malach. Then I will be exposed for both my former sins and my current deceit. I will read this out after the noonday service. See that everyone, especially the clergy and religious, are in attendance." They nodded gravely and left me.

The anticipation in the air during the service was intense, making concentration on worship nearly impossible. Father Sechnall read the scriptures, Father Gosacht delivered the sermon, leaving me to administer the feast of the Lord. Brother Ninus and Benignus stood near the front of the sanctuary, Mother Scothie stood near the back with Father Malach and Father Auxilius. The church was full. The last prayer prayed, the last hymn sung, I unrolled the proclamation.

"Brothers and sisters, please hear and carefully consider this communication," I instructed.

" 'A Public Proclamation from the Council of Bishops and Clergy, to be read aloud in every church throughout Ireland and Britannia.

"'It has come to our attention, that before being ordained a priest, Patricius Magonus Sucatus, defiled the sanctuary of our Lord by... vilely...'" Brother Ninus's warning echoed in my mind, "So many fragile souls look up to you." But there was nothing to be done for it now. The murmurs of confused brothers and sisters rose like a wave through the hall. I tried to read once more, but grossly overestimated my emotional reserve.

"Ninus," I called soundlessly.

Brother Ninus hurried to my side. I handed him the proclamation and took his place beside Benignus. Brother Ninus began to read.

"'It has come to our attention, that before being ordained a priest, Patricius Magonus Sucatus defiled the sanctuary of our Lord by vilely raping... an innocent Christian virgin within its sacred walls."

Whispered exclamations breathed throughout the congregation. Ninus paused thoughtfully, then glanced toward me. I nodded. He resumed the reading.

"'Discovered violating his victim... Discovered violating his victim by Father Molue, an elderly blind priest, Patrick set the priest's robes ablaze and fled with the girl, leaving the dear saint to die horribly in the flames.'" Ninus paused. Oppressive heaviness weighed on us all in the silence. *"'Upon learning that she was with child, Patrick later compounded his already heinous crimes by pushing the girl he had violated and his unborn child to their deaths.'"*

The entire body gasped as one, then was hushed. My shame made lifting my head impossible. The truth would have been terrible enough. Yet how skillfully the writer had embellished my villainy. Still, I was guilty of all, in spirit if not in letter.

"Patrick..."

"Read on, Ninus, or I'll have to," I insisted without meeting his eyes.

"'The Roman authorities never apprehended and punished this criminal, only because he was shortly afterwards carried outside the realm of Roman law. Had the bishops known this terrible truth, they would never, could never, have ordained a man with such a monstrous capacity for evil, his subsequent conversion notwithstanding. In light of this revelation and in consideration of more recent charges of misconduct... an investigation is underway to determine what must be done, whether it is even conceivable that Patrick would remain Bishop of Ireland.'"

For several moments the hall was silent.

"Lies, all of them. Do they think we will be influenced by their slander?" Father Sechnall posed.

"Where is a better man than Patrick?" Father Gosacht shouted.

"He's a good man! a saint! a holy man! How dare they speak against him?" the hall erupted in accolades.

"Think of the marvelous things Father Patrick has accomplished in Ireland! Churches in every kingdom, respect from every king..." Benignus championed.

I stepped beside Brother Ninus. The people fell silent. "What *GOD* has accomplished in Ireland is the result of God's goodness... Not mine."

"What are you saying, Patrick?" Father Gosacht queried.

"Can I say there is no truth to these charges? No. I cannot defend myself. Nor will I appear in any way to justify what I did, by taking issue with the clever wording of this letter."

Murmurs rose as shock, anger, pity, and contempt were reflected variously in their faces. They were troubled, hurt, scandalized. Some glared with disgust, not just at me, but at the altar and crucifix, before turning to go. 'Oh, Father in Heaven, no! Let no souls be lost to you because of my villainy!' I grieved.

"Will you hear me a moment longer?" I urgently begged.

The hall grew still and silent again. Endeavoring to overcome the enormous lump in my throat, I began, "How can I answer for a beardless boy, not yet sixteen, his heart dark and godless; his acts as vile, base, and criminal as was his soul? Such was I. I admit that with terrible shame and humiliation.

"But know that I did receive my punishment, though not from Rome. I spent *six... long... years...* in Hell. Hungry, naked, abused, and that daily, shamefully humiliated and beaten almost past living. That wicked, wretched boy died, for God changed him. *Changed him into a man who loves God and His people more than his own life.* How often I have repented with rivers of tears for the sins of my youth. But still I bear on my soul the scars of that sin, as surely as I bear on my back the scars of my punishment."

My eyes met Scothie's, luminous with tears.

"Even changed, I confess I have not lived a life of perfection, as other believers have. But, God knows, I do try. And when I fail, I confess my sins to God. I am not ashamed in His sight. And if it counts for anything, know that from my youth until this moment, though every day, *every day* I expect assassination, or treachery, or reduction again to slavery, still, *I have kept the faith*! As to the charges that I have used the office of bishop for personal gain, personal glory, and personal licentiousness, you all know me. Judge me if you must, and I will not dispute your judgement.

"Only, ...may it never happen that I see you fall away. You may despise me. I can't, don't, ask for your respect. But, please, do not, because of me, despise *God* and all that *he* has done. ...It is Patrick that fails."

Too overcome to say more, I laid a hand on Ninus' shoulder and turned toward the side door. One thing remained. I searched their tragic and confused faces, then forced a final comment from my heart.

"Unworthy as I must be, *GOD* has called me. The church may revoke my title. It cannot revoke the authority I receive from God to tell his story, and I will... as long as I have breath."

I stepped through the doorway and wandered to the spring, leaving the congregation to heatedly discuss the issues. The cool water felt soothing on my face, hot from tension and wet with tears. As I sat on the worn stone bench, Mother Scothie approached and silently sat beside me. I was both embarrassed and comforted by her presence. We stared together into the clear flowing water, its purity a painful contrast to the murkiness I saw within me, not a blackness like that of my youth, but blood red.

"Can there be a man worse than I, Scothie?" I honestly inquired.

"No, Patrick," she sighed heavily, "none worse." Leaning her head against my shoulder she added, "nor is there any man better." The bleeding stopped. I smiled sadly and rubbed my bearded cheek against her head as she tenderly took my hand in her own.

CHAPTER THIRTY
The Gift of God

In spite of my humiliating exposure, the Irish church was never ashamed of me. "Bishop or not," they proclaimed, "Patrick is our father in the faith. If he is judged a bastard, then we'll all be bastards together, for the glory of God!" A fine, colorful people, the Irish! They are given to fighting and drinking, and are such skilled liars that the yarns they spin are not to be believed, but the Irish are big hearted and honest at the core. I have not seen their equal in the depths of their love, in their strong sense of justice, in their reverence for the nobility of one man's sacrifice for the common good, and in the willingness of so many to be just such a man or woman. I pray that in the day of the Lord, God may not assign the Irish to some other, but will charge their judgement to this man, who has come to love them as much for their faults as for their virtues.

The council of bishops in Britannia never again addressed the issue of my office, or if they did, I was not informed. Communications between the two islands had become increasingly difficult, as Irish raids on the coasts of Britannia, instigated by King Diarmuid, and encouraged by their weak defenses, excelled even those of my youth. My old friend, Samson, did get a message to me. It read:

"Now Bishop Patrick, they're saying all manner of things about you here, but don't let that worry you none. Most shepherds don't smell any better than the sheep they shepherd. That's all right, long as they keep them sheep fed and watered. You go right on making honey, praying man, and let these hornets stew in their own vinegar.

" I thought a note from someone who still thinks mighty highly of you would be helpful under the circumstances. My angel's fine, a bit testy cause her womb's drying up, but I'll love her on past that. I'll never forget the good you did for me, Patrick. God bless you in all the good you are doing now. Your old and most faithful friend, Samson. "

God is always so good to send just the right word from just the right person. Samson failed to date his letter but it came just months after the proclamation was read. I pray Samson received the warm letter I wrote him in response.

I continue to wonder why Bishop Amicus, Ami, my dearest friend for so many years, had so hurtfully violated my confidence, encouraging my brothers to despise me, and spurring Coroticus to hate me so completely. And what threats had King Coroticus made on the churches under his protection, that they chose to champion a butcher and butcher a man of God? God, help the church "when men of faith become, instead, men of power." How completely divorced from my kinsmen I had now become.

I have learned from King Diarmuid over the years, that Britannia has become a country overrun by Saxon and other savages, marauding bandits, undisciplined deserters from the legions of Rome, and of course, Irish raiders. The fine Roman villas, baths, markets, schools, have been abandoned and are overgrown. "Oh, how the mighty are fallen!"

Without Roman order, the British church will be as isolated as our Irish church has been, but by God's grace she will survive. Her good people, like my friend Samson, will keep her alive. On the continent, Valentinian III conferred on the Bishop of Rome sovereign authority over all the Christian churches in the Western Roman Empire. That was in Anno Domini 445. Our crumbling communications with the empire insured that that had little immediate effect on us.

Here in Leinster a powerful church grew from the blood of her martyrs. Her oversight was no longer as critical as the churches in the north, where Picts continually harassed, clan wars constantly threatened, and greedy brehons measured their justice to Christians by the weight of the tribute in their hands. So we returned to Lord Dichru's barn north of Meath, where I could quickly address the needs of the surrounding kingdoms.

And so it went. I was happily isolated in Ireland, a country I was never to leave again. Year after year the same trials had to be met, especially whenever a new king was chosen in any kingdom. At least a half a dozen more times my life was at peril, and the lives of my companions as well. And how many tens of thousands I baptized in the faith! There was much more that could have been told. For thirty years I was Bishop of Ireland, shepherd of two hundred fifty churches. At seventy-five it was time to give it up.

So many dear friends had gone before me. The persistent inquiries I made among the Picts concerning Rioc were answered with the same silence Scothie had received when trying to locate Julia years earlier. Yet I had peace. I saw, in my mind's eye, every time I prayed for him, Julia and Rioc and Totmael, white robed, standing together around God's throne, martyr's crowns upon their heads. He had achieved what I never could, and how much more preferable than suffering twenty grueling years in slavery.

Father Malach died of fever in Anno Domini 457. Father Auxilius passed two years later. But faithful Sechnall, and my orphan son Benignus remained. Gosacht, too. Ninus, my most dearly loved friend and companion, was my companion still, and Scothie, my very heart, still beat at my side.

"Patrick, give your pen a rest. I want you to see something," Scothie insisted.

Obediently I returned my pen to the well. Benignus and Sechnall helped me to my feet and across the room, where my window opened to the gentle slope of the hillside and the valley below.

"Dear God!" I breathed. How many hundreds of people lined the valley floor, camped on either side of the stream at her heart. Those near enough to see clearly, were pleasantly visiting. Some were praying. As I strained these faulty old ears, I could make out a hymn being sung. A number of fire pits were being readied for the evening meal.

"I hope they've brought their bodhrans and bones," I quipped lightly. "I fancy going out on the strains of a jig or two."

"They heard you were dying, Patrick. They've come from all over Ireland to let you know how very much you are loved," Scothie explained sadly.

How badly I had wanted to imitate Christ. But the Good Lord never saw fit to grant me a martyr's crown, though I had given him every opportunity. Had I been sawn asunder and my body parts thrown to the wild boars I would not have this multitude to worry me.

"Why are you downcast, Patrick? Doesn't their devotion touch your heart?" Scothie asked.

"It is *GOD* I want them to love with such devotion," I asserted. "Ninus, Gosacht, all of you listen to me. I will have no monument, no shrine, to encourage the devotions of dear misguided people. Promise you will do exactly as I have instructed."

"Of course, Father," Benignus spoke up. I had to smile. He was such a strong, handsome man, nearly forty now, and a good priest for some fifteen years.

"Sechnall, bring me my shepherd's crook," I insisted. As he laid it in my hand, I held it out to Benignus, my other hand resting on his head. Benignus knelt. "As Elijah to Elisha, Benignus, let my mantle fall on you. And may God be as close to you as your next breath and as warm as every ray of summer sun, even as he has been all these years to me."

Father Sechnall, Father Gosacht, and Brother Ninus added their prayers to mine, their hands upon his head. I felt the anointing flowing into, through, and out of me, filling Benignus, filling the entire room with the warmth and comfort of purest love. And I felt the life within me rising out of myself to meet it.

"Sit me down quickly, old friends. I have but one more thing to write, and my strength fades fast."

And so I take the pen in hand and, by God's grace, I close:

I beg that whoever shall receive this writing,
will never say that it was I, the ignorant sinner,
if I have achieved any small success
through God's good pleasure.
Rather you are to earnestly and sincerely believe,
that it was the gift of God.

And this is my confession before I die.

Patrick

ADDENDUM
No Shrine, No Monument

I pray that Patrick will not object to the few words I add to his record. I have loved him more than anyone can ever know. I have been for him what he needed me to be, never too close and never too distant. Even Ninus didn't know his heart as well as I. And so, though I am a woman, I boldly take up his pen to finish this account.

Patrick left us before the ink had dried on his last word. We laid his body on the bed, and I began to dress him for burial. As he had spoken, only half in jest, the pipes and bells, bodhrans and bones, played pleasantly outside the window. I washed his wrinkled old face and combed his white beard, and I couldn't help but kiss him, releasing a flood of tears.

I didn't weep for Patrick. His blessed Lord, the very object of his passion, his love, his deepest devotion, now enveloped him in such glorious rapture that who could weep for him? No, I wept for the emptiness I felt in my own soul at his absence. I was embarrassed for the men to see me so, until one by one each bent down and kissed him, too.

Having finished my ministrations, the men rolled Patrick's body in the blankets, and, under cover of night, placed him on an oxcart. Just as Patrick had instructed, they yoked the cart to two contrary oxen that had never pulled together. Benignus covered the body with straw and loaded several shovels onto the cart. The oxen began to pull. No one directed the oxen. They pulled against each other and fought, wandering here and there, sometimes in circles. But just as Patrick had said, in time they came to walk peacefully together. We followed by the light of the moon until the blackness of night faded to predawn purple and the oxen stopped to graze on the lush grass at the side of a spring. The field was full of flowers, and the spring gurgled melodiously as it tumbled over its banks and into a pebble filled stream. It was here, in this valley, that we were to bury him, near where the oxen fed. What more appropriate place could we have chosen?

Benignus and Sechnall dug the grave deep. Gosacht and Iserninus carefully lowered the body into it's resting place. We filled it in, then generously covered the fresh turned earth with straw, as we had been directed. After saying the prayers and singing the hymns that Patrick most preferred, we celebrated mystic Holy Communion with each other, Patrick, and all the saints gone before. I would have lingered, but there was nothing more to be done.

As we rode the oxcart out of the valley, I glanced briefly at the place we had lain him. A few straws blew across the top of his grave. In a few weeks the grass would grow, the straw would blow away, and there would be nothing to mark the bones of God's man in Ireland, just as God's man had intended.

Still he couldn't help but leave a monument. It was that fire that no man could quench, that consumed all Ireland in a single lifetime, filling her people with love for the God of a humble, holy man we called Patrick.

Thanks be to God!

Mother Scothie

AUTHOR'S DISCLAIMER

There is a vast amount of historical truth to be found within these pages. Many actual statements from Patrick's <u>Confession</u> and his "Letter to Coroticus" are carefully woven into this narrative. However, this novel, in its entirety, is a work of fiction. The only factual individuals recorded are Bishop Patrick, Bishop Palladius, Calpornius, Potitus, Coroticus, Amicus (the name is fictitious, he was simply referred to by Patrick as "my dearest friend"), the brothers from Gaul, and Scothie (again, the name is fictitious as was her very personal relationship to Patrick. She was simply referred to as "a noble lady, full of age and beautiful." One of the few individuals, and the only woman, specifically mentioned in his <u>Confession</u>.) Every other character was taken from the large body of legend and folklore or this author's imagination.

The balance I tried to maintain between good and evil, noble and ignoble, among those of the British race, the Irish race, the practitioners of Druidism, and the Christians, will, I hope, prove that it was not my intention to disparage or glorify any of these. We are all equally capable of both generous nobility and supreme wickedness. The history of every race and religion attests to that. The Picts suffered the most indignity in these pages, only because Patrick, who admitted to suffering "humiliations, nakedness, hunger, and that daily... and those things which I cannot describe in words," never said a critical word about his captors, yet, when enumerating the immoral indignities slaves were made to suffer in primitive bondage, he specifically identified the Picts as "the lowest, vilest outlaws." My goal was to present the story as nearly as possible from Patrick's perspective, and so I did. Many great families have descended from Pictish stock to whom I can only say, we were all savages once.

In the historical records of the church in Rome there is a brief statement about large numbers of people being converted to the Christian faith in Ireland. The evangelist responsible for this is not mentioned nor probably known. It is my assumption that Patrick was that man. Five years later the church in Rome ordained Palladius as Bishop of Ireland and sent him north. These facts are recorded. There is no record of Patrick's ordination in the Roman church. We only know of it from his writings. Records do get lost. It is possible the Bishop of Rome did send Patrick, but much more probable that he was ordained and commissioned by the British church. We can claim in Patrick the roots of Catholic, Celtic, and Anglican Christianity in Ireland, all three so alike in their foundations, like three rivers branching from one source.

Patrick was an uncultured country evangelist, a rugged individualist, easily identified with the pioneer preachers of the old west and missionaries the world over. His witness belongs to all Christians, Protestant, Anglican, Roman, Evangelical. His was the universal message, "God loves you."

Audrey's Lament

Words and music by S. Lavenia Swinnea

GLOSSARY

Arian Heresy - The doctrines of Arius who taught that Jesus Christ was not the embodiment of the very substance of God, but a created being, exalted above all others. This was rejected by the early church in that any being, exalted or otherwise, that accepts the worship of men, as did Christ, is a god. "Hear O Israel, the Lord our God is One." Christ had to be God, the same in substance and equality, as did the Holy Spirit, or the Christian religion would no longer be monotheistic.

Beltane - (1 May) A fire festival. Cattle were driven through fires of purification before sending them out to summer grazing. Horse racing was always a feature of this celebration, as was, in some kingdoms, bestial copulation with the mares. According to legend, no fires were to be ignited the eve of Beltane until the king had set the ceremonial structures ablaze.

Julius Caesar, a credible historian, recorded of the Celtic Druid practices, that people were forced into huge human-shaped wicker cages which were then set on fire. Condemned criminals were the usual victims unless the supply was inadequate. Whether or not this was part of the Beltane ceremony or another is debatable. Some choose to believe that human sacrifice was never practiced in Ireland as there is little recorded in Irish texts. However, the ancient Irish recorded little of anything, and the study of bones from the period suggests it was occasionally practiced there, too. To believe that their baptism in the Irish sea as they crossed from Europe and Britain to Ireland transformed the Irish Celts into more civilized tribes than their forebears is a stretch of the imagination too broad for any but a true Irishman.

bard - An ancient Celtic poet and singer of epic poems, who accompanied himself on the harp; a praise-poet who studied for seven years to learn his craft and belonged to the elite class accordingly.

bodhrans and bones - The bodhran is a large, shallow drum, held almost vertically by one hand, and played by striking alternate ends of a short, thick stick (bone) which is gripped in the center by either fist or thumb and forefinger of the other hand.

brehon - A freeman and member of the class of lawyers and judges in ancient Ireland.

Ca bhfuil an brabach? - Where is the profit?

Cad e sin duinne cad a dheanfaidh se? - What does he matter to us?

curraugh - An ancient flat-bottomed, skin-covered boat equipped with oars and sails, varying in size from smaller fishing vessels to larger ships capable of carrying upwards of forty men and cargo.

Dagda - The Irish tribal god, protector, giver of all that was good, leader in battle, judge, and mate of the tribal goddess, lord of the Otherworld feast. Each tribe had its own Dagda. When the tribe moved, Dagda moved with them, but their goddess remained with the land, to be killed or mated with another tribal god. Gods and goddesses were not inviolable.

decurion - Usually a local noble who was authorized as an official of the Roman government to collect the allotted taxes from the landholders or nobles of a province. Compensation for any deficit was to be supplied from his own resources.

Druid - Druid seems to mean "knowledge of the oak". Among the Celts the oak was held in special awe. As a class, Druids ranked immediately below the nobility and were designated among the men of arts or special gifts. They were exempt from the obligations of war and taxes. At least 12 years of memorization were required to become a Druid in Irish society. More usually one would study 7 years the bards' curriculum, 7 more the filids' curriculum, and another 7 to become 'knowledge-master' or 'oak-knower'.

Like the gods, the Druid priests were thought to be shape shifters, able to transform into animals and back into men. Their sanctuaries were sacred oak groves. According to Julius Caesar's account of European Druid practices, the oak trees were carved into grotesque shapes and sprinkled regularly with human blood. Snakes slithered through the roots of the trees, and the clearings were piled high with hideous offerings. Ghastly groans emanated from the groves so that birds refused to perch in the trees. Even Druid priests dared not enter except at certain times of the day when the terrible Celtic gods were believed to be absent. To Julius Caesar's chagrin, the famous Roman Legions refused to enter as well, until Caesar's own feet were first to trod the heart of the grove and his own eyes were witness to this record. It must be remembered that these or similar religious practices were not uncommon in most primitive societies. The Celtic Druids were without question the intellectual elite, men of science and art, math and music, literature and history in the society of their day.

filid - The filid was more than a storyteller in ancient Ireland, but a prophet or 'seer' as well. He was well learned, having studied and memorized both the epic literature of the bards and all the historic, scientific, and sacred chronicles as well. It took 14 years altogether.

Patrick had completed two levels of Roman education, equivalent to our elementary and high school experience. At Lerins, study would have been integral to monastic life. And his studies in pursuing the priesthood and the office of bishop would have guaranteed him an education comparable in breadth and scope, if not in substance, to that of the filid. He was certainly a prophet, and must have been an admirable storyteller. However, he would never have been recognized as a filid in Irish society, except possibly poetically, like our honorary doctorates today. As the author I have taken the license to so honor Patrick.

Pelagian heresy - The doctrine of Pelagius, a religious brother from Britannia, and his followers. Pelagianism proposes that God chooses those who choose him and loves those who love him. This is in direct contradiction to the doctrine that God loves all, and that it is God who initiates reconciliation, not man. Pelagianism also proposes that as man has free will, he can love, trust, and believe of his own free will, or he can be bitter, prideful, fearful, prejudiced of his own free will. Since he can be free of willful sin if he chooses to be, any willful sin is unforgivable. The great doctor of the church, Saint Augustine of Hippo, responded, "This is too hard for men." Thus, 'we are saved by grace through faith (faith that God also bestows) not through our own merit but according to God's love', became the accepted doctrine of the early church.

Picts - The word 'pict' meaning 'painted' was the Roman word for those tribes of people living in the northeastern area of Ireland and the land known today as Scotland. (At this time in history the tribes known as Scots were inhabitants of Ireland.) These painted warriors were noted for the elaborate, terrifying, and artistic decorations that covered every inch of flesh, their paint being their only covering. Rather than conquer these fierce opponents, the Romans built Hadrian's wall across the island of Britannia from the Irish sea to the North Sea, protecting the southern inhabitants from their aggression. Patrick was particularly appalled at their barbarity in the early fifth century.

rath - A primitive earthenwork fortress comprised of graduated circular mounds and ditches to which the scattered population would flee when attacked or would gather for celebrations. Like a fort in time of war and a fair ground in time of peace, but not at all similar to a village. Towns were nonexistent in primitive Ireland.

Samhain - (November 1 and the night before) A sacred time when barriers between mortal and immortal were down. Inhabitants of the Otherworld became hostile and dangerous, played tricks on mankind, caused panic and destruction, then had to be appeased. Sacrifice and correct performance of ritual were practiced to keep sinister gods at bay. Those venturing out during dawn or twilight might accidentally cross over to the Otherworld and not find their way back. The dead could freely pass into the world of the living, and be seen by foolish wayfarers as well. Any breach of the public peace was punishable by death during Samhain. In addition to sacrifices and ritual observance, courts were in session, markets were held, games played, public bardic competitions enjoyed, races run, and feasting relished. Often the festival lasted several days.

Scots - A Gaelic people who migrated from Ireland to northern Britannia beginning in the fifth century. Their new homeland came to be called Scotland. During Patrick's lifetime, however, whenever Scots were written of, the reference was to the people of Ireland.

shillelagh - Gaelic for 'oak'. Oak trees were sacred to the Druids. Walking sticks, cudgels, and clubs cut from oak wood were thought to have special properties. In time all walking sticks were called shillelagh. The shillelagh came to represent a kind of scepter of authority which was passed from father to son when the parents retired to the 'good room' and the son and his wife became the new master and mistress of the family property.

thrace - The flat, slender, pivoting portion of the chariot extended between the two wheeled body and the yoke.

tinker - An itinerant individual and his family members who traveled like gypsies from place to place working as jack-of-all-trades as they went.

BIBLIOGRAPHY

Aesop's Fables translated by V. S. Vernon **Jones**, Gramercy Books, A Random House Company, Inc. 40 Englehard Ave., Avenel, New Jersey 07001

An Raleabhar Gaeilge or The Irish Phrase Book by Diarmuid **O'Donnchadha**, Mercier Press, Dublin and Cork, Ireland, 1993

Ancient Costumes of Great Britain and Ireland by Charles Hamilton **Smith**, Arch Cape Press, Distributed by Crown Publishers Inc., 225 Park Ave. South, New York, NY 10003, 1989

Atlas of the Roman World, Facts on file, Inc., 460 Park Ave. South, New York, NY 10016

Augustine of Hippo by Peter **Brown**, University of California Press, Berkley and Los Angeles, CA, 1969

Augustine - Major Writings by Benedict J **Groeshel**, Crossroad Publishing Company, 370 Lexington Ave., New York, NY 10017, 1995

Butler's Lives of the Saints compiled by Herbert J. **Thurston**, S. J., and Donald **Attwater**, Christian Classics, Inc., P.O. Box 30, Westminster, MD 21157 1981

The Celts in Myth and Legend by Timothy R. **Roberts** Metro Books, Michael Friedman Publishing Group, Inc., 15 West 26th St., New York, NY 10010, 1995

Celtic Mythology by Proinsias **MacCana**, Peter Bedrick Books, New York, NY 1983

The Christians by Bamber **Gascoigne**, William Morrow and Company, Inc., 105 Madison Ave., New York, NY 10016, 1977

Chronicle of the Roman Emperors, Thames and Hudson, Inc., 500 Fifth Ave., New York, NY 10110, 1995

Clans and Families of Ireland by **Clucas**, **Gibbon**, and **Maguire**, The Willfleet Press, 110 Enterprise Ave., Seaucus, New Jersey 07094, 1994

Classic Coastal Walks of Britain by Martin **Collins**, The Promotional Reprint Company, Ltd., Deacon House, 65 Church Street, London SW3 5BS, 1995

Confessions by Saint **Augustine**, Barnes and Noble, Inc., and Penguin Books, USA, 1992

The Confession of Saint Patrick edited by D. R. Howlett, Triumph Books, Liguori, Missouri 1994

Dictionary of Celtic Myth and Legend by Miranda J. Green, Thames and Hudson, Inc., 500 Fifth Ave., New York, NY 10110, 1992

Dictionary of Faiths and Folklore by W. C. **Hazlitt**, Bracken Books, Studio Editions, Ltd., Princess House, 50 Eastcastle Street, London WIN TAP, England, 1995

Encyclopedia of the Roman Empire, Facts on File, Inc., 460 Park Ave. South, New York, NY 10016, 1994

Flame Over Tara by Madeline **Pollard**, Doubleday and Company, Inc., Garden City, New York, NY, 1964

A History of Christianity, Volume I, Beginnings to 1500 by Kenneth Scott **Latourette**, Harper and Row, New York, Hagerston, San Francisco, London, 1975

The Hymnal 1982 according to the use of The Episcopal Church, the Church Hymnal Corporation, 800 Second Avenue, New York, NY 10017

In The Steps of Saint Patrick by Brian De **Breffny**, Thomas and Hudson, Inc., 500 Fifth Ave., New York, NY 10110, 1982

Knights of God by Partricia **Lynch**, Holt, Reinhart, and Winston of Canada, Limited, 1969

The Life and Writings of the Historical Saint Patrick by R. P. C. **Hanson**, The Seabury Press, 815 Second Ave., New York, NY 10017, 1983

The Living Legend of Saint Patrick by Allanah **Hopkin**, St. Martin's Press, 175 Fifth Ave. New York, NY 10010, 1989

Man, Myth, and Magic, The Illustrated Encyclopedia of Mythology, Religion, and the Unknown, Vol. 8, Marshall Cavendish, Publisher, New York, London, Toronto, 143 West Merrick Road, Freeport, Long Island, NY 11520, 1983

New Catholic Encyclopedia, Vol. 10, The Catholic University of America, Washington, D. C. 1967

The New English Bible With The Apocrypha, Oxford Study Edition, edited by Samuel **Sandmel**, M. Jack **Suggs**, and Arnold J. **Tkacik**, Oxford University Press, New York, NY 1972

Patrick of Ireland by Wilma Pitchford **Hays**, Longman's Canada Limited, Toronto, Canada 1970

Religious Holidays and Calendars by Adam **Kelly**, Peter **Dresser**, and Linda M. **Ross**, Omnigraphics, Inc., Penobscot Building, Detroit, MI 48226, 1993

The Steadfast Man by Paul **Gallico**, Doubleday and Company, Inc., Garden City, NY 1958

Tales of Saint Patrick by Eileen **Dunlop**, Holiday House, Inc. Pllobeg Press, Ltd., Dublin, Ireland 1995

Traditional Irish Recipes by John **Murphy**, Outlet Book Company, Inc., Random House Company, 225 Park Ave. South, New York, NY 10003

A Treasury of Irish Folklore by Padraic **Colum**, Wings Books, 225 Park Avenue South, New York, NY 10003, 1992

Who Was Saint Patrick? by E. A. **Thompson**, St. Martin's Press, Inc., New York, NY 10010, 1986

The World's Great Folktales edited by James R. **Foster**, Galahad Books, A division of Budget Book Service, Inc., 386 Park Avenue South, New York, NY 10016, 1994